An Introduction to Sociolinguistics

Also available from Continuum

An Introduction to Conversation Analysis: Second Edition, Tony Liddicoat
An Introduction to the Nature and Function of Language, Howard Jackson and
  Peter Stockwell
Linguistics: An Introduction, William McGregor

An Introduction to Sociolinguistics

Society and Identity

Sharon K. Deckert
and
Caroline H. Vickers

continuum

Continuum International Publishing Group

The Tower Building   80 Maiden Lane
11 York Road   Suite 704
London SE1 7NX   New York, NY 10038

www.continuumbooks.com

British Library Cataloguing-in-Publication Data
A catalogue record for this book is available from the British Library.

ISBN: 978-1-4411-5023-3 (HB)
        978-1-4411-0028-3 (PB)

Library of Congress Cataloging-in-Publication Data
A catalog record for this book is available from the Library of Congress.

Typeset by Newgen Imaging Systems Pvt Ltd, Chennai, India
Printed and bound by CPI Group (UK) Ltd, Croydon, CR0 4YY

Contents

Introduction to Sociolinguistics: Society and Identity

1.1 Sociolinguistics and identity

Sociolinguistics is a field that looks at how people use language in their everyday lives across a variety of life events and language experiences. In this text, we address sociolinguistics in its broadest sense. The "linguistics" in sociolinguistics indicates that we are really focusing on how language is used. The "socio" in sociolinguistics indicates that we are looking at how language is used in social contexts—at how it is used when people interact with one another on interpersonal levels and in larger group, cultural, national, and international levels. In sociolinguistics, then, we begin with the recognition that the language that each of us uses can be different in different situations and with different people. That's a lot of difference, and it's typically referred to as *variation* in studies that look at language use. This sounds obvious enough, but the fact that we humans are complex social creatures means that studying anything we do with language will also be complex. It is this complexity in relation to everyday life that makes studying sociolinguistics both fascinating and personal.

It is important to recognize that the term *sociolinguistics* can be used in more than one way (Koerner, 2002; Gumperz & Cook-Gumperz, 2008). In a more narrow definition of the term, it can refer to work that looks at dialects and varieties of language and addresses how these are used in relation to social, economic, and even political structures. So it is possible to discuss how the use of a particular variety of English, for example, can indicate the area that an individual comes from, as well as his or her socioeconomic status. The use of one variety might mark someone as being from the southern states in the United States, for example. The use of another variety of English might indicate that someone is from the North of England. An individual's social status might be marked by certain types of language choices. Particularly within the United States, the term sociolinguistics represents work from dialectology, historical linguistics studies, as well as bi- and multilingualism work. It is quite often marked as beginning with the work of William Labov. This definition of sociolinguistics considers language variation and change, and it is most often viewed as a subfield of linguistics.

In this textbook, however, we are really looking at sociolinguistics in its broadest sense. So here, we will consider both the work just mentioned within the field of linguistics, but also the work in other fields of study such as sociology, linguistic anthropology, conversation analysis, and the sociology of language. These fields share a great deal in common, and in many cases they have developed in relation to one another or share research agendas and methodologies. This much broader use of the term sociolinguistics represents work from a wider range of fields that consider how languages, dialects, and varieties of languages are used in social, political, and economic ways. In particular, this text will consider how language can be used to signal and construct particular aspects of identity.

Language is one of the many systems of signs that humans use to communicate with one another, and since language is systematic, we can ask systematic questions about the different choices that we make when we talk with one another. So, for example, we can ask questions, such as William Labov did in the early 1960s, about whether sales people in different types of New York department stores talked in the same way (Labov, 1966). They didn't. Then, using sociolinguistics, we can talk about the systems of social stratification that affect the workers' choices. We can also ask questions about why it is that many U.S. movies portray people with southern accents in rather negative ways, or why it is that school systems argue about what variety of English their students should be allowed to use, or even why it is a requirement in many universities around the world that students pass English proficiency exams. We can ask questions about how some speakers of a language insist that there is a "standard" version of their language that is somehow "better" than other versions when those other versions are themselves completely formed operational languages. As you can see, sociolinguistics covers a very wide range of ways to look at and ask questions about language. Sociolinguistics, with all of its variety of applications, can provide ways to explore both the positive attitudes that people hold in relation to some forms of language and the negative attitudes that some hold toward other forms of language. In addition, it provides frameworks for discussions of the complex notions of power and identity that are connected with those attitudes.

Since sociolinguistics looks at language in its social contexts, we can explore how social contexts shape the ways that we think about language. We can examine how political, social, and cultural ideas about language shape how we think about the languages that we speak and the languages that others speak. At one level, then, we can look at how the power relations between people shape concepts of language value, and on a more intimate level, we can look at how language affects interpersonal relationships. We can look at how the choices we make when we use language in any given situation shape how people think about who we are. In essence, then, sociolinguistics allows us to look at how we create, or construct, our identities in any given situation. To be a bit more precise, since language choices are made by the speaker in relation to the people they are interacting with in any given moment, we can say that the speaker's choices both affect and are affected by the interactions with other people in the ongoing interaction. We can say, then, that the speaker's identity is both constructed and co-constructed in that interaction. Co-construction sounds a bit like cooperation, but each of us can recount interactions in which we were either misunderstood or interacting with people who were in some social sense more powerful than we were. We can find that in our interactions with them, the conversation has constructed us in ways that didn't seem to represent us or that didn't feel like we had much say in the matter. As the "co" in co-construction implies, it does mean that more than one person is involved in the construction, but it doesn't necessarily mean that the construction was cooperative in its most positive sense. So, for example, in moments with our best friends, we can feel that the co-construction creates powerful, positive identities for us, and in moments with people that don't know us well or have other motives in the situation, we can find the identity that has been co-constructed a very frustrating one. It's much more complex than this, of course, because we construct and co-construct all kinds of particular aspects of our identities throughout the day in all our interactions with others. At a larger social level, these kinds of ongoing constructions affect how large groups of people think about their group, ethnic, or national identities as well.

If we go back to Labov's (1966) classic New York Department store study, we can see how identity can be seen in language. In this study, Labov collected data in three different departments stores: Saks, Macy's, and Klein's. He chose these three as representations of different social strata to see how sales persons would pronounce the sounds of /r/. In particular he looked at the two /r/ sounds in the ways that the different sales clerks pronounced "fourth floor." Some people pronounced the two /r/ sounds in "fourth floor" and some people did not, producing a pronunciation something like "foath floah." Labov argued that the pattern of how different people pronounced /r/ was not random, but was socially stratified. He showed that people within different social stratas pronounced words in similar ways within the social group but in different ways across the social groups. What we want to point out here is that something as seemingly simple as the way that someone pronounces the /r/ in certain words can be a signal to what social strata the person occupies—or wants to appear to occupy. Although Labov does not specifically make the claim that the pronunciation of /r/ is a part of identity construction because sociolinguists were not framing questions in that way at the time, we can say that the pronunciation of certain sounds, like the /r/ Labov looked at, can signal a person's social status, and constructs that person's identity in certain ways. Many sociolinguists study variation in the sound systems of language and may address issues such as regional variations of language. Other variations in language are also considered. For example, shifts of style, or differences in gender, age, and social class are often associated with the study of sociolinguistics.

In addition, we can argue that linguistic signals such as those that signal gender identity, institutional identity, national identity, language identity, ethnic identity, and learner identity, to name a few are part of the sets of linguistic signals that we use to construct our own complex identities in various contexts.

It is important to note that signed languages are also full-fledged languages, which exhibit similar forms of variation by geographical region, age, ethnicity, and gender, to name a few parameters, in the same way that other languages do, and sociolinguists study these languages as well (Swisher, 1989).

1.2 Chapter overviews

In Chapter 2, "Identity as a Central Theme in Linguistics," we begin to look at the notion of identity and its various aspects. Identity, as it will be looked at in this book, is not a static quality of an individual, but it is a flexible, fluid, and multi-aspected co-construction that is only partially (if at all, in some instances) representative of an individual's sense of self. In this chapter, we examine the idea that identity is co-constructed in ongoing interactions in very complex ways with a single interaction often being used to co-construct multiple dimensions of identity. In particular, we examine notions related to identity construction, such as gender, discussing the idea that in interactions it cannot be taken as a simply binary construction. We look at expert-novice identities and their constructions in different types of events. Finally, we examine issues related to national, ethnic, and migration identities recognizing that some of these are highly contested and take place in third space and non-place contexts.

In Chapter 3, "Language Variation," we begin with a look at some of the earliest work done in sociolinguistics and at how it made connections between language use and daily life and how, although this work did not explicitly address notions of identity, it did pave the way for modern discussions on the connection between language and identity. We also examine how language contact contributes to language change including the creation of pidgins and creoles. We also explore the social implications of languages in diglossic relationships. Finally, we discuss code-switching and mixing as societal-level phenomena.

In Chapter 4, "Language Development," we look at the idea that from a sociolinguistic perspective, language development is inherently tied to social contexts. People develop language within these social contexts. Consequently, the language we develop becomes a part of our understandings of our social environments to the point that quite often we are completely unaware of some of the language choices we make relative to these environments. In examining how speakers acquire a range of languages and varieties as well as different styles, registers, and a vast verbal repertoire, we look at language from a social perspective and examine the Language Socialization framework to specifically address language development processes. We then examine the notion of a Community of Practice and relate it to the Language Socialization framework because a Community of Practice model provides a mechanism—its different types of participation and interactions with more experienced group members—to account for how socialization processes can occur.

Finally, we briefly examine the notion of literacy practices with an emphasis on the consequences of what happens when the literacy practices of one group are superceded by the literacy practices and demands of another social group.

In Chapter 5, "Language and Social Interaction," we examine how individuals use language in their interactions with one another, and in this way it addresses the idea that talk is action. This chapter includes an overview of Goffman's constructs of face, footing, and participation frameworks and relates these to notions of politeness. In particular, it looks at how individuals orient themselves to various conversational frames and addresses how shifts in frame can affect the various footing an individual takes. This chapter also examines what happens when people from different cultural and language groups come to an interaction using different contextualization cues and how divergent ways of doing contextualization can account for different interpretations. Finally, this chapter addresses how Conversation Analysis has contributed to understandings of the micro-interactions that contribute to larger societal constructs including identity.

In Chapter 6, "Language, Power and Micro-Interactions," we look at how power is enacted at the micro-interactional levels in various social settings. We discuss indexicality as one basic mechanism for conveying social relations through language. We examine how power and authority are enacted in various ways in family life. We examine how power is enacted in bureaucratic settings, including various types of gatekeeping encounters, medical encounters, and legal encounters. We address how research in these areas provides opportunities for both clearer understandings of the micro-processes of interaction in language, as well as provides the potential to affect social change.

In Chapter 7, "Language, Power and Macro-Societal Issues," we explore conceptions of language, ideology, and identity at the macro-societal level. This chapter includes a discussion of language ideologies and the social, cultural, and political hierarchies that help to create and maintain them. In particular, it examines the nature of language hierarchies and how the language used in the media and in political discourses reinforces both these hierarchies and understandings of particular language dialects and varieties. The chapter also provides discussions of how one type of globalized economic phenomenon, the outsourced customer service call center, connects linguistic resources to economic benefits. Finally, we discuss how notions of language and national identity are ideologically based in relatively fixed associations between languages and national identities.

In Chapter 8, "Sociolinguistics: Methods and Approaches," we look at how research related to sociolinguistics can be done. We provide an in-depth examination of the practices and fundamental empirical approaches to doing sociolinguistics. In many ways, this chapter is very different from other chapters in the book. First, it can stand alone as a chapter that introduces techniques, such as transcription, and provides a more in-depth introduction to methods and approaches such as corpus linguistics, interactional sociolinguistics, narrative analysis, ethnography of communication, and conversation analysis. Second, it can be used by instructors as supplemental material related to the specific activities that are provided throughout the text.

1.3 Final thoughts

Finally, this book recognizes that as speakers of more than one language or variety of language, each of us has a great deal of personal experience and knowledge about how language works at the social level. Some of this knowledge may be very conscious due to personal experiences. Many of us, for example, have had experiences in which our languages or language varieties have been questioned by others. We may have experienced our language as either ratified as powerful, or labeled as inappropriate or non-powerful. These kinds of experiences can occur not only at the personal level, but also at the national or political levels. Much of this knowledge, however, is part of our competence as language speakers and often remains unexamined and unexplored to the point that we are often unaware of the complex knowledge we have and use when we make choices as we speak.

This book is written from the perspective that sociolinguistics is not something to read about—it is something to do and discover. From this perspective, sociolinguistics, like language itself, is an activity and not just a product. This text is organized so that you have the opportunity not only to read about ideas and issues important to the broad fields of sociolinguistics, but also to discover these things for yourself through various types of activities designed to get you thinking about and discovering many of the concepts that are important to considering language from a sociolinguistic perspective.

In the activities throughout this text, you will often be asked to examine data that you have collected from conversations or other interactions with your friends or other willing participants. You may also find that your instructor and fellow students are willing to have parts of class periods recorded for data-gathering purposes. Not all of this data needs to be transcribed for you to consider some of the questions that are posed. However, there are times that certain questions ask you to look beyond elements of the conversations or interactions that are analyzable by referring to your conscious awareness. Much of what happens with language can occur at more subtle levels or as a matter of course. These elements of language, things that we often do without any conscious effort, still can tell us a great deal about human interactions and about how we use language.

As the authors of this text, we hope that explorations of the ideas presented in these chapters will enhance your own awe of the languages and varieties that you speak and increase your awareness of the complexity of the competence you wield as you make the minute choices you do as you use language at every level of social interaction.

2 Identity as a Central Theme in Linguistics

Key Terms: *language competence; marked and unmarked; gender; expert-novice; crossing; code-switching; categorization processes; construction; co-construction; L2 user; multicompetence; Third Space; non-place identities*

This chapter provides an overview of the central role that identity plays in sociolinguistic scholarship. To begin, the chapter provides a discussion of the construct of identity, including its history and significance in academic thought. This overview includes perspectives on sociolinguistics and identity that have emerged from sociolinguistic studies of a range of types of identity. This chapter emphasizes the importance of looking at language and identity construction from an interactional, dialogic perspective that includes notions of construction and co-construction.

As discussed in Chapter 1, the early traditions of sociolinguistics did not specifically reference the notion of identity. These works began the process of arguing that language varied not only by region and dialect, but also by social categories such as class and gender (Labov, 1972; Trudgill, 1972). Even in this early work, we can see notions that relate to identity and to the idea that identity is connected to language use. Certainly work on social status addresses notions of identity. In using the language of a particular class, as the sales clerks did in Labov's department store study discussed in Chapter 1, the clerks were constructing particular aspects of their identities. Similarly, in using language that reflects a particular gender, individuals are constructing particular aspects of identities. So the field of sociolinguistics has always addressed issues related to notions of identity.

2.1 The construct of identity

The idea of identity is a somewhat familiar one. We all know something about our identities and the identities of others. We've heard about the threat of identity theft. Within fields of study that look at society and language, however, the notion of identity is used in a different way. First of all, the types of identities that we are discussing are typically not something that can be stolen. In cases of identity theft, what individuals are usually stealing is our legal identification information, and, consequently, access to our financial and other critical information. However, the definition of our identities, as a form of legal identification, is typically not what we are talking about in language studies when we use the word "identity;" though, of course, they can be related. In looking at language in use, we do talk about legal identities—our identities as citizens in a particular country, for example. These identities say something about who we are, and we perform these identities by behaving in certain ways. For example, we pay taxes, or speak or learn a language related to the social structure of the country, or behave in the many other ways that are appropriate to the social environment of a particular country. In each of these, we can be said to be performing the identity of a "citizen," which also happens to have an important legal aspect to it, of course. Clearly identities can be very complex constructions.

The term *identity* is also not equivalent with concepts of self. It is possible, for example, in an interaction with others to have identities constructed that do not at all reflect the way individuals think about themselves. Consider for example, the consequences of a guilty verdict in a court of law. Quite often this can construct an aspect of identity for someone that they do not accept. They may not want to accept the identity of a thief, for example.

2.1 Doing Sociolinguistics: Thought Exploration

Have you ever left a situation thinking that you had been represented in a way that did not reflect how you think about yourself? How do you think this identity was constructed in that event?

Greg Matoesian (1993; 2001) examines a different type of identity that can be constructed in the ongoing interactions of a trial event. Witnesses in rape trials can be constructed as victims by one side of the argument and as willing participants by the other side. Certainly one of these two identities is not a welcome construction. Neither is it equivalent to the witness' sense of self or the witness' self-concept. We can see in the research looking at language and in our own linguistic performances that the ideas of identity and self are not synonymous. Owens (2003) notes this distinction while maintaining the idea that they are related, "Self and identity are complementary terms . . ." (p. 206). But the example from Matoesian, above, shows that while the terms might be related, the constructions do not always align. The notion of identity as we will be using it in this text is strongly linked to notions of performance (Austin, 1975; Briggs, 1988; Butler, 1997). As Schiffrin (1996) has defined it, "social identity is locally situated; who we are is, at least partially, a product of where we are and who we are with . . ." (p. 198).

2.2 Doing Sociolinguistics: Thought Exploration

Consider the ways that you construct your own identity with different groups of people. Do you present yourself in exactly the same ways, or reveal the same sets of aspects to your identity in every situation? How might the different situations allow you to construct different aspects of your identity?

Identity is performed, or constructed if you will, in particular language interactions. This means that identity is not a static characteristic of an individual, and this is part of what makes it distinguishable from "self" in some ways. Identity, as a performed construct, is dependent on the contexts of that construction. This means to paraphrase Gallagher and Marcel (1999) that "in my various activities, I am many different [identities] to many different social groups" (p. 19).

Identity, as it will be looked at here, is not a static quality of an individual, but it is a flexible, fluid, and multi-aspected co-construction that is only partially (if at all, in some instances) representative of an individual's sense of self.

Co-construction is the "joint construction of a form, interpretation, stance, action, activity, identity, institution, skill, ideology, emotion or other culturally meaningful reality" (Jacoby & Ochs, 1995, p. 171). It is important to notice, however, that while the "co-" prefix does imply that more than one individual is responsible for the construction, it does not imply that all of the constructions are necessarily affiliative or supportive.

In this section, we have discussed how identity is very much dependent on the contexts of the interaction in which it is constructed. While it may be related to an individual's sense of self, it is not equivalent to it, as examples in which an unwanted aspect of identity is constructed reveal. Identity, then, is co-constructed in ongoing interactions in relation to the specific contexts (relational, social, cultural, ethnic, political, etc.) in which the particular interaction is occurring.

2.1.1 Style and identity construction

Most of us have a very good idea of what we mean by style when we are talking about clothes or room decorations. We instinctively see the difference in style between something traditional and something contemporary, for example. In literature there is one meaning of style that is somewhat like these distinctions. We can talk about how different writers have their own styles. So we can easily see how the writing in William Shakespeare's plays is very different from Virginia Woolf's novels. Style is related to what makes up both the differences and the similarities. Shakespeare and Woolf both wrote in English, though very different forms of English: Shakespeare spoke and wrote in Early Modern English, and Woolf used a more contemporary version of English. In addition, the plays and novels represent different genres. The plays are written for their performative qualities, the novels less so. So their writing is distinguished by time, genre, and situation of intended use, to name a few of many differences.

In sociolinguistics when we are looking at style, we are asking about somewhat similar notions. We know that we don't all speak the same way. Even when we are speaking English, we aren't necessarily speaking the same variety, and we make choices about the levels of formality of language that we use in different situations. So as researchers who look at language, we can begin to ask why people who can speak more than one variety choose to talk in one variety or another in different situations; we can look at how they choose certain levels of formality; we can look at the ways that people carry out face-to-face interactions; we can even look at the types of words that people use in different situations for different purposes. Most of us have a clear sense that we use certain vocabulary items in certain situations and other vocabulary items in others. Our abilities to make these types of choices are known as our *language competence*. In displaying the appropriate types of language choices for the context, we are not only performing our language competence, we are also performing our identities within each of those contexts as, among other aspects, competent speakers.

2.3 Doing Sociolinguistics: Thought Exploration

Think of different types of situations that you negotiate on a regular basis. These might be in your job, in class, relaxing with friends, for example. How do you use language in different ways in these different situations? Are you consciously aware of making these choices? How much of your language competence do you think is the result of conscious choices? How much do you think is the result of socialized practices?

In this section, we discussed how language choices related to the linguistic styles needed for various types of interactions help construct aspects of your identity in these situations. We have also discussed the fact that displaying these appropriate style choices in the right events both reveals your language competence and constructs you as a competent language speaker.

2.1.2 The co-construction of identity through language

As speakers, we do more than perform our language competence in a variety of ways. We also construct aspects of our identities in interactions. These constructions are very complex. More than one aspect of identity can be constructed in the ongoing interaction of an event. Cecilia Cutler (2007), for example, looks at the MC verbal battles that occur within the hip-hop culture. In these events, competing MCs are given a specific amount of time to take the microphone and, in time to a rap beat, improvise a rhyming verbal sequence of ritual insults at one another. Since a majority of MCs in these events are African American, which is congruent with the typical performers of rap music, the ethnicity of white performers is the marked category of performer. A theory of marking allows for the ability to talk about how some categories, whether those be groups of people or particular pronunciations of a sound, are perceived and constructed as the norm and seen as *unmarked*, and others are viewed as being different from the norm, and seen as *marked* in some way. Cutler's work shows that the categories that are marked or unmarked depend on the context. In the case of MC verbal battles, whiteness is the marked category.

On one level, these verbal battles construct as the whiteness of particular competitors; on another level, they construct these competitors as legitimate members of the hip-hop community. Example 2.1 (Cutler, 2007, p. 19) shows a segment of one of these competitions in which Shells, an African American native of New York City is performing his "spit," against Eyedea, a White skate kid from Minneapolis.

Example 2.1
14. And you talk about my teeth, talk about my flow.
15. I'm a hot ((skimity)) cat.
16. Me mad nice.
17. I'll be damned to lose against Vanilla Ice. //Eyedea throws up his hands and
18. rolls his eyes//
19. Hold up, don't try to save my lines
20. 'Cause it's like 1-800 nuttin' but hot lines.
21. Hold up, you better slow up.
22. This dude's so ugly, I about to throw up.
23. //Shell turns to the audience. //You Ø sayin' I'm wack cause my man's ((White))
24. And guess what, I'm here (( ))
25. And I can fight, and I don't care.
26. We can do this forever,
27. You like fake jeans and you fake . . . //buzzer sounds//

In this excerpt, we can see Shells construct his opponent's whiteness in line 17 when he indexes a connection between his opponent and Vanilla Ice. In the same spit, however, we can see that although he constructs his competitor's whiteness, he also constructs him as a worthy opponent in the spit. In line 26, for example, "We can do this forever," he constructs his opponent as capable of carrying out this challenge. In this language event, then, we can see that identity construction can be complex involving more than one aspect of an individual's identity. A second issue that can be considered in relation to this example is the notion of crossing. *Crossing* occurs when individuals use a variety of language that is typically seen as not belonging to them (Rampton, 1995, 2005, 2009). It can be seen as a form of switching languages or language varieties, often referred to as *code-switching*, in a manner that reflects movement across perceived social or ethnic boundaries. The individual who crosses is faced with challenges to their legitimacy and must typically negotiate this legitimacy in the given context. In this example, then, we can see Shells highlighting Eyedea's act of crossing when he references his whiteness, but we can also see that he performs part of Eyedea's identity negotiation in the context when he constructs Eyedea as a worthy opponent.

In this section, we examined the idea that identity constructions are complex with the possibility that multiple aspects of identity can be co-constructed concurrently in ongoing interactions. We have also discussed the distinction between marked and unmarked categories and showed some actions that can be defined as crossing.

2.2 Gender identity

Early work in the field of sociolinguistics presented a concept of gendered language that made claims that men and boys and women and girls had gendered speech styles and used language differently. Labov (1972), for example, found differences in the ways that women and men used language and in how they generated language change. He claimed that "the sexual differentiation of speech often plays a major role in the mechanism for language change" (p. 303). Trudgill (1972) argued, for example, that women in his study in Norwich used more language forms that were associated with prestige language, while men tended to give preference to working-class forms.

Also in this tradition of looking at gender, Lakoff (1975) argued that certain types of language use were more characteristic of the language of women than the language of men, with women tending to use more hedges, super-polite forms, tag questions, speaking in italics, empty adjectives, hypercorrect grammar and pronunciation, direct quotations, special lexical items, and question intonation in declarative contexts.

Further work in this area, however, challenged these notions about gendered language by finding that these language forms are not exclusive to women. O'Barr and Atkins (1980) and O'Barr (1982), for example, examined the speech of individuals who were familiar with or not familiar with court situations and determined that individuals who were not familiar with the types of powerful language required in court environments, whether they were men or women, used the forms of language that Lakoff mentions. O'Barr and Atkins reframed the discussion of these forms as one between powerful and powerless language rather than one between men's and women's language use.

Tannen (1990, 1994), while pointing out that it is not entirely possible to conclusively associate particular forms with either men or women, argued that men and women can be seen as using different interactional styles while communicating, with women using an interactional style that is focused on constructing solidarity and intimacy, and men using an interactional style that is focused more on individuality and independence. Consider Example 2.2 from Tannen (1990, p. 51).

Example 2.2
1. HE: I'm really tired. I didn't sleep well last night.
2. SHE: I didn't sleep well either. I never do.
3. HE: Why are you trying to belittle me?
4. SHE: I'm not! I'm just trying to show that I understand!

Tannen explains the breakdown that is evident in the man's response in line 3 as one that is based in the asymmetries of men's and women's styles of communicating. She argues that the woman's response to the man's comment about being tired and not sleeping was one that attempted to establish solidarity and understanding. This is indicative of, Tannen argued, the woman's conversational goal of intimacy. The man, however, interprets this move in a very different way as evidenced in his response in line 3, "Why are you trying to belittle me?" in which he indicates that he did not take the move as a supportive one. Instead, working from a communicative style that acts out of notions of independence, he reacts as if his independence has been challenged. In line 4, the woman's response highlights the fact that the man's interpretation is a misunderstanding of her intent. Tannen explains that these types of misunderstandings arise out of two different communicative styles. She compares these misunderstandings that arise out of different conversational styles as similar to those that can occur in cross-cultural interactional events.

There are several things to consider in relation to the approaches that these earlier works in sociolinguistics took in relation to men's and women's language. As sociolinguists it is important to make sure that we consider the context of such work. First it is important to consider the fact that these earlier studies that considered gender tended to focus on white individuals in western cultural contexts, and, therefore, the studies cannot be said to represent all women and men everywhere.

In this section, we have looked at work that shows that there may be differences in the ways that groups of people speak, in particular in the ways that gendered groups speak. However, we have also noted that these studies have looked at a very narrow set of speakers and, as we will see in the next section, used a rather rigid definition of gender.

2.2.1 Gender, social, and cultural identities

Current work in gender identity recognizes gender as a social construct. Notions of what constructs an individual as a "man," for example, are socially and contextually dependent. In a recent episode of HGTV's *Don't Sweat It*, a man was learning how to veneer the raw edges of a bookshelf he was building. This process of veneering included using a hot iron to heat press a thin strip of veneer to the edges of the bookshelf. As he was using the iron, the man said to his instructor, an experienced woodworker, "My wife would laugh if she could see me right now." This comment reflects an example of a social construction of gender identity. Clearly, this man was operating with the cultural under-standing that "ironing is something that women do" and therefore "real men don't iron." In his comment, then, he is referencing these notions as a way to construct himself as someone who typically does not participate in this gendered activity, and therefore, can still be seen as having the appropriate qualities of a man. The experienced woodworker did not respond in kind to this comment, possibly because within the woodworking field, using an iron is a typical way to heat these veneering strips. This example illustrates the idea that certain actions, such as ironing, can for certain segments of the culture be associated with the category of female, but for other segments of the culture be seen in a more neutral way. We can see, then, that part of the man's gender construction was based on the fact that certain actions are seen as correlated with particular categories (Sacks, 1992). The fact that for the woodworker, the same action was associated with a different category shows that the asso-ciation of the action to the gender category is not a natural one, but is a socially constructed one that is differentially constructed in various speech commu-nities (Bucholtz, Liang, & Sutton, 1999; Eckert, 2000a; Hall & Bucholtz, 1995; Livia & Hall, 1997; Milroy, 1987, among others).

Categorization processes represent social processes that can be examined to identify how gender is socially constructed in particular speech communities. The notion of a category must be taken carefully, since the contents of a par-ticular category can vary by speech community and even by a given speech situation. The idea of group homogeneity must also be taken carefully since it can be used to imply that members of groups, such as those connected to gender, class, ethnicity, or language, for example, speak in ways that are consistent across the group. As the example above illustrates, particular groups may have different categories. This means that the categories themselves are not static but are affected by the ongoing processes of individual interactions. In this way, gender construction in a particular event cannot be evaluated simply in relation to perceptions of larger social categories but must be seen as constructed in the event itself.

2.4 Doing Sociolinguistics: Thought Exploration

Think carefully about your own constructions of gender. Do you construct aspects of your gender in exactly the same way with different groups of people? Do you construct your gender differently at a sports event in comparison to when you are out to dinner, for example?

Gaudio (1997) considers a social context where a subordinate group uses language both to forge their mutuality and understanding as a group and to confront and affect the larger social understandings of their bigendered performances. The *Yan daudu* are a group of men within a conservative Muslim Hausa community. *Yan daudu* display womanlike behaviors in their speech patterns, their occupational choices, and occasionally the form of dress they choose. Consequently, within their larger conservative culture, they face social repercussions, often violent ones, that members of the culture employ to maintain the rules and understandings of that culture. In order to negotiate these consequences, *Yan daudu* employ a complex set of linguistic resources in which they use multiple meanings to communicate within their group and outside of their group to those who have various types of relationships with them, their complex understandings of gender, as well as their sexual positioning within the community. These individuals, then, represent a population who challenge the language-use researchers' assumptions that speech communities are homogeneous. They also reinforce a recognition that gender is a social construct that may or may not align with the assumed binary of male and female.

This section has discussed the idea that gender is not a simple binary. It is a social construction that can be used in various ways by individuals to construct complex aspects of their gendered identities in different social and cultural environments.

2.3 Expert-novice identities

A set of identity relationships that provide for interesting discussions of identity constructions are those between people who are constructed as experts and those that are considered novices. These expert and novice identities are typically categorized as representing a binary pattern. For example, we are familiar with doctor-expert/patient-novice, teacher-expert/student-novice, and lawyer-expert/client-novice binary patterns, to name a few.

When we think of these roles, we often consider the expert-novice relationship to be a predetermined, static one. It's assumed, for example, that the doctor always enacts the role of expert, while the patient enacts the role of novice. However, sociolinguistic research has demonstrated that these expert-novice relationships are neither as static nor as obvious as they may seem at first. Jacoby and Gonzalez (1991), for example, discuss how expert identity is achieved in ongoing interactions.

In looking at interactions between physics professors and their graduate students, Jacoby and Gonzalez found that the individual who is constructed with the expert identity is fluid and shifting in the course of conversational interactions. It was not unusual in their data, for instance, for the physics graduate students to achieve an expert identity, subordinating the professors they were interacting with in particular sequences of an ongoing discussion. Jacoby and Gonzalez found that during these discussions, the expert identity could shift from one person to another, depending on the topics within the conversation. Their work demonstrates that expert-novice identities are not simply tied to people enacting predetermined roles; they are also tied to individuals' expertise as they discuss certain topics in ongoing interactions.

2.5 Doing Sociolinguistics: Thought Exploration

Think of your own varying levels of expertise in different areas. How do you use this expertise in interactions with others in ways that construct you as the expert? How do you negotiate your understandings in interactions with others whom you view to have more expertise in a given area?

The "native speaker"/expert and "nonnative speaker"/novice assumption is also shown to be problematic when we examine interactions in which first language (L1) users and second language (L2) users talk to one other about topics other than language learning. Vickers (2007), for instance, argued that when engineering students who are L1 and L2 users talk to one other about engineering, conversational participants orient toward engineering expertise rather than to L1 and L2 user status.

On the other hand, societal-level assumptions about expertise can heavily influence the interactional achievement of expert status. Vickers (2010a; 2010b) showed that the achievement of expert identity in ongoing discussions is complex. For example, within a single interaction, each participant can be orienting to a different aspect of identity. In Example 2.3, adapted from Vickers (2010a, p. 132), David, an L1 engineering student, interacts with Jun, an L2 engineering student. In the course of the interaction, David continually orients toward his engineering identity. Jun, on the other hand, often orients toward his language learner identity.

Example 2.3: D=David; J=Jun

1. D: we're gonna have to do this debug and test the board and debug and test t the software and so probably put after we . . . we have to I think I skipped a few steps here let's put in we routed the board build . . . up board and debug and test board . . . bug test board (whispers) . . . debug and test software should be down here (0.5) test (whispers) (0.5)
2. J: what's here? Manufacture?
3. D: route
4. J: ah route
5. D: that means when you actually cut a board out
6. J: yeah
7. D: there's a milling machine you call that mill board or milling mill board uh route I think I spelled that correctly kind of interchangeable mean the same thing [mill or route
8. J: [yeah uh] how can I spell that
9. D: uh
10. J: do you
11. D: I'd just say m-i-l-l board
12. J: oh oh yeah
13. D: it's like when you cut traces into the board there's a machine we have that does it cuts the circuit board out start out with uh copper
14. J: oh yeah
15. D: copper board it's usually somewhere around a twelve inch square it's double sided copper
16. J: yeah
17. D: there's a machine that comes along and cut first you after you've done your software layout
18. J: yeah

19. D: loaded it into the this uh routing milling machine he'll come along cut the traces out?
20. J: yeah
21. D: and you put your components in the board [and]
22. J: [oh] yeah oh that's hard work
23. D: is it hard work? or it is hard work
24. J: basically I think it's really hard
25. D: well ah it it's a little time consuming and kinda you have to think about where where to put things so it it's I've done it quite a bit so it's not too bad
26. J: ok ok
27. D: if you were to try to just do it for the first time yeah it'd be very very hard so that's probably one of things I'll work on

In this interaction, Jun asks David, in turn 8, how to spell either "mill," "route," or "millboard." After David supplies a spelling, he launches into a long explanation of routing/milling, clearly constructing his expertise in this area. Jun, however, does not display this expertise, though it is not at all clear that he lacks it. In turn 22, for instance, when Jun says "yeah, that's hard work" potentially constructing his knowledge of the process, David's return in 23, asks if Jun is asking a question or making a statement, essentially disrupting this construction. In turn 24, Jun restates his claim displaying that he was making a statement, but David again constructs his own expertise in turn 25 by reframing Jun's definition of "hard" as related to time consumption and essentially returning to his discussion of routing/milling.

Vickers (2010a) argues that Jun's orientation toward his identity as a language learner in turn 8 when he asked about spelling is in conflict with David's orientation toward engineering. David, therefore, took Jun's question about spelling as an indication of Jun's novice engineering status. Evidently, David assumed that if Jun did not know how to spell the word, he didn't know the engineering process the word referred to either. This is clear in David's hefty explanations throughout Example 2.3. Jun, on the other hand, provided minimal responses to David's explanations, so it was unclear what he knew. In this example, Vickers argued that Jun's orientation toward language learning led to the construction of his novice engineering identity in this interaction with David.

This example demonstrates that expert-novice identity constructions can be complex. First, it is possible that interactants may not be orienting to a single expert-novice dimension. Second, it is possible that one participant's constructions may not be effective, essentially constructing an identity that might not reflect an appropriate level of expertise. In these co-constructions, then, we can see that it is possible that co-constructions are not necessarily cooperative (Jacoby & Ochs, 1995).

This section has examined how the notions of expert-novice can be used to reveal the processes of identity construction. It also demonstrates that just as we saw in relation to gender, expert-novice identities are not simple. Within the same event, for example, more than one dimension may be in play at the same time, affecting ongoing co-constructions.

2.4 Language identities

National identities, those that are constructed in relation to a nation state, are most often equated to notions of citizenship. National identities can be constructed through political rules and regulations, such as those determined by laws in relation to birthplace or immigration policies. However, not all identities that would seem to be national ones are limited to national boundaries. As we discuss in more detail in Chapter 7, Gal (1989) provides an example of Romania in the late 1980s, in which the language a particular group of individuals spoke was correlated to their understanding of their group's national affiliation. In the case of Romania, individuals who spoke German considered themselves German nationals even though their families had lived in Romania for centuries alongside Romanian speaking people. German speakers, then, were identified as German and Romanian speakers as Romanian. As this example illustrates, life within the boundaries of a nation state is not equivalent to ethnic or national identities. Hanauer (2009) argues that the politics of multicultural identity push migrants, for example, into an identity in which their ethnic identity is defined by either a past or present connection to a national identity.

We can see the distinctions between ethnic and national identities as politically and ideationally complex; and the fact that these distinctions have often been a point of great contention politically, in some historic and current cases, leading to wars, only highlights the difficulties and emotions inherent in these distinctions.

2.6 Doing Sociolinguistic: Thought Exploration

Choose an event in history in which there has been conflict between people that involved both nationality and ethnicity. How do you think these notions were related to language? How do you think understandings of identity affected the interactions?

Rather than try to distinguish between these types of identities, we will consider how these identities are constructed through language in ongoing interactions. The complex group interactions in Guatemala provide a political landscape for examining these constructions. The people of Guatemala include Ladinos, individuals who would identify as non-Indigenous, and roughly "20 indigenous ethnolinguistic groups belonging to the family of Mayan languages" (French, 2001, p. 157). Members of these indigenous groups see themselves as both different from Ladinos and as distinct from the other Mayan ethnolinguistic groups. So while all of these groups could be said to be national Guatemalans, within that category there are a number of distinct ethnic groups who maintain and construct particular group identities. The social status of these groups is not equal, Ladinos are typically Spanish speakers and, as a whole, hold a higher social status in the country. This does not mean, of course, that this would be true in every cultural context. In Chapters 3 and 7, for example, we consider an ideological preference that has evolved among the multilingual population in Mexico for the use of Spanish in public domains and the use of Mexicano in private domains (Messing, 2007).

For the Guatemalan area studied by French (2001), in the public domain of the market, Spanish speakers generally hold higher status. This status is constructed by both the Ladino buyers and the Mayan sellers in bargaining exchanges. French's analysis of this status negotiation, however, shows examples in which Mayan women use Spanish to resist these cultural constructions of their lower status by manipulating aspects of the Spanish language to signal their resistance. Spanish, like many other languages, has two ways to address an individual. When addressing those who are unfamiliar to the speaker, the form *ustéd*, with its verb conjugation patterns, is used. When addressing those who are familiar, the form *tu*, with its verb conjugation patterns, is used. This distinction between forms, however, can also be used to signal relative social status. Those who are in a higher status would expect to be addressed using the *ustéd* forms. This means that these forms are available for the constructions of social status in the ongoing interaction. In 2.4 (excerpted from French 2001, p. 179), we can see the vendor, a member of one of the Mayan language groups often considered to hold lower social status interacting with a customer, a Ladina who it is assumed has greater social status. In the vendor's choice of *ustéd/tu* forms, we can see her conforming to and using the expected *ustéd* forms; however, we can also see her resisting this cultural expectation, and constructing herself as an equal by addressing the customer using the *tu* form at a crucial point in the interaction. Example 2.4 shows a point in the conversation after the typical opening sequences have been performed.

Example 2.4: V=vendor, C: customer, and C2 a second customer/onlooker.

24. C:	No quiero esto, o pero en blanco ¿Cual es lo ultimo de este aquel?	C:	I don't want this, but rather in white. What is the (lowest) price?
25. V:	Yo pido setenticinco, ¿Cuánto ofrece?	V:	I ask 75, How much do you (U) offer?
26. C:	Cinco. ((Clients laugh.))	C:	Five. ((Clients laugh.))
27. V:	¡¡Ay la gran chucha!!/	V:	Ay, the big dog!
28. C2:	¿Te pusiste bien enojada?	C2:	Did you (T) get really mad?
29. V:	¡No! (5)	V:	No! (5)
30. C2:	¡Hijo! ((C2 to C1))	C2:	Son of . . ! . .
31. V:	¿Cuánto ofreces?	V:	How much do you (T) offer?
32. C:	¿En otro color no hay?	C:	These aren't any in another color?
33. V:	Hay en rojo, hay en blanco, está esté en blanco, est esté en morado.	V:	There are (sweaters) in red, in white, This one in white, this one in purple
34. V:	¿O,Qué tal? Buenas tardes ((to someone passing by))	V:	How's everything? Good afternoon. ((to someone walking by))
35. V:	Éste, éste en rojito y en negro	V:	This one, this one in light red and in black
36.	Pues sí seño. ¿No se lo lleva?		Well, Ms. Aren't you (U) going to take it?
37. C:	Fíjese que es blanco si no consigo en blanco//	C:	Look, (U) it is white that I want, if I Don't find it in white//
38. V:	Vaya, está bien.	V:	Okay, that's fine.
39. C:	Gracias.	C:	Thanks
40. V:	No tenga pena.	V:	Don't you (U) worry about it

In the beginning of the interaction, where the early greetings and opening sequences were performed, the vendor addressed the customer with the *ustéd* forms that signaled her higher status. The accepted bargaining culture of these markets requires certain moves from each participant. For example, before serious bargaining can begin, the two negotiators must establish a top and bottom price, and both of these must be seen as reasonable starting positions. The customer, however, performs an unacceptable and rude form of negotiation in line 26, when she offers to pay five quetzals in response to the vendor's opening statement that she would sell the sweater for 75 quetzals. In asking for this opening offer, the vendor had used the expected *ustéd* form— "¿Cuánto ofrece?" (*How much do you (U) offer?*). However, after the customer has offered a completely unacceptable low price, the vendor repeats the question in a form that addresses her as someone of equal status in line 31, "Cuánto ofreces?" (*How much do you (T) offer?*). This negotiation then breaks down into a discussion of sweater color choices and the customer's decision not to buy is framed as one about color. At this point, the vendor returns to the expected *ustéd* form as part of the closing of the unsuccessful negotiation. It is important to notice that language choice, here, was used to display to the customer that the vendor was not accepting the customer's expected social superiority throughout the entire negotiation. The fact that the opening and closing sequences were in the expected forms, does not negate the resistance and equal status constructions.

In this section we have looked at the idea that different aspects of identity such as citizenship, ethnic group, and language are at constant interplay with one another, often in highly contested ways. These include the individual instances in which group members use language both to create dominance and to resist that dominance.

2.4.1 Identity and multicompetent speakers

When speakers of more than one language meet there can be social assumptions about which language to use that are connected to larger societal preferences. This means that often multilingual individuals must negotiate the language they choose to speak, particularly when one of the individuals belongs to the majority language.

Consider Example 2.5 from Vickers's data in which two speakers negotiate their language use as multicompetent speakers in a Southern California medical clinic that caters, in part, to a Spanish speaking clientele. This excerpt begins after a patient at the clinic, Timoteo, has had a second interview with the nurse in which his medical history was taken. Although Timoteo had spoken Spanish in the first section of this clinic visit, he spoke English during this second section. The following segment begins as the researcher attempts to find out why Timoteo made this decision.

Example 2.5: T=Timoteo, C=the researcher

1.	C:	so why do you choose English..instead of Spanish? I'm just curious—			
2.	T:	oh I thought because..y—you you—			
3.	C:	oh per—cuz of me?=			
4.	T:	=yeah=			
5.	C:	okay..porque hablo español	5.	C:	okay..because I speak Spanish
6.	T:	oh muy [bien]	6.	T:	oh [great]
7.	C:	[@] ((C: and T: laugh))	7.	C:	[@] ((C: and T: laugh))
8.	T:	yo no [sabía] aустéd	8.	T:	I didn't [know] you
9.	C:	[@]	9.	C:	[@]
10.	T:	por la para no sentirse que dice que mal ustéd	10.	T:	for the so you wouldn't feel what is it bad you
11.	C:	no no no..no	11.	C:	no no no..no
12.	T:	okay	12.	T:	okay
13.	C:	no..sí okay um pero está bien en en ingles también?=	13.	C:	no..yes okay um but is it fine in in English too?=
14.	T:	=s:í	14.	T:	=ye:s
15.	C:	sí?	15.	C:	yes?
16.	T:	mhm	16.	T:	mhm
17.	C:	okay=	17.	C:	okay=
18.	T:	=sí..yo con ella me me puedo comunicar en los dos	18.	T:	=yes..I I can communicate in both with her
19.	C:	=mhm=	19.	C:	=mhm=
20.	T:	vine aquí de El Salvador [y:]	20.	T:	I came here from El Salvador [and]
21.	C:	[mhm]	21.	C:	[mhm]
22.	T:	vine aquí despues de que terminar high school vine aquí a estudiar en [la]	22.	T:	I came here after I finished high school to study here at [the]
23.	C:	[mhm]	23.	C:	[mhm]
24.	T:	universidad y..aprendía el inglés bien=	24.	T:	university and..I learned English very well
25.	C:	sí sí habla inglés muy muy bien..mejor que yo..hablo @español @sí ((C: and T: laugh))	25.	C:	yes yes you speak English very very well..better than I..speak @Spanish @yes ((C: and T: laugh))
<<Lines skipped--Later in the conversation they return to this issue>>					

31.	C:	oh..um es más cómodo tener las consultas en ingles or español? (1.5)	31.	C:	oh..um is it more comfortable to have consultations in English or Spanish? (1.5)
32.	T:	eh: para mi: (2.0) eh yo me siento más cómodo en español=	32.	T:	eh: for me: (2.0) eh I feel more comfortable in Spanish=
33.	C:	=okay=	33.	C:	=okay=
34.	T:	=pero: no sé uh porque en la casa mi mama todos hablan espanol entonces=	34.	T:	=but: I don't know uh because at home my mom everyone speaks Spanish so=
35.	C:	=mhm=	35.	C:	=mhm=
36.	T:	=es es natural para mi en español=	36.	T:	=it's it's natural for me in Spanish=
37.	C:	=sí=	37.	C:	=yes=
38.	T:	pero cuando la necesidad tengo que hablar en inglés	38.	T:	but when it's necessary I have to speak in English

In the beginning of this excerpt, part of C's introduction of the question about why Timoteo chose to speak in English is partially due to her concerns that her research presence has affected Timoteo's interaction in the medical event. In addition, it allows her to move to a statement, seen in turn 5, in which she establishes in Spanish that she speaks Spanish. This construction establishes her identity as a Spanish speaker in both the declarative statement and in the choice to make that statement in Spanish. Timoteo also constructs himself as a multicompetent speaker in turn 18, for example, when he refers to his interactions with the nurse by saying, "yo con ella me me puedo comunicar en los dos" (*yes..I can communicate in both [languages] with her*) establishing his ability to speak in either language in the medical setting. To add to this construction of competence, he narrates a brief story of his coming to the United States to study at a university to improve his English. C ratifies his English abilities in turn 25, when she says with some laughter, represented by the @ sign, "sí sí habla inglés muy muy bien..mejor que yo..hablo @español @sí (*Yes, yes, you speak English very very well..better than I..speak @Spanish @yes.*)

Finally, it should be noticed that part of what is negotiated in this interaction is the *meaning* of Timoteo's choice to speak English in the previous medical interaction. The interactants first negotiate the idea that Timoteo made a particular choice choice based on C's presence so that she could understand the interaction. Once Timoteo realizes that C's Spanish is sufficient for understanding the interactions, he assures her that his construction of her as someone who might not understand Spanish, as evidenced in his choice to speak in English in the medical event, was not meant to make her feel bad. This leaves Timoteo free to construct himself as someone who would prefer to interact with the doctor in Spanish. In this interaction, then, we can see a multilayered negotiation—a redefining of identities and a negotiation of language preferences in the medical setting.

2.7 Doing Sociolinguistics: Thought Exploration

Consider your own use of language. Do you use multiple languages or varieties? How do you decide which language or variety to use in particular situations?

In this section, we have discussed how multicompetent speakers negotiate the use of each of their languages. We have shown that the choice of language is a reflection of the speakers' identities but also of their sensitivity to the local interactional situation.

2.4.2 Critiquing the native-nonnative speaker dichotomy

Issues of the types of terms used to refer to speakers of languages who also speak English or are in the process of learning English provide an interesting site for considering the processes of identity construction. In one sense, the labels that have been created for these speakers have arisen not out of the everyday lives of various people, but out of the academic world that studies the processes of acquiring a second language. The history of this academic discussion had its beginnings in countries that are primarily English speaking with a preference for monolingualism. This could be part of the reason that the labels "native speaker" and "nonnative speaker" are not neutral with respect to one another. Current critiques of the field of applied linguistics, in fact, address how this assumption of monolingualism has affected understandings both of second language acquisition and of individuals acquiring a second language (Birdsong, 2005; Kachru, B., 1994; Ortega, 2010; Valdés, 2005, among others).

The labeling process itself can be seen as relevant to co-constructions at different levels. It can be seen at the societal level as a type of co-construction that is the result of interactional processes within the larger academic conversation on the topic. It can also be seen on the individual interactional level of co-constructions of individual speakers who choose to adopt or resist these labels. Consider, for example, Paul Kei Matsuda's (2003) TESOL Matters Viewpoint article "Proud to be a Nonnative English Speaker." In this article, Matsuda is challenging the negativity of the term "nonnative" speaker. He argues that for a term like "nonnative" to be considered a negative term, its counterpoint, "native," would have to be considered a positive term and adds that ". . . the assumption that *native* is somehow more positive than *nonnative* that needs to be challenged" (italics in original, p. 15). This article is an example of the process of co-construction in action. Matsuda's title frames the discussion at an individual level; however, his publication for an academic audience also frames this interaction at the larger societal level. Like most societal level constructions, these processes are not power neutral. The term "native speaker" is closely linked with both notions of ownership of language and with the notions of monolingualism. It can be argued that these notions lead to a deficit model construction of these language users as people whose language use does not achieve monolingual competence. Cumming and Abdolmehdi (2000) provide a useful definition of a deficit model of learning as "one that faults the baseline learners for what they lack—suggesting that their deficiencies should form the basis for instruction, but without knowing if instruction addressing such lacks would really be effective" (58). Notions of "nonnative speakers," have meaning in relationship to a metaphorical "native speaker" competence, and the uses of this metaphor can be evaluated in terms how it establishes the power of a particular type of language speaker: in this case, those who are monolingual (Radwanska-Williams, 2008).

Other linguists have also challenged the labels in terms of their descriptive accuracy. Vivian Cook's (1991; 1992) seminal challenge to consider second language acquisition in terms of the notion of *multicompetence* and to recognize that the multiple languages of bilingual and multilingual speakers are not entirely distinct from one another in human perception, challenges second language acquisition theorists and sociolinguists to reconsider their theories of acquisition and their labeling of second language speakers. These works along with Hall, Cheng and Carlson (2006), among others, provide challenges to reconceptualize our understandings of language knowledge. Other recent work in the field of applied linguistics (Birdsong, 2005; Kachru, B., 1994; Ortega, 2010; Valdés, 2005, among others) also challenges applied linguists to consider how we evaluate multicompetence in relation to monocompetence. Ortega argues, for example, that one of the problems with much of the second language acquisition research is that it compares second language speakers with monolingual speakers rather then with bilingual speakers. Finally, Cook (1999) promotes the term "second language user." His conception of multi-competence also provides for the term "multicompetent" speaker.

In this section, we have examined how labeling processes are not neutral. They both reveal particular understandings, such as the monolingual bias seen in some second language acquisition research, and construct ongoing understandings of individuals. This section has proposed that more neutral labels such as second language user or multicompetent speaker reflect the positive aspects of individuals' abilities to speak more than one language.

2.5 Third space, migration, and non-place identities

Multicompetent speakers of languages represent the changing cultures of the world as individuals interact in multilingual environments, some of them the result of colonial and post-colonial conditions, and as individuals work in multicultural environments or immigrate to other areas of the world. Bhabha (1994) provides a discussion of the types of environments in which culture is defined by the interactions between cultures found in these environments. In these environments, he argues that it is not the diversity of cultures in these spaces, but the hybridity of cultures that define these cultural spaces. He defines such situations as examples of *Third Space*, a place where we "may elude the politics of polarity and emerge as the others of ourselves" (p. 56). Augé (1995) also considers aspects of place, arguing that there are spaces that are the result of supermodernity. He argues that spaces can typically be defined by their relations to other places, by their histories, and by their individual identities; but he argues there are supermodern spaces, which really do not have these types of individual histories, relationships to other places, and specific identities. These places can include airports, supermarkets, hotel rooms, fast food restaurants, or motor ways, for example. In other words, these non-places, as he labels them, are the types of places that feel they are generally interchangeable with other such places in other environments.

Researchers looking at the experiences of transient individuals, such as migrants, use these notions to discuss the types of identities individuals adopt in relation to their circumstances. Migrants can be constructed, for example, as existing outside of the typical narratives of national identity. Hanauer (2009) examines British citizenship texts. He finds that aspects of these texts focus on notions of mobility that are linked to economics and that, in some respects, present an understanding of citizenship for immigrants that is distanced from a more typical knowledge of national life. According to Hanauer, this distinction lends itself to individuals' understandings of their non-place identities as migrants. Krzyzanowski and Wodak (2008) examine similar identity issues in relation to migrants. In this case, they examine migrants' experiences and discourses as representing a struggle for both recognition and a sense of belonging and membership. This struggle for recognition and belonging in the new country affects migrants understandings of attachments to their original home communities. Krzyzanokowski and Wodak conclude that migrants' identities are "inherently ambivalent and constantly subject to inherent and continuous change" (p. 115).

This section introduces the ideas that migration processes are complex ones affecting both individuals' self-perceptions and their constructions of their personal, linguistic, cultural, and national identities.

2.6 Doing sociolinguistics: research activities

1. Record a short conversation that involves people of different genders. Analyze the different ways that these individuals construct their genders in the interaction. Remember to get the consent of the individuals involved.

2. Find a television show that takes place in an environment where there would be experts and novices, such as doctors and patients or lawyers and clients. Analyze the ways that the writers of the show construct expert and novice identities. You could, alternatively, record an interaction that you feel represents an expert-novice relationship. Make sure, however, that you have the permission of each individual to record such interactions.

3. Find an area where you can see the effect of more than one culture merging. This could be in a particular part of the area where you live. It could be realized in signs, particular newspapers, and in the use of a variety of languages. Choose one aspect of this cultural merging to analyze how each group is constructed or co-constructed.

2.8 Suggested further reading

Briggs, C. L. (1988). *Competence in performance: The creativity of tradition in Mexicano verbal art.* Philadelphia: University of Pennsylvania Press.

Bucholtz, M., Liang, A. C., & Sutton, L. A. (Eds.). (1999). *Reinventing identities: The gendered self in discourse.* New York: Oxford University Press.

Cutler, C. (2007). The co-construction of whiteness in an MC battle. *Pragmatics, 17*(1), 9–22.

French, B. M. (2001). The symbolic capital of social identities: The genre of bargaining in an urban Guatemalan market. *Journal of Linguisitic Anthropology, 10*(2), 155–189.

Gaudio, R. (1997). Not talking straight in Hausa. In A. Livia & K. Hall (Eds.), *Queerly phrased, language, gender, and sexuality* (pp. 416–429). New York: Oxford University Press.

Hall, K., & Bucholtz, M. (1995). *Gender articulated: Language and the socially constructed self.* New York: Routledge.

Jacoby, S., & Gonzales, P. (1991). The constitution of expert-novice in scientific discourse. *Issues in Applied Linguistics, 2*(2), 149–181.

Jacoby, S., & Ochs, E. (1995). Co-construction: An introduction. *Research on Language & Social Interaction, 23*(3), 171–183.

Livia, A., & Hall, K. (Eds.). (1997). *Queerly phrased: Language, gender, and sexuality.* New York: Oxford University Press.

Owens, T. J. (2003). Self and identity. In J. D. DeLamater (Ed.), *Handbook of social psychology* (pp. 205–232). New York: Kluwwer Academic/Plenum Publishers.

Rampton, B. (2005). *Crossing: Language and ethnicity among adolescents.* London: Longman.

Sacks, H. (1992). *Lectures on conversation.* Oxford: Blackwell.

Schiffrin, D. (1996). Narrative as self-portrait: Sociolinguistic constructions of identity. *Language in Society, 25*(2), 167–203.

3 Language Variation

Key Terms: *language varieties; observer's paradox; intraspeaker variation; interspeaker variation; social capital; language change; diachronic change; synchronic change; language contact; intensity of contact; pidgin; creole; Lingua Franca; diglossia; code-switching; ethnolect*

3.1 Language variation

This chapter provides an overview of language variation and its relation to a wide range of sociolinguistic issues. We begin the chapter by looking at early variationists' work and examine their analyses of sociolinguistic patterns that led to new understandings of how language varied, not only by dialect, but also by variables such as age, gender, and social class, to name a few. We also include a look at how these early sociolinguists collected and analyzed their data. We then move to a discussion of variation and examine the notions of standard and non-standard language within a wide range of linguistic contexts. We provide an analysis of how variation is related to language change. In looking at change, we examine language contact and the linguistic and social results of that contact.

3.1.1 Labov and the early variationists

Language variation began as soon as groups of people moved far enough away from one another, socially, or geographically, for their young generations of speakers to develop their languages independently from the young people in the other groups. The groups might begin to pronounce their words slightly differently, create different sets of new words, even eventually develop different sentence patterns. With enough time and distance, of course, the groups' languages might become distinct enough to be unintelligible to other groups. Now we may label these as separate languages. According to *Ethnologue: Languages of the World*, there are 6,909 living languages in the world (Anderson, 2004). Most languages also have a number of different varieties. Consider English, for example. There are differences between the Englishes of Great Britain, Canada, the United States, and any number of other major varieties of the language in other English speaking countries. Even within a given country, there are different varieties of English. These different Englishes and varieties, however, are not held in equal social standing due to centuries of history, and in some cases, the effects of colonialism. People are very aware that the way people use language varies from place to place and from social group to social group, and this awareness is part of our understanding of identity. People hold personal preferences for some varieties over others, although from a linguistic perspective, they are equally well formed. In fact, as we will discuss in this chapter, an intrinsic aspect of studying language use is analyzing the attitudes individuals and groups hold toward particular language varieties.

The study of sociolinguistics began as a pursuit to understand language variation and its relationship with the social life of the language users. In the United States, the work of William Labov is typically considered the beginning of sociolinguistics in its classic, narrow definition. His work, however, was not the first work to look at variation in languages. Dialectologists such as André Martinet, Sever Pop, and Uriel Weinreich, among many others, studied sociolinguistic patterns of language use in a variety of sociolinguistic domains (Gumperz & Cook-Gumperz, 2008; Koerner, 2002).

Labov's (1963) early sociolinguistic work was conducted on Martha's Vineyard, an island community off the coast of Massachusetts in the United States. Labov went to Martha's Vineyard to study the unique language variety that occurred there. He found a distinctive sound pattern that occurred on the island. Many people there tended to say words like *fight*, *hide*, and *sky* in a way that was different from the way many English speakers say these words. The difference was in the way that many people on Martha's Vineyard pronounced the *diphthong*. A diphthong is a vowel sound that is pronounced by quickly moving from one vowel position to another. If you say the word, *I*, in a way that begins with a very short "ah"-like sound and ends up with the "ee" sound of *see*, then you use the diphthong /ay/. This is the diphthong that many people use when they say words like *fight*, *hide*, and *sky*. If you, like those studied by Labov in Martha's Vineyard, however, say this diphthong starting in a more central position that sounds more like the "u" in "cut," and still end on the "ee" sound of see, then you use the diphthong, /əy/. In this case, the "ə," called a *schwa*, represents the "u" in "cut" sound.

Since the /a/ sound is pronounced low in the back of the mouth and the /ə/ is pronounced more toward the center of the mouth, linguists say that the /əy/ diphthong of Martha's Vineyard speakers is more *centralized* than the /ay/ of other speakers.

For many people in Martha's Vineyard, this centralization means that a word like "fight" was pronounced with the diphthong beginning with /ə/ sound and ending with /y/. This would sound something like "fueet," if you say the diphthong quickly. Labov also found that many people on Martha's Vineyard also centralized the diphthong /aw/ that you can hear in "pout" and "found" pronouncing it more like /əw/.

Labov, however, was curious to know why many people on Martha's Vineyard had this pronunciation. When he looked more carefully, he found that the centralized vowels occurred only in particular linguistic contexts. In other words, they only occurred in combination with particular consonants. For example, if the diphthong was followed by the consonant sounds /t/, /s/, /p/, or /f/, it was more likely to be centralized. In "fight" and "pout," then, the diphthongs were likely to be centralized. If, however, the vowel was followed by the consonant sounds /l/, /r/, /n/, or /m/, it was less likely to be centralized. In "pine" or "crown," then, the diphthongs were less likely to be centralized.

The story, however, does not end there. Labov considered variables such as where the individuals lived, what they did for a living, whether they lived on the island full time or part time, and, of course, their ages. What he found was that the people with centralized diphthongs were typical of people who lived in rural areas of the island full time, who typically fished as their profession, and who were in their 30s and 40s. In other words, these were people who lived and worked on the island and took pride in being from the island community. Their way of talking made them stand out as individuals who sounded uniquely like people from Martha's Vineyard. Although Labov did not discuss these language sounds as markers of identity, we can see that individuals who used these sounds constructed themselves as valid members of the island community. Their language constructed their identities as people who came from the island.

It is also interesting that Martha's Vineyard has been the site of studies of bilingualism as well. In this case, due to the high numbers of individuals who were born deaf due to hereditary patterns, (Groce, 1985) a large number of people in Martha's Vineyard, particularly in the more rural areas, were bilingual in English and in the local sign language. Sign language, like any other language, shows variation. There are variations in relation to geographic area, age, race, gender, and particular schools (Swisher, 1989). Although as Lucas, Bayley, Valli, et al. (2001) note, there is not yet a complete understanding of all of the units that may vary in American Sign Language, for example, or of how these variations interact with other variables such as age, race, and gender. Variation in sign languages can be see in relation to a number of linguistic units, including lexical, phonological, morphological, and syntactic units. In a study of how gestures can be used to accompany signed language story telling, Quinto-Pozos and Mehta (2010) examined the variation of gestures across settings and audiences. They found that these gestures that accompanied constructed action stories occurred across all of the registers they examined, including formal registers, but that there was variation by setting and audience. Essentially they found how the different body parts used to support constructed action patterned differently across audiences and settings (p. 577).

3.1 Doing Sociolinguistics: Thought Exploration

How is your language different, for example, when you are talking to your professor in office hours than when you are talking to your friends?

In this section, we have looked at some of the earliest work in sociolinguistics. We have seen how this early work made connections between language use and social life. Though much of this early work, such as that done by Labov, did not explicitly discuss identity, we can see that his early work paved the way for modern discussions on the connection between language and identity. In looking at this early sociolinguistic work, we've discussed examples from Martha's Vineyard. In particular, we've looked at how Martha's Vineyard has been the site of sociolinguistic studies of variation. And finally, we've examined how this community has also provided examples of variation in sign language as well.

3.1.2 Early variationist sociolinguistics, data collection, and analysis

At this point, you might be wondering how these early sociolinguists collected their data. The usual method for collecting data was for the researcher to conduct a sociolinguistic interview. Sociolinguists were interested in collecting examples of peoples' day-to-day speech. The difficulty was that in conducting these interviews, sociolinguists were creating a situation that was not typical in people's daily lives and which affected the formality of the speech they used. Labov called this the *observer's paradox*. The observer is trying to observe everyday speech, but the researchers' presence meant that people changed their speech for the situation. This means that researchers had to create different ways of interviewing. They assumed that when participants were paying attention to the quality of their speech, they were more likely to monitor their speech, which resulted in a more formal speech sample. They found, for example, that eliciting speech read out loud produced the most monitored, formal speech sample. However, asking people to talk about very emotionally laden moments in their lives, such as times when they almost died or times when they got into a fight produced a much more day-to-day level of speech. Researchers realized that when people became emotionally involved in talking about these sorts of topics, they were less likely to monitor their language and more likely to speak informally. Questions asking people about times when they had almost died or when they had been in a fight seemed to allow people to become involved in their stories and engage in the more informal language the researchers were hoping to collect. In this way, the type of question had an effect on the observer's paradox.

Early variationist work was usually quantitative in its orientation. It was typical to look for variables, such as the vowel sounds of Martha's Vineyard, and to identify their variants. To do this, Labov and others doing sociolinguistics engaged in variable rules analysis. This kind of analysis was designed to determine the probability of the use of a particular linguistic feature taking linguistic and social context into account. The mathematicians, Henrietta Cedergren and David Sankoff (1974) and Sankoff (1978) developed a computer program, VARBRUL, that allowed quantitative sociolinguists to carry out variable rules analysis quite easily.

This program, and its counterpart Goldvarb, can be used to find relationships among independent variable and a range of dependent variables. Norma Mendoza-Denton (2008), for example, examined the variation in the language used by two specific groups of Latina high school girls' group affiliations; Norteñas and Sureñas. In particular, she examined their use of various vowel sounds. She used ten independent and one dependent variable group to determine the relationships between, among other things, speaker individuation, social affiliation, realization of the phoneme, the preceding and following phonological segment, as well as phrase-level and topic-level code-switching. After running the Goldvarb program and analyzing the results of the step up and step down regression processes, she found that the girls from the two groups used language in very particular ways. She also found that as girls move their affiliation from one group to another, they shift their pronunciation to more closely match the pronunciation patterns of their target groups. Mendoza-Denton found that the particular way in which the girls spoke marked their membership in a particular group. This work shows that the variables in interactions can be very complex as individuals construct particular identities.

3.2 Doing Sociolinguistics: Thought Exploration

Consider your own language use. Come up with some words that you use that are connected to your affiliation with particular groups. Also, consider what your variety sounds like. Do you recognize other people as from your home area based on the way that they sound? Which particular sounds help you make the distinction?

In this section, we have discussed early work in sociolinguistics. We have seen that early sociolinguists recognized the observer's paradox and developed ways to collect data in sociolinguistic interviews, which could be designed to elicit speech at different levels of formality. Early sociolinguistic work tended to be quantitative in orientation, analyzing variables to determine their patterns of use.

3.1.3 Language variation and social life

In looking at the way that people speak, we can talk about *interspeaker variation*: the ways that people speak differently from one another. The Martha's Vineyard study of vowel sounds, for example, looked at interspeaker variation. We should note, however, that we can also see *intraspeaker* variation as well. This variation can be seen in the ways that single individuals speak in different ways in the various social and linguistic contexts of their lives. For instance, the sociolinguistic interviews that we discussed earlier considered intraspeaker variation in terms of whether people read aloud or were asked the danger-of-death or been-in-a fight types of questions. It was assumed that their language would vary in formality according to the level of monitoring that they engaged in. The level of formality of speech affects the sounds, vocabulary, and grammatical structure of what is said. For instance, in a formal utterance, an individual might say a greeting as, "Hello. How are you?" In an informal greeting, the same individual might say, "Hey. How's it goin'?" People don't speak in exactly the same way all the time. Our language variation is determined by the social situation. We use particular varieties in conjunction with the person we are talking to, the topic, the setting, and even our mood.

As you read in Chapter 2, language variation is one of the ways that people construct their identities through language. The fact that there are various ways of speaking has important implications for identity construction. For example, in Chapters 6 and 7, we will look at the relationship between language variation and constructions of power.

In this section, we have discussed the fact that both interspeaker and intraspeaker variation occur. We discussed the link between language variation, identity construction, and constructions of power.

3.2 Language varieties: standard and non-standard language

Society has created different values for different varieties of language labeling some of them as standard and some as non-standard. Standard and non-standard language labels, however, are not linguistic labels. They are social labels. Languages that are constructed as the standard variety of any given language exist all over the world. From a linguistic standpoint, these standard varieties are no more fully developed or well formed than any other variety.

Lippi-Green (1997a) has written about the "standard language myth." In her work, she presents the myth of standard U.S. English as the language that is spoken and written by persons

- who have no regional accent;
- who reside in the Midwest, far west, or perhaps some parts of the northeast (but never in the south);

- with more than average or superior education;
- who are themselves educators or broadcasters;
- who pay attention to speech, and are not sloppy in terms of pronunciation or grammar;
- who are easily understood by all;
- who enter into a consensus of other individuals like themselves about what is proper in language (p. 58)

Lippi-Green labels the notion of a standard language a "myth" because it does not actually exist. There is, for example, no such thing as unaccented language. All language speakers have an accent, even sign languages can be said to have accents (Lucas, et al., 2001). The point is that some people's language is socially constructed as sounding "normal" and others' language by default is constructed as sounding "accented." It is also possible to take the list above and use its opposite to more fully understand the biases inherent in the use of a standard language. The notion, or myth, of a standard language is used by some people to pass certain kinds of judgments on the language of others.

The notion of a standard language is maintained in part because it is normatively enforced by the educational system. Blommaert (2005) affirms that children from elite backgrounds typically control the standard language, and the educational system systematically attributes higher value to the standard language (p. 13). A clear function of the written system of languages is to enforce or sustain standardization (Milroy & Lesley, 1985). The maintenance of a standard language provides for the social production and reproduction of linguistic capital for people who are invested in it. As Lippi-Green puts it, "The myth of a standard language exists because it is carefully tended and propagated. Individuals acting for a larger social group take it upon themselves to control and limit spoken language variation, the most basic and fundamental of human socialization tools" (2007a, p. 59).

In some countries, there are even particular academies that have been legally established to protect the standard language. Consider for example, the Real Academia Española or the Académie Française whose purpose is to maintain a particular version of Spanish and French respectively. As these academies show, while there is nothing linguistically superior about standard language, it is socially constructed as superior.

Since the notion of a standard is socially constructed, we should be able to see it functioning as individuals use it in particular ways. This is, indeed, the case. Reyes-Rodríguez (2008), for example, examined how politicians' control of standardized varieties of Spanish provided them with legitimacy, social capital (Bourdieu & Nice, 1980), and finally "authority" in their political speeches.

As seen in Reyes-Rodríguez's work, the idea that standard languages are social constructions, then, means that their use has social consequences. Bourdieu (1977a), examines the social economics of particular types of language use. He uses the notion of *social capital* to talk about the social consequences of particular language uses. Since the standard variety of a language is socially constructed as the language of the elite and the educated, for example, the control and use of a standard language in contexts where it is socially constructed as the proper form to use has positive social value. It represents social capital. The choice of the non-standard variety in the same circumstances can be seen as having a lower social capital. The use of varieties, however, can also signal group membership and solidarity, a different kind of social value. So the interactions between standard varieties, and the social constructions about them, are complicated by various groups' dynamics and the values that they place on their individual varieties for particular purposes.

3.3 Doing Sociolinguistics: Thought Exploration

Consider how you talk when you are interacting with family members. Is your language use exactly the same as it is when you are speaking in a presentation in class? How does this show your understandings of different linguistic contexts?

As languages, like English, become world languages, the standard and non-standard distinction and the power issues related to the distinction, become even more complicated. In this post-colonial era, these issues of standard and non-standard types of languages take on additional layers of meaning. Particular languages are no longer identified with one nation-state but can be identified with several places. English, for instance, is used worldwide as a first language. People learn it as a first language in Singapore and India, among other places. Therefore, several varieties of World Englishes have developed. In some contexts, particular varieties of English may be considered standard. However, outside of that context, the same variety is often constructed as "non-standard." For example, Indian English is normative in its use within India. However, outside of India, the variety is considered to diverge from the standard. Standard British English and Standard American English, for instance, are considered standards worldwide, though they are neither identical nor consistent among speakers, whereas Indian English is considered non-standard to some English speakers outside of India.

In this section, we have discussed concepts of standard and non-standard language. We have seen this as a social rather than a linguistic distinction. We have also looked at world language varieties in terms of how they provide a more complex understanding of these notions as socially constructed.

3.3 Language change in progress

Work in the history of languages has demonstrated that changes have occurred in languages. For instance, if we look at the history of English, it is easy to see that Old English is very different from the Englishes that are currently spoken today. As noted in Chapter 1, we can see that Shakespeare's English was different from the English of Virginia Woolf representing changes over the past 400 years or so. This does not mean, of course, that the study of language change is only a historical venture. It is also possible to see language change in progress.

Labov (2007), for instance, has shown that it is possible to see change in progress in the work that has been done on the Northern Cities Vowel Shift by a number of sociolinguists. This shift represents changes in vowel sounds in a number of cities in the northern region of the United States. Labov talks about this shift extensively in the PBS series *Do You Speak American?* In that series, he discusses one rather salient example in which a northern cities speaker says a word that to other speakers sounds like "bosses." When the word is contextualized within an utterance, "I remember the bosses with the antennas," people who do not have this vowel shift might have a difficult time figuring out this utterance taken out of its larger conversational context. However, the utterance is a clear example of the vowel shift. What sounds something like "bosses" here is actually "busses." For these speakers, the vowel in bus, /ə/—that schwa sound we saw in the example of Martha's Vineyard—which is typically made in the center of the mouth has shifted to the "ah" sound in boss. In this shift their word "boss" has also changed sound. In a longer conversational context, speakers from these regions are clearly understood, of course. They are just typically perceived as having an accent from that region. What is important to understand about vowel shifts is that they are patterned.

Eckert (2000a) explored how social identity was constructed in a Detroit suburban high school, Belten High, located in a northern city that is part of the area in which the Northern Cities Vowel shift can be seen. She examined the language of high school students and considered how they used these vowel sounds as part of the way that they distinguished themselves as part of different high school social groups: the "jocks," the "burnouts," and the "in-betweeners."

Eckert notes that one important finding of her study was an understanding of the small extent to which the speech of Belten High students reflected their parents' socioeconomic characteristics. She identified two major variables that could be used to define the difference she saw in the speech of these student groups. One of these variables was gender, and the other was the students' group affiliation. This means, that while Eckert examined a number of speech variables, such as (aeh) raising, (o) fronting, (oh fronting), (e) backing, and (ay) monophthongizing, to name a few, what she found was that some of these categories of change correlated with gender, such as the (aeh) raising and the (o) fronting, while others such as (e) backing correlated with group affiliation. Some, of course, correlated with both gender and group affiliation. Eckert's work shows that the language change in progress in the larger community can be used in different ways by different groups to distinguish themselves and their group memberships.

3.5 Doing Sociolinguistics: Thought Exploration

Consider how you talk as compared with how your grandparents talk. Which linguistic features differ between you and your grandparents, or other older members of your family? These could include sounds, vocabulary, or grammatical constructions.

In this section, we have discussed the fact that it is possible to see change in progress and that these processes are patterned. The types of changes that give any region its trademark accent are really the result of certain types of language changes. Essentially, where there is variation, there is change.

3.4 Language contact and language change

Situations in which languages come into contact with each other arise all over the world. In fact, language contact is a major factor in language change. At this point, we will discuss language contact *diachronically*, across time, including how it contributes to language change as well as *synchronically*, at a given time, including the social implications of language contact. *Language contact* is a term that refers to a situation in which language users within a particular geographic area are exposed to more than one language variety in their daily lives. Such language contact can be high intensity, meaning that speakers of languages in contact have many opportunities to engage in social interaction with each other. For most speakers of signed languages, for instance, the language contact with various verbal languages is often high intensity. For example, high intensity contact between American Sign Language and American English affects the syntax of American Sign Language, among other things (Swisher, 1989).

Low intensity contact, on the other hand, describes situations in which speakers of languages in contact do not have many opportunities to engage in social interaction with one another. The intensity of the contact is very important in understanding the implications of language contact. As you can probably imagine, situations of high intensity language contact often result in more extreme shifts, such as pidginization (see the discussion in section 3.4.1). Low intensity contact, conversely, often results in less extreme shifts. Duration of contact is also an important determinant of how the contact situation influences language change. In situations of high intensity contact that continue for long periods of time, new varieties may emerge. In situations of low intensity contact that last for a short duration, there may be no shift or very little shift, such as the adoption of a few loanwords.

3.6 Doing Sociolinguistics: A Thought Exploration

Consider varieties in contact in the region in which you live. What is the duration, intensity? How have the various varieties spoken in your region been affected by contact with other varieties?

In the Southwestern region of the United States, Spanish and English have been in contact for centuries. This is a situation of long duration of contact. However, the intensity of the contact between English and Spanish in this region is variable. In some cases, the contact is high intensity. Intensity of contact can also include socioeconomic and often political pressure on one of the contact language groups to shift to the other language (Paredes & Valdes, 2008). For instance, for most primary Spanish speakers in the Southwestern United States, contact with English is high intensity, although higher intensity for some than for others. For primary English speakers in the United States, on the other hand, contact with Spanish is likely to be low intensity, though lower intensity for some than for others.

There are several results of this contact, depending on the intensity of the contact. The long duration, yet low intensity of contact with Spanish has resulted in the use of Spanish loanwords in English. In many cases, since the words have been incorporated into the English language for such a long period of time, they take on English phonological characteristics. For instance, the word "patio" is a loanword from Spanish, but its pronunciation, /pærio/, follows the rules of the English sound system. English words have been borrowed into Spanish as well. Again, because of the long duration of the contact between Spanish and English, the loanwords often take on the phonological characteristics of Spanish. It is not uncommon to hear Spanish speakers in the Southwestern United States say "parquiar" for "park" as in "park the car."

However, "parquiar" takes on Spanish morphology as we can see as well as Spanish phonology as it is pronounced /parkiar/. This is evidence that "parquiar" is a relatively new borrowing into Spanish. It is typical for borrowings to be adapted to the language that they are borrowed into.

In any contact situation, there is a power dynamic that results in a hierarchical differentiation between languages. In the Southwest United States, English is the language of power. It is higher in the power hierarchy than Spanish is. Because of this, Spanish speaking children in the Southwest United States learn English when they begin school. English is the language of the elite, of education, of power. In situations in which Spanish speaking families immigrate to the United States, this power differential leads to Spanish language use diminishing the longer families live in the United States. The first generation of Spanish speaking immigrants might be primarily Spanish speaking. However, by the third generation, the family is often monolingual English speaking. Therefore, the contact with Spanish becomes lower intensity through the generations.

The story, however, is often more complex than that. In situations of high intensity contact, it is not unusual for new language varieties to form. Let's consider the case of New York Spanish. Otheguy, Zentella, and Livert (2007) demonstrate that New York Spanish speakers' participation in various speech communities in their daily lives has led to the formation of a new New York Spanish speech community. Otheguy et al. (2007) focused on the variable use of subject pronouns in the language variety associated with the New York Spanish speech community. The corpus of language use that they collected came from people born and raised in New York with familial origins in six Latin American countries as well as newcomers to New York from the same six Latin American countries. One finding is that the second generation New Yorkers used more overt subject pronouns when speaking Spanish. Note that Spanish is a language in which the subject pronoun can be dropped. In English, the subject pronoun is obligatory, or overt. The following sentences in English and Spanish demonstrate the difference.

English: I eat fish.
Spanish: Como pescado

In Spanish, the morphological marker –o indicates that the verb is first person singular. English, on the other hand, has no morphological marker to distinguish first person singular. The overt subject pronoun makes the distinction. However, for the second generation New York Spanish speakers, contact with English has made it more likely that New York Spanish speakers will include the overt subject pronoun, so that "I eat fish" would be "Yo como pescado" with the overt first person singular subject pronoun, "yo."

New York Spanish is also characterized by the contact between Spanish speakers from different countries. The result is the formation of a New York Spanish that combines features of the various Spanish dialects used within the city. Clearly, high intensity contact is a driver of dramatic shifts in the way that people use language. Another interesting finding that Otheguy et al. discussed is the fact that Caribbean Spanish speakers in New York tend to shift in the direction of the more prestigious Spanish spoken by Spanish speakers from the mainland. In contact situations, the power relationships between languages can have an important impact on language development at the societal level.

3.7 Doing Sociolinguistics: Thought Exploration

Consider the language varieties that you encounter on a daily basis. Can you identify any instances of one language or variety affecting another? How do the linguistic features associated with these language varieties influence one another?

In this section, we have considered how language contact impacts language change. We have seen that these types of contact are often mediated by issues such as duration, intensity of contact, and power hierarchies. We have also seen that language contact can result in the formation of entire new varieties, as was the case with New York Spanish.

3.4.1 Pidgins and creoles

One of the dramatic shifts that occurs as a result of high intensity contact is the development of pidgin and creole languages. A pidgin language develops when groups of people who speak different languages have a relatively sudden need to communicate with each other. Historically, a major driver for the development of pidgin languages has been economic. Groups of people who speak different languages yet need to engage in economic exchange with each other must find a way of communicating. These instances, then, become ripe for the development of pidgins.

Pidgins become Lingua Francas within the regions where they are spoken. We can define a Lingua Franca as a common language that people who come from different language backgrounds use in communication with each other. Lingua Francas can be languages other than pidgins. For instance, English is considered a Lingua Franca in certain parts of the world, including India, Nigeria, and Singapore. English is often used as a Lingua Franca for international business, science, and technology, and it is almost always the Lingua Franca for aviation.

It makes sense that pidgins tend to become Lingua Francas because they develop in response to the need for a Lingua Franca. They develop when people who speak different languages come into contact and have a typically economic incentive to communicate with each other.

Interestingly, all pidgins share some common features. For instance, all pidgins are formed when features of at least two languages combine. One important factor in the formation of pidgin languages is the fact that the contributor languages combine in such a way that the language or languages of the more powerful group or groups usually provide much of the lexicon, or vocabulary. In relation to the pidgin, then, the language that provides the lexicon is called the *superstratum*. The language or languages of the less powerful group usually become the syntactic, morphological, and phonological elements of the pidgin. They are called the *substratum* of the pidgin. Therefore, the languages that contribute to the formation of the pidgin are in a superstrate-substrate relationship. The superstratum languages are the lexifiers, and the substratum languages are donors of syntactic, morphological, and phonological structure to the pidgin.

Another crucial characteristic of all pidgins is that no one is a first language user of a pidgin language. All users of pidgin languages speak another language or languages as their first language. They are, then, second language users of pidgin. This is always the case because pidgins develop when people who already speak other languages need to communicate in economic transactions. Pidgins are not the language of the home and family. They are the language of business and trade.

Scholars often refer to pidgins as simplified languages (Romaine, 1999). However, this classification may have more to do with the fact that pidgins are used in limited contexts, such as in particular kinds of trade. Users of pidgins are multilinguals who have multiple linguistic resources available to them in their daily lives. It may be that people only use the pidgin for trade purposes, but they use other varieties for their other life functions. The fact that the pidgin is used for such limited communicative needs would contribute to it having a simpler structure and fewer vocabulary words than linguistic varieties that meet a wider array of communicative needs.

Pidgins, like any other linguistic varieties, meet the communicative needs of their speakers. When they fail to meet those needs, they become expanded. Pidgins typically begin with a *jargon phase*. During this jargon phase, there is quite a bit of individual variation in the use of the pidgin, and pidgin varieties are quite simplified in their structure and contain quite reduced vocabularies at this stage. As the pidgin becomes the wholesale linguistic variety for people engaged in economic activity, there comes to be less individual variation and more standard grammatical, phonological, and lexical features. This is termed the stable pidgin phase. Stable pidgins often have reduced vocabularies, sounds, and grammars. However, as pidgins come to be used in more contexts in people's daily lives, they become expanded grammatically, phonologically, and lexically. This is the expanded pidgin phase. People who use pidgins are capable of adapting these varieties so that they can meet their communicative needs. It is highly unusual to see societal linguistic varieties that are not well suited to the communicative needs of the people who use those varieties.

Scholars often differentiate pidgins and creoles with the distinction that creole languages develop when children of pidgin users begin to use the pidgin as their first language. However, in multilingual societies, this can be difficult to decipher. Children in multilingual societies may use the pidgin from early childhood or they may not, depending on the languages that their families use in the home. However, one crucial element seems to exist as a variety moves from expanded pidgin to creole, which is that the variety comes to be used in more contexts in daily life. It becomes a means by which people construct identities, not only for economic purposes, but also for the purposes of building personal relationships and providing cohesion for a speech community. As the variety comes to be used in more nuanced and complex human ways in people's daily lives, the variety itself becomes more nuanced and complex. This often corresponds with the variety becoming the language of the home and a first language for children.

Pidgins and creoles have arisen in multiple places throughout the world. Sebba (1997) defines pidgins as being of seven types: military or police pidgins, seafaring and trade pidgins and creoles, plantation pidgins and creoles, mine and construction pidgins, immigrants' pidgins, tourist pidgins, and urban contact vernaculars. Sebba (1997) asserts that the first known pidgin was Sabir, a military pidgin, which was spoken among soldiers in Southern Europe during the Crusades. Sebba also lists Russenorsk, a Russian-Norwegian pidgin that developed as a seafaring and trade pidgin.

In nineteenth-century Hawai'i, a plantation pidgin, Pidgin Hawai'ian, developed. Kanahele-Stutz (2009) indicates that immigrants came to Hawai'i from China, Portugal, and several Pacific Islands. As these immigrants began to oversee plantations and as speakers of several languages labored together, they developed Pidgin Hawai'ian in response to the need for a Lingua Franca. The superstrate and lexifier was Hawai'ian. The other languages acted as substrates and contributed to the grammar and phonology of the pidgin. As Kanahele-Stutz indicates, the Hawai'ian monarchy was quite powerful in the eighteenth century, allowing the indigenous population to maintain sovereignty. Therefore, Hawai'ian language maintained a prestigious status. Sakoda and Siegel (2003, p. 6) cite examples of the difference between Pidgin Hawai'ian (PH) and Hawai'ian.

Example 3.1
PH   Kela lio oe hele hauhau lela palani wau ma ka ponei.
            (That horse you[rs] went eat that bran I [my] in the last night.)
Hawai'ian   Ua hele kou lio e 'ai i ka'u palani i ka po nei.
            (Went your horse to eat my bran [last] night.)

From this example, it seems clear that Hawai'ian is the lexifier. However, as English speakers increasingly came to Hawai'i from the mainland, English came to be used more often in eighteenth-century Hawai'i. It, too, became a substrate in a changing Pidgin Hawai'ian. As Kanahele-Stutz (2009, p. 20) explains it, the overthrow of the Hawai'ian monarchy by American business people (assisted by American marines) led to English replacing Hawai'ian as the official language in 1896. These events dealt a blow to Hawai'ian sovereignty and eventually to Hawai'ian identity. Pidgin Hawai'ian gave way to Pidgin English. By the mid- twentieth century, the variety was no longer known as a pidgin but as Hawai'ian Creole English. Kanahele-Stutz provides an example of Hawai'ian Creole English from a Hawai'ian concert-goer in 2009 (p. 22)

Example 3.2: Modern Day Hawai'ian Creole English
Eh, you bettah watchyo mowt, yo maddah goeen geev you
likens if she catchyou talkeen Pidgin laidat.
(Hey, you had better watch your mouth, your mother is going to give you physical punishment if she catches you talking Pidgin like that.)

Hawai'ian Creole English was born out of colonization. Kanahele-Stutz conducted a survey among Hawai'ians living in the mainland United States. She found that Hawai'ian Creole English is an important identity marker for Hawai'ians. Its use allows Hawai'ian people living in the mainland United States to form a group identity as "Hawai'ians living on the mainland." However, they also consider Hawai'ian Creole English to be inferior. They find its use in schools, government, and professional contexts to be inappropriate. As such, a colonized indigenous Hawai'i remains and is indexed through the use of Hawai'ian Creole English.

3.8 Doing Sociolinguistics: Thought Exploration

Consider how colonization has led to the formation of other language varieties besides Hawai'ian Creole English. What do people's attitudes toward these varieties tend to be? How do these attitudes reflect the prestige that these varieties carry?

In this section, we have looked at the development of pidgins as a result of high intensity contact. We have also discussed the distinction between pidgin and creole languages as being rooted in the range of communicative uses. Finally, we discussed the development of Hawai'ian Creole English, and its present day importance of an identity marker for Hawai'ians.

3.4.2 Multilingualism

The contact situations discussed in section 3.2.1 are the result of societal multilingualism. Most places in the world exhibit societal multilingualism. People who live in multilingual societies are multicompetent. *Multicompetence* is a term that refers to multilinguals' ability to use more than one language (Cook, 1991, 1992, 1999). One of the important realizations that has come out of work in multilingual communities is reconceptualization of what it means to be a native speaker of a language (Canagarajah, 2007, among others). The term becomes irrelevant in multilingual contexts for several reasons. First, there may be a case in which a person learned several languages from birth. However, for identity purposes, that person may associate most with one language in some contexts of use and with other languages in other contexts of use.

The slippery nature of the native speaker construct is especially clear in the literature on Lingua Franca English. Though it may be the case that nativized varieties of English, such as American, British, Indian, and Singaporean English, are used as Lingua Francas in particular contexts, Lingua Franca English refers to situations of societal use of English as a second language. Seidlhofer (2001, 2004) argues for a "conceptual space" for Lingua Franca English so that it can be studied in its own right, not just in terms of how it deviates from standard Englishes. As Seidlhofer argues it is not necessary to define second language users of English as learners. Instead they can be categorized as competent users of Lingua Franca English.

As Canagarajah (2007) asserts, there are currently more users of English as a second language than there are users of English as a first language. In these global uses of English as a second language, English is a contact language, which speakers of other languages use to communicate with people world-wide. The purpose of communication could be professional needs, such as business transactions, academic publication, and aviation. However, the purpose could also be related to one's personal interests, including online gaming, blogging, and tweeting. The use of Lingua Franca English may be face-to-face or it may be written, but Lingua Franca English is not contained within a particular region. Canagarajah refers to it as a *virtual speech community*. Users of Lingua Franca English, then, share a particular kind of communicative competence. This competence cannot be predefined, however, as it is a shifting competence that is dependent on its context of use. Users of Lingua Franca English are adept at negotiating the appropriate forms of the language to use in order to effectively communicate with their interlocutors. Users of Lingua Franca English, like multilinguals more generally, are highly adaptable and adept at employing aspects of their communicative repertoire that meet their communicative needs.

Multilinguals are generally able to understand which language code to employ with particular interlocutors at any one time. In multilingual societies, language is fluid and shifting to meet the needs of everyday situations. This is very different from monolingual ideology in which language is seen as static and monolithic. According to Canagarajah (2007), multilinguals have the advantage of being more interactionally adaptable in communicative situations. Monolinguals tend to view their linguistic resources as static and as residing within the individual. Multilinguals, conversely, tend to align their linguistic resources to meet the communicative need at hand and to construct their identities. This idea of using linguistic resources to meet communicative needs is illustrated in multilinguals' ability to employ different varieties in different domains, in their ability to code-switch, and in the use of ethnolects.

3.9 Doing Sociolinguistics: Thought Exploration

Consider situations in which you have interacted with someone whose accent is substantially different from your own. How adept are you at negotiating communication in these situations? Do you come from a monolingual or a multilingual background? How do you think that background affects your ability to communicate in such situations?

In this section, we have discussed a re-imagining of multilingualism as multicompetence in order to make clear that people who know more than one language are not limited but that they can use more than one language. We have also shown that multilingualism can lead to the development of Lingua Francas. Finally, we talked about the fact that multicompetent language users are highly adept at communicating with people who come from different backgrounds and use language in different ways than they do.

3.4.3 Domains and diglossia

Multilingual people typically use their various languages in distinct domains in their daily lives. In order to construct an insider identity, multilingual people have know to when, where, and with whom to use the various language codes that they control. Early research on domains of multilingual language use was conducted within the framework of diglossia (Fishman, 1967). This early work conceptualized the different languages that multilinguals use as being in a hierarchical status relationship. Particular varieties that multi-linguals used were labeled as highly valued (H), while others were deemed as lowly valued (L). The H varieties were considered to be those that were used in "official" contexts, such as educational contexts and governmental offices. The L varieties were considered to be those that were used for "unofficial" purposes, such as communications among intimates and communications on the street. These H and L varieties were described by researchers, such as Fishman, as being in a diglossic relationship since they were used in distinct, separate domains in the daily life of the multilingual. The H variety is typically the colonizing language, such as English or Spanish. The L variety is typically the language of the indigenous people of the area.

More recent research still asserts that multilinguals use their different varieties in distinct, separate contexts. However, modern understandings of multilingual language use complexify the H and L distinction. Modern research on multilingual communities demonstrates that this is a shifting distinction, which is dependent on the context of language use. Messing (2007) illustrates the contextual nature of highly and lowly valued varieties through her study of Mexicano (also known as Nahtual)-Spanish bilingualism in central Mexico. Among the group of Mexicano-Spanish bilinguals that she studied, Spanish is considered to be a public language, while Mexicano is considered to be a private language. Spanish is highly valued for use in public contexts, such as public meetings and school. However, Spanish is lowly valued and Mexicano is highly valued in private contexts of language use in which all participants are users of Mexicano. For this reason, attempts to introduce Mexicano into the school context have been met with some resistance by indigenous Mexicano language users. For them, Mexicano is highly valued as a private language, not as a public language. An ideological preference has evolved among this multilingual population for the use of Spanish in public domains and the use of Mexicano in private domains. It is not uncommon in multilingual societies for the colonizing language to take on high public value and for the indigenous language to take on high private value.

3.10 Doing Sociolinguistics: Thought Exploration

Think about languages in contact in your area. Which varieties are highly valued and for what purposes? Which varieties are lowly valued and for what purposes?

In this section, we have discussed the fact that languages in contact can be in a diglossic relationship, which means that there is a highly valued variety and a lowly valued variety that are used in distinct domains in daily life. However, we have also complicated the story by demonstrating that the terms highly valued and lowly valued are relative and shifting.

3.4.4 Code-switching and mixing

Code-switching has been defined as two or more languages spoken interchangeably by the interactants within the same text, whether written or spoken (Bamiro, 2006; de Klerk, 2006; Heller, 1992; Myers-Scotton, 1993). Bamiro (2006) explained that "code-switching is used to mark identity, solidarity, region, exclusion from an in-group membership, status manipulation, and social and communicative distance" (p. 30). In the same vein, Panayiotou (2004), studying the effects that "switching codes" exerts on the speakers' emotions, argued that certain experiences can occur only within the context of a specific language. Code-switching is an interactional resource in multilingual contexts that allows multilingual people to most readily build relationships and mutual understanding (Auer, 2005) in interaction with each other. Halmari and Smith (1994), for example, demonstrate the code-switching that occurs between two Finnish-English bilingual girls living in the United States. As the girls played with dolls together, they were able to contextualize whether they were in direction giving mode or in the midst of play. Directions, such as "now we'll pretend grandmother is talking to mother," were given in Finnish. On the other hand, the actual play, pretending that the grandmother was talking to the mother, took place in English. The two girls were easily able to know which mode of talk they were in because of their ability to code-switch.

Code-switching is a prevalent feature of most productive multilingual communities. In multilingual contexts, the use of multiple languages and code-switching has been referred to as third space (Bhabha, 1994; Bhatt, 2008). In this third space, code-switching allows for a unique construction of meaning and identity because for multilinguals, different languages are differently suited to different expressions of experience. Example 3.3, from Bhatt (2008, p. 191), presents an extract from an advertisement for Coca Cola in India.

Example 3.3
Just add Santa Claus
And you'll never know
Summers hit New Delhi.
Fun 'n' food presents its summer long Snow Theme
Life ho to aisi! (Life should be like this!)
Coca Cola

Bhatt argues that this advertisement indexes a third space, as discussed in Chapter 2. It indexes the very hot summers of the local context, New Delhi, intermixed with a global symbol, Santa Claus. The advertisement then switches to Hindi (*Life ho to aisi!*), mixing the global language, English, with the local language, Hindi. This advertisement only makes sense within the local context among multilinguals who participate in both the global and the local context. The hybridization, as Bhatt calls it, forms a new social world. The people who live in this social world are both global and local. They are users of Hindi and of English. The two languages used together allow the construction of identities and meanings that are connected to participation within that social world.

3.11 Doing Sociolinguistics: Thought Exploration

In your experience, when have you encountered code-switching and mixing? How do people feel about it? Do they look down on it as an inferior way of talking? Do they take pride in their ability to switch between languages? How aware do they seem to be that there are switches between languages?

In this section, we have discussed code-switching and mixing as a societal-level phenomenon. We have shown that code-switching and mixing are used in ways that reflect a unique social world.

3.4.5 Ethnolects

Ethnolects are language varieties that are used in multilingual communities by members of particular ethnic groups who come from a particular language background. Majewicz (1996) claims that at minimum, there are 20 different ethnic groups in Poland and that these various ethnic groups use language varieties associated with their ethnicity. In that sense, their language variety indexes their ethnic identity. Majewicz (1996) details the Kashubs, an ethnic group from the Kashuby region of Poland, which is located in Northern Poland along the Baltic Sea. The Kashubians distinguish themselves as a separate ethnic group but also align with the Polish nation-state, considering themselves both Polish and Kashubian. Much of what distinguishes these individuals as Kashubian is the use of the Kashubian ethnolect. This is an ethnolect with ancient roots. The Kashubians are descended from the Pomeranians, who inhabited the area along the Baltic Sea in the early middle ages. Therefore, the Kashubians are a historically embedded people. Their ethnolect has surely developed and changed, but some Kashubian language variety has existed for a long time. At this point, the Kashubian ethnolect is endangered. The children became embarrassed to speak it because of its relatively low status. The Kashubians are traditionally farming, rural people without a lot of economic prestige. When the children stop using the ethnolect, the ethnolect becomes in danger of death.

Other ethnolects, on the other hand, are quite new and vital. One example is the language of the Maltese population in Australia as discussed by Bovingdon (2004). Maltese immigrants in Australia have developed a new ethnolect, Maltraljan, which is used by Maltese-Australians. As Bovingdon explains it, as soon as people who spoke standard Maltese emigrated to Australia, they laid the way to the formation of a new ethnolect. This is because they became part of a new linguistic ecology. British English and Italian were in contact with and influenced Maltese in Malta. In Australia, the linguistic ecology was different. Bovingdon asserts, ". . . while still retaining their British English and Italianate language structures, Australian English and the new social environment take over and the process of development of a new ethnolect begins" (p. 173). Maltraljan has been formally legitimized in many ways, as it is used for media broadcast and for print publications instead of standard Maltese in Australia.

Chicano English in the United States (see Fought, 2006) developed when second and third generation Mexican immigrants formed their own variety. Some second and third generation immigrants from Mexico in the United States do not speak the immigrant language, Spanish, like their parents or grandparents do. In many cases, they become monolingual speakers of standard American English. In other cases, these children of immigrants begin to use Chicano English, an ethnic variety that is mutually intelligible for speakers of standard American English, yet is sufficiently different. The use of Chicano English marks an identity as a Mexican-American.

3.12 Doing Sociolinguistics: Thought Exploration

Consider the relationship between ethnolects and identity. How does an ethnolect serve as a marker of identity?

In this section, we have looked at the formation of ethnolects. We have seen that in some cases, ethnolects become legitimized as evidenced through their use in the mass media. In other cases, however, these varieties are given low societal status.

3.5 Doing sociolinguistics: research activities

1. Develop 8–10 questions related to how people think they index facets of identity through their language use. Interview about five of your classmates and analyze how they talk about indexing facets of their identity through language.
2. Consider when you hear standard and non-standard varieties in public forums, like the media. Analyze the types of spaces that display or use standard language and the kinds of spaces that display or use non-standard language. Analyze what the differentiation you find says about their social constructions. Remember to consider the importance of context.
3. Develop a survey in which you create 8–10 questions to explore people's attitudes toward a particular ethnic variety. Survey 10–15 people to gain a range of responses. Be careful to avoid yes/no questions. Try to make sure that your questions are not leading questions.

3.6 Suggested further reading

Bourdieu, P. (1977). The economics of linguistic exchanges. *Social Science Information, 16,* 645–668.

Canagarajah, S. (2007). Lingua Franca English, multilingual communities, and language acquisition. *The Modern Language Journal, 91*(Focal Issue), 923–939.

Eckert, P. (2000). *Linguistic variation as social practice.* Oxford: Blackwell Publishers.

Fishman, J. (1967). Bilingualism with and without diglossia: Diglossia with and without bilingualism. *Journal of Social Issues*, *23*(2), 29–38.

Fought, C. (2006). *Language and ethnicity*. Cambridge: Cambridge University Press.

Labov, W. (1963). The social motivation of a sound change. *Word*, *19*, 273–209.

Labov, W. (2007). Transmission and diffusion. *Language*, *83*(2), 344–387.

Lippi-Green, R. (1997). *English with an accent: Language, ideology, and discrimination in the United States*. London: Routledge.

Lucas, C. (Ed.). (2001). *Sociolinguistics of sign languages*. Cambridge: Cambridge University Press.

Mendoza-Denton, N. (2008). *Homegirls: Language and cultural practice among Latina youth gangs*. Malden, MA: Blackwell.

Myers-Scotton, C. (1993). *Social motivations for codeswitching: Evidence from Africa*. Oxford: Oxford University Press.

Reyes-Rodríguez, A. (2008). Political discourse and its sociolinguistic variables. *Critical Inquiry in Language Studies*, *5*(4), 225–242.

4 Language Development

Key Terms: *Activity theory; communicative competence; communicative expertise; community of practice; developmental imperative; ethnography of communication; language development; language socialization; legitimate peripheral participation; literacy development; multicompetence; speech norms; verbal repertoires; zone of proximal development*

In sociolinguistics, the study of language development considers both the individual who is acquiring the language and the societal influences that affect the individual. From a sociolinguistic perspective, language development is intertwined with human development on the one hand and with the development of individual and group identities on the other hand. Learning a language is a social process. As the sociolinguist Penny Eckert (2000b) puts it, ". . . the construction of social meaning and the construction of language are one and the same" p. 43). Children, for example, are not simply learning the languages of their parents; children's language development is strongly affected by the language of their social groups. In fact, the major influence on the dialect children learn to speak is their peers (Labov, 1972). Eckert (2000b) explains that "all childhood is, among other things, learning to be the next step older . . . Social status among one's peers requires demonstrating new 'mature' behaviors, a continual move beyond the childish—a need to be age appropriate that amounts to a *developmental imperative*" (2000, p. 8).

In this discussion of language development, therefore, we do not address the typical language acquisition questions of whether the human brain is specifically set up to acquire language. Rather in looking at language development from a sociolinguistic perspective, we are addressing the social aspects of language development. In particular, we will demonstrate the tension between individual language development and its connection to social aspects of life and the ways in which we construct aspects of our identities. First, we will look at the notion of a speech community as it has been developed in a framework called Ethnography of Communication. Within the Ethnography of Communication an important concept we will discuss is *communicative competence*. After this, we will discuss a theory, *Language Socialization*, that has grown out of these types of ideas. In particular, language socialization introduces concepts of *Community of Practice* that are more fluid and less static than the notions of *Speech Community*. Next we will consider the fact that many people in the world speak more than one language and develop *multicompetence* in language.

4.1 Doing Sociolinguistics: Thought Exploration

We can begin by considering the meaning of the word "development." Do you think of development as holistic? Or do you think of it as occurring in parts? What about intellectual development, athletic development, or emotional development? Are these completely unrelated to each other? Are they related but separate? Or are they absolutely integrated? How does the development of group identities happen?

4.1 The speech community and the ethnography of communication

One way to look at language development within its social domains is by its relation to the notion of a *speech community*. One simple definition of a speech community is given by John J. Gumperz (1982): A speech community is a group of people who share the same rules and norms for using language. This notion of speech communities is a central construct in a framework for studying language developed by Dell Hymes, a linguistic anthropologist. This framework, called the *Ethnography of Communication*, is concerned with what it means to be communicatively competent in a particular speech community. Within this framework, *communicative competence* is defined as a speaker's ability to use language in a way that is appropriate to a given situation. As Hymes (1972) states, "language is not everywhere equivalent in role and value; speech may have a different scope and functional load in the communicative economies of different societies" (p. 39). If we think about language competence in terms of embodied experience in the world, which includes the various activities that people perform, then what we are really discussing is language competencies that are developed as we perform activities in everyday life. Language competence is multiplicitous, situated, and tied to our embodied experience in the world. Joan Hall, An Cheng, and Matthew Carlson, (2006) stated, "language knowledge has its roots in socioculturally contextualized activity" (p. 229) and "*all* language knowledge is socially contingent and dynamic no matter how many language codes one has access to" (p. 230). In other words, monolingual language users, like multilingual language users, have different language competencies, or what they term different areas of *communicative expertise*, which are developed in particular contexts of use. Similarly, Suresh Canagarajah (2007) argued that language development is multidimensional and that verbal repertoires are expanded and strengthened as people move into new contexts of language use.

There are many examples that each of us can recall in which we have moved into new contexts of language use. If this is your first course in sociolinguistics, you are being introduced for the first time to the sociolinguistic jargon and sociolinguistic ways of talking about the world. You are, then, in the process of expanding your verbal repertoire by adding a new register. When you complete this course, you will have developed a new area of communicative expertise.

4.2 Doing Sociolinguistics: A Thought Exploration

How is the language that you use when you are out to a movie with friends different from the language you use when you are making a presentation in class? If you are multilingual, what are the unspoken, but understood, rules you use when you choose one language or another language?

In a Speech Community framework for looking at how people use language, the kinds of questions that you just considered are exactly the kinds of questions that are explored through research. Notice how difficult these questions can be to answer by simply doing a "Thought Exploration" about them. Quite often in looking at languages, we find that much of what we do is the result of seemingly unconscious choices. We, very often, are not aware of how we actually *do* language. This is one of the reasons that we need to do more active explorations about language use. From the perspective of the sociolinguistic researcher, the method for deciphering what it is that communicatively competent members of a speech community know and are able to do with language is conducting an *Ethnography of Communication*. Such ethnographic work not only results in an understanding that is contextual and specific to the speech community being focused on, but it is also generalizable as far as gaining an understanding of the intricate connection between language use in everyday social life and communicative competence. So it is important that researchers do field work to get what Clifford Geertz (1973) calls a "thick description" of the particular speech community and the speech genres, speech events, and speech situations that take place within that community. "Thick description" means that the researcher gathers a very rich set of data that reflects the ways that the members of the speech community organize the world. Hymes developed the Ethnography of Communication to create a framework for gaining thick descriptions of the uses of language within the speech community. Using Ethnography of Communication allows us, as sociolinguistics, to understand the particular speech community's typical ways of communicating in particular situations and events as well as the layers of diversity at work within the speech community. The Ethnography of Communication will be more thoroughly detailed in Chapter 8, so at this point, we can turn our discussion to considering the notion of the speech community itself.

As noted, a speech community is a group of people who share regular patterns of speech for particular communication purposes, but there are different ways of using language depending on the various life functions that people engage in within a particular speech community. These different ways of using language are not random. They form regular linguistic patterns specific to the particular group of people. We call these regular patterns the *speech norms* of the group.

One aspect of the linguistic diversity inherent in any speech community is how distinct ways of using language take on symbolic meaning within that particular group. This means that people in the group can make very specific choices about language, which contributes to their ability to construct their identities through language. As members of a speech community, we know the symbolic meaning of these various ways of talking, even if each individual does not engage in all of the forms of talk possible within the speech community. We can competently discern how people construct identities as they engage in ways of using language that are unique to particular functions of their lives. We also have intuition about the appropriateness of particular people's uses of language within the speech community, which contributes to our interpretation of language and of people.

As children develop language, they become socialized to use the various codes associated with the roles in which they participate within the speech community. Children also learn to recognize the codes that are associated with the roles that they are exposed to within the speech community even if they do not use or control these codes. As Elaine S. Anderson (1990) has demonstrated, children are sensitive to speakers' power relative to one another. In this work, for example, Anderson had children whose ages ranged from 4 years 7 months up to 6 years 10 months use puppets to act out various scenarios with different types of speakers. Children modulated their voices in different ways using higher pitch for children and lower pitch for adult males. They also used different types of speech in relation to fathers and mothers. So, for example, in enacting children asking for ice cream from their fathers, children had their puppets use indirect requests, such as "Might we be able to get some ice cream?" but in enacting children asking for ice cream from mothers, the requests would look more like direct statements or even imperatives "Gimme some ice cream." Anderson's work also demonstrates that at rather early ages children are aware that there are certain ways that various professionals speak. They show awareness of register. In this study, children used puppets to imitate the language of doctors, for example. Even the younger children used particular vocabulary items to mark the doctors' roles. While not always accurate in their use of the terms, they used words like "thermometer" or "temperature" or other words that we would associate with doctors, such as a "cast" in relation to something "broken." Anderson's evidence illustrates children's ability to differentiate the codes associated with various roles within the speech community. As these children engaged in play with their puppets, they took on the roles of mothers, fathers, and doctors, imitating the language that goes along with these roles.

These are not, of course, the only roles that children can enact. Susan M. Hoyle (1991) demonstrated how adeptly young children are able to enact the language of sportscasters. When the children in her study played sportscaster, they demonstrated their communicative competence in sportscaster register, which includes frequent use of simple present and passives and ellipsis of subject pronouns and verbal elements. In Example 4.1, a young boy, Ben, commentates on his friend's computer basketball game.

Example 4.1

Ben: Doctor J with the ball
Bird steals it and slams it ho-ome

One minute six seconds left
in the third quarter
A stuff!
But Dr. J gets the rebound
It's another stuff
He takes it out of his hand! (pp. 437–438)

In Ben's example, we can see some of the features common to sportscasting. It is clear that Ben is able to differentiate sportscasting from other registers and that he is able to employ it appropriately. Clearly, this is a boy who has participated in watching a lot of sports and who has engaged in this kind of play with his friends before.

In this section we have looked at the ideas that from sociolinguistic perspectives, language development is inherently tied to social contexts. We develop language within these social contexts, and it becomes such a part of our understandings of our social environments that quite often we are completely unaware of some of the language choices that we make relative to these environments. This is part of our communicative competence—that ability to use language in an appropriate way in a given social environment. In order to look at these types of issues, sociolinguists often do ethnographies of communication and gather thick descriptions of how different groups of people actually use language. In particular, the framework of Ethnography of Communication and the notion of Speech Community have provided ways to talk about how people have communicative competence relative to particular speech communities and can move between them in appropriate ways. Finally, we've looked at examples of children acquiring communicative competence in ways that indicate they are aware of socially relevant language issues, such as those related to the relative power between speakers and the appropriate use of language for particular types of social events.

4.2 Speech communities and language codes

Within the speech community, people enact various language codes that go along with their various life functions. The definition of language code includes language varieties, which encompasses distinct languages and dialects. However, language code can also refer to registers and styles, as discussed in Chapter 3.

Because of the different roles that people play within a speech community, different language codes are used in the enactment of these roles. All of us are able to do this. We are able to decipher the internal diversity within our speech communities and recognize who is able to use which language codes as well as when, where, and how to use them.

It is not, however, that speech community norms exist in a vacuum. For example, consider the work of H. Samy Alim (2004) who looks at the Hip Hop Nation speech community. His work shows how this speech community has developed unique norms for communication that set it apart as distinct from other speech communities. Alim demonstrates the style shifting that takes place within the speech community based on race, gender, Hip Hop cultural knowledge, and interactional style. Within a speech community, members have access to particular language codes and have a repertoire of codes with which they enact their day-to-day interactions. For example, Alim argued that the use of "O-kay!" to indicate full agreement seems to be a symbolic marker of black female identity within this particular community. This argument is based upon the fact that in his data, Alim finds the use of "O-kay!" only among black females, and he does not find inappropriate uses of "O-kay!" in his data. Users of Hip Hop Nation Language have a tacit awareness of when and how to say "O-kay!" to mean full agreement. They also know when it is appropriate to make these linguistic choices. In Example 4.2 taken from Alim (2004, p. 219), Speakers A, B, D, and F discuss the dangers of spending Halloween night in a town that Alim calls Shadyside.

Example 4.2

A: One year somebody put a razor blade in like this candy apple thing and a kid . . .

D: Mm-hmm!

A: . . . bit into it and they tongue got cut off

F: Over in Shadyside?

A: Yep!

D: Yep . . .

F: You gotta watch out cuz sometimes that's where the loonies be at . . .

D: Mm-hmm!

B: Hell yeah, rapists and stuff . . .

A: O-kay!

As Alim explains the data example, A's emphatic "O-kay!" in the final turn of this data example shows strong agreement with the description of Shadyside that these speakers have co-constructed in this conversation. This "O-kay" is different from other uses of "O-kay." As anyone from this particular group would note, it is said with a particular pitch pattern, and in each case, as in the above data example, female speakers use it to emphasize that they strongly agree with or support the content of their interlocutors' contributions to the conversation.

Such knowledge is constituted by a lifetime accumulation of socializing experiences. All of the participants in Alim's study were fully socialized members of the broader Hip Hop Nation speech community and therefore knew when to say what to whom. As Alim (2004) states, "these rules of interaction, or communicative norms, are learned in and through language socialization within a community of speakers. They are unwritten and largely subconscious ways of speaking that authenticate one's membership within a given speech community" (p. 225). Therefore, part of the nature of being a member of a speech community is adherence to speech community norms. The internal diversity within the speech community allows for members to show alignments with one another and create particular identities through their ways of using language. In the case of "O-kay!" for full agreement, black female identity is indexed precisely because black females use that form. In the same way, particular forms may be used in interaction to index masculinity, youth, educational status, and many other affiliations.

4.3 Doing Sociolinguistics: A Thought Exploration

Think about ways that you use language to create facets of your own identity. How do you use language with people in your "in" group in ways that show you are a part of that particular group? Would you use this same language with an entirely different group of people who have different interests?

In this section we have looked at how individuals demonstrate a particular type of highly socialized language competence that enables them to use distinct languages and dialects as well as registers and styles to enact their memberships in particular language communities.

4.3 Speech communities and verbal repertoires

Members of a speech community control particular sets of language codes that are associated with their life experiences and activities. These can be called their *verbal repertoires*. Importantly, part of our language competence is that we know when and where it is appropriate to employ the different sets of codes that are part of our verbal repertoire.

Though we may primarily affiliate with one speech community, most people participate in multiple speech communities in their daily lives. Participation in multiple speech communities does not necessarily mean full membership in these speech communities. We participate in speech communities that we are not fully socialized to participate in. This is commonly the case in more bureaucratic settings, such as the school, the courtroom, and the hospital. It can be very difficult for people who are not socialized to participate in these bureaucratic speech communities to navigate effective language use. In these situations, as less experienced members in these settings, we are somewhat at the mercy of the experts who are fully socialized members, such as teachers, lawyers, and nurses, to guide us. We may also participate in non-bureaucratic speech communities without being fully socialized members. In diverse urban areas, people may participate in many different types of speech communities without necessarily gaining full membership. If participation within a new speech community is prolonged and frequent, it is likely that we become socialized through time, allowing for fuller membership.

Consider the example of social groups within a high school environment. Most of us experienced the formation of several types of social groups in the high schools we attended. Eckert (2000b) explored how social identity was constructed in a Detroit suburban high school, Belten High. She looked at the way that individuals in different social groups, the "jocks," the "burnouts," and the "in-betweeners" lived their lives. They dressed and behaved differently, and used language to construct themselves as individuals and as members of a group, but it is important to notice that in doing this, they were constructing social meaning. "The burnouts and the jocks are not simply two visible social groups, but they embody opposing class-related ideologies, norms, trajectories, and practices of all sorts" (p. 3).

In examining the group patterns of these individuals, Eckert found strong correspondences between the parents' socioeconomic status as well as the education of both parents. In particular, she found correlations between the father's occupation and socioeconomic status and the particular individual's high school group membership. Saying that students' group memberships had correlations with their parents' socioeconomic status, however, is not at all the same as saying that they spoke like their parents. As Eckert notes, perhaps the most important finding of this study is the small extent to which the speech of Belten High students reflects their parents' socioeconomic characteristics. Two major variables seemed to express the speech of these students. One was gender, and the other was their group affiliation. So while Eckert examined a number of speech variables, such as (aeh) raising, (o) fronting, (oh fronting), (e) backing, and (ay) monophthongizing, to name a few, what she found was that some of these categories of change correlated with gender, such as the (aeh) raising and the (o) fronting, while others, such as (e) backing, correlated with group affiliation. Some, of course, correlate with both gender and group affiliation. What this work shows, then, is that during adolescence the ways that people speak are affected by language constructions that have the purpose of constructing particular aspects of identity such as gender and group affiliation. Norma Mendoza-Denton (2008) looks at specific groups of Latina high school girls' group affiliations. One important finding of her work is that as girls move their affiliation from one group to another, they shift their pronunciation to more closely match the pronunciation patterns of their target groups. The way that they speak, in other words, marks their membership in a particular group.

Benjamin Bailey's (2001) work also illustrates how people can construct their identities both as individuals and as members of groups as they participate in and hold partial membership in multiple speech communities. In his ethnographic study of Dominican American language use, Bailey demonstrates how the Dominican American participants tend to affiliate with several different communities and how in these interactions they create and show different facets of their identity. A single individual in this group may self-identify on different occasions in different contexts as American, Hispanic, Black, a female New Yorker, and Dominican, to name a few. For example, one participant, Maria, showed different facets of her identity by making part of a statement directly address her affiliation. Bailey calls these "self-ascriptions." So, for example, Maria would say things like "And us Americans, we know what you have to go through . . ." or "I'm from New York . . ." (p. 194) in which she defines herself as an American by showing that she is part of the "us" and the "we" that makes up the group "Americans." She defines herself as being part of the group of people that make up New York, in her statement "I'm from New York." These examples of Maria's self-identification are quite explicit. Almost anyone from any group would recognize Maria's identifications as both American and from New York.

However, there are other ways that people make facets of their identity clear. Consider again the use of "O-kay" that we looked at earlier in Alim's

(2004) work. Without explicitly saying "I'm a member of the hip hop community," the use of this particular form of "O-kay" said in the appropriate place in the conversation using the appropriate pitch, demonstrates an identity as a member of the hip hop community.

In much the same way, Bailey's (2001) look at the linguistic resources of Dominican Americans demonstrates how the linguistic repertoire of members of the Dominican American speech community contains linguistic resources that allow its users to index facets of identity, which have been formed by their contact with multiple speech communities. Therefore, even though they may be primarily Dominican American, there are other facets of their identity, including their affiliation with the Black American speech community, various Hispanic speech communities, mainstream American speech community, among others. Dominican Americans, then, can use these linguistic resources to index facets of their identity. This indexing may occur by using words and expressions that are associated with a particular variety of language, including Spanish words. It may also be that a particular syntactic form is used. Bailey (2001) gives the example of one of his participants, Janelle, using habitual *be*, a syntactic feature characteristic of African American Vernacular English (AAVE), to describe a place as hot all the time.

For example Janelle says " I just wear something comfortable, because it's—cause it be hot in there" (p. 202). It is interesting that Janelle self-corrects, switching from a construction with a form of *be* that would not indicate a condition that is long term, to the AAVE habitual *be* in order to emphasize that it is habitually hot. Notice that this self-correction does more than one thing. First, of course, it changes the meaning of the sentence. Second, because it is a syntactically appropriate way to express this idea in this particular community, her adeptness in using this form indexes her membership in the Black American speech community. At the same time it also distinguishes her from other groups of English speaking Americans who are not adept in using AAVE. As multicompetent speakers, it isn't only in relationship to English that Dominican Americans construct their group identity. Dominican Americans may also use Spanish words, expressions, and syntax to index their identity as part of the Spanish-speaking world, thus differentiating themselves from Black Americans. At other times they may also mock Dominican Spanish, thus disaffiliating with people who still live in the Dominican Republic or who are recent immigrants from the Dominican Republic. Their complex set of linguistic resources allows them to construct facets of their identity as they affiliate with particular groups but also disaffiliate with other groups to create a unique Dominican American identity.

As this example illustrates, it is most typical for people to have at least partial membership in multiple speech communities. This may play out in the formation of a distinct societal speech community, in the way that it does with the Dominican American speech community, or it may play out in other ways. For example, individuals who are part of mainstream cultural groups, such as white, middle-class Americans, are influenced by contact with the speech communities associated with subcultures like Hip Hop, surfing, or even use of social network technologies, such as texting.

4.4 Doing Sociolinguistics: A Thought Exploration

Think about your own complex set of linguistic resources. What group affiliations have contributed to your linguistic resources? How do you think you use these resources in regard to your affiliation with that group and/or disaffiliations with other groups?

As individuals, we each gain partial or full membership in a slightly different set of speech communities. Two people may be from Southern California, for instance. They may both be students in Southern California, be members of the same peer group and participate in many of the same activities. Let's suppose one of these people becomes heavily involved in Hip Hop and the other in snowboarding. Each of them will probably adopt some of the norms for communication from these speech communities with which they have contact. Therefore, their linguistic repertoires will become different. Their ways of talking may be mocked or rejected by their peer group, or their ways of talking may be accepted or even adopted. In any case, they come to develop their own individual repertoires that may at times be at odds with the linguistic expectations of the peer group. On the other hand, the unique linguistic repertoire contributes the unique identity of individuals. Participation in multiple speech communities, then, becomes the catalyst for our socialization into the various speech community norms and the basis for the formation of individual identity.

What the works examined in this section show is that language development is closely tied to identity construction and group membership. Monolinguals and multilinguals alike control and use a variety of registers, styles, and possibly dialects in their daily lives. Therefore, any person's verbal repertoire, whether multilingual or monolingual, consists of multiple language codes, which means we are all multicompetent.

4.5 Doing Sociolinguistics: A Thought Exploration

What speech communities do you have contact with in your everyday life? How do you distinguish your identity as you interact with people from various speech communities?

In this section, we discussed how part of an individual's communicative competence includes a vast linguistic verbal repertoire. Monolingual individuals typically control, if not a variety of languages or dialects, a variety of registers and styles that they can use to move from one group to another marking their group membership with particular linguistic choices. Multilinguals have the ability to do the same things with the addition that they can use choices of more than one language to mark group membership in very complex ways. This means that part of the abilities of language speakers is the socially acquired competence to mark both group membership and group non-membership in very complex ways.

4.4 Language socialization and community of practice

Sociolinguists tend to view all aspects of language development as connected to our daily life experiences. Furthermore, sociolinguists tend to understand language development as deriving from social context. For this reason, many sociolinguists who are interested in language development have utilized a *Language Socialization* (LS) paradigm because it allows for the study of language development as connected to other aspects of human development and as derived from social life. In studying language development from an LS perspective, identity is a central theme as language development is intimately connected to the development of one's social identity.

Jack P. Shonkoff and Deborah A. Phillips (2000) argue that aspects of development, including language development, are all part of a larger process of human development and that this process is dependent on our interactions in social life. This perspective allows us to study aspects of development separately but with an understanding that all aspects of development are connected to overall human development.

To examine language development, the anthropological linguists, Elinor Ochs and Bambi Schieffelin, developed a Language Socialization (LS) framework. Language socialization is typically conceptualized as a process of gaining competence in the language of a speech community. Ochs (1993) defines socialization as "a dynamic interactional process between participants in expert and novice roles who develop cognitively through their activity, thereby changing over interactional time" (p. 1). Importantly, Ochs' definition of socialization suggests that *both* the expert and the novice develop in the process of jointly participating in an activity.

The LS paradigm has been quite useful in explaining first language development, a process by which young children develop language. Within the LS paradigm language socialization is understood as connected to the larger process of human development.

Vygotskian theory also provides a framework for studying socialization processes. However, an important difference between Vygotskian views of development and views of development espoused within the LS paradigm developed by Ochs and Schieffelin has to do with individual autonomy. While Vygotskian scholars argue that development leads to internalized, autonomous knowledge, LS scholars typically argue that knowledge can never be internalized or autonomous. Rather, an LS perspective takes as a premise that all knowledge is socially constructed and constituted. Even when we have gained expertise, that expertise is still contingent upon the dynamic, ever-changing social world within which it is embedded.

However, Vygotskian theory encompasses some important constructs that contribute to an understanding of human development as a social process, such as Zone of Proximal Development, scaffolding, and the distinction between scientific and everyday concepts. Each of these tells a slightly different story when it comes to the development of competence. In one sense, the Zone of Proximal Development and scaffolding are interrelated terms. The *Zone of Proximal Development* is the distance between the problem solving abilities of a person working alone and the problem solving abilities of that same person working with a more experienced, expert, competent person. The idea is that the more experienced person can scaffold the performance of the less experienced person. This scaffolding entails other-mediated, other-regulated performance of an activity. As Patricia Marks Greenfield (1984) points out, the goal of all that scaffolding is self-mediation and self-regulation in the performance of the activity. This, then, would define competence.

Another way of conceptualizing the Zone of Proximal Development is the distance between scientific and everyday concepts (Vygotsky, 1978). The idea here is that scientific concepts are understood, usually through instruction, whereas everyday concepts are developed in everyday experience. Mariane Hedegaard (2001) argues that the knowledge gained through everyday experience is owned knowledge, while knowledge gained from instruction is understood knowledge. Presumably owned knowledge and understood knowledge can merge so that one's owned, everyday knowledge base contains a stock of scientific concepts. This merging of the scientific and the everyday would then define some types of competence.

James V. Wertsch (1985) argued that participation in activities is mediated by cultural models. The Zone of Proximal Development is conceptualized as the distance between people's culturally informed ways of participating in everyday activities and the social transformation in the cultural model guiding performance of that same activity. Accordingly, competence becomes a dialectic between the social world and the social actors. Our very participation in an activity can bring on a slight change in what it means to perform that activity. This activity theory conceptualization of the Zone of Proximal Development is helpful in that it provides a framework for understanding how the social world influences individual cognition and how individual everyday participation in the social world can transform that social world. Competence, then, is a dynamic, negotiated construct.

Illustrating activity theory in action, Karen Ann Watson-Gegeo and David W. Gegeo (1999) demonstrated that children's "cognitive and linguistic competence" is tied to cultural models. For instance, the young Kwara'ae child they studied, Ruana, demonstrated both cognitive and linguistic competence in terms of the Kwara'ae cultural model of sharing. Ruana was given instructions by her mother to take bananas to a relative's house, but not to accept any gift in return. The mother invoked the Kwara'ae cultural model of sharing (Family members share without any expectation of return) as opposed to the cultural model of reciprocal exchange, which would be done to reconcile a dispute. Such dispute reconciliation is often done by children in Kwara'ae culture, so there could easily be confusion between sharing and dispute reconciliation in this particular instance.

As Ruana performed the sharing activity, the relative offered Ruana two tins of tuna. This caused a dilemma for Ruana because the activity became more like reciprocal exchange than sharing. Her mother had instructed her to share. In confronting this highly complex dilemma, she invoked several cultural schemas—sharing, politeness, meals, and debate. She demonstrated knowledge of the Kwara'ae cultural models of sharing and of debate as she went about refusing the tins of tuna. She also demonstrated knowledge of cultural models of politeness in knowing that two refusals would be highly offensive (the relative again offering the tins of tuna after the first refusal). She also showed an understanding of the need for protein at mealtime. Her family, stricken by poverty, had been living mostly on rice. In eventually finding a compromise and accepting one tin of tuna from the relative, Ruana demonstrated a sophisticated level of competence in navigating various cultural models. Perhaps most importantly, the activity that was co-performed by Ruana and the relative was still defined as sharing, so Ruana's performance of the activity was understood as being what her mother instructed. Ruana's case illustrates how individual interaction with the social world can cause transformation in the cultural model guiding the performance of an activity, in this case sharing.

Activity theory provides a framework for understanding how individual actors interact with the social world to create social transformation. This, then, allows for different kinds of performance of competence and for a dynamic understanding of competence relative to the social world. Language competence is tied in many ways to more general practical competence that comes with the experience of participating in various activities, and language socialization is one aspect of a process of human development in which we come to understand how to engage in activities in particular social contexts.

The construct of communicative competence was born out of the Ethnography of Communication and linked to membership within a speech community. However, as Paul B. Garrett and Patricia Baquedano-Lopez (2002) assert, the construct of speech community assumes static norms for language use. To gain an understanding of communicative norms as shifting and dynamic and to theorize the ongoing tension between individual identity and group identity, we have to move beyond speech community. The construct, *Community of Practice*, allows for a more intricate look at the relationship among socialization, competence, and identity.

In this section so far, we have looked at how linguists looking at language from a social perspective, have proposed the Language Socialization framework to specifically examine language socialization processes. In these processes, more advanced, expert members of communities, such as adults, interact with novice members of the community, such as children, in very intricate, dynamic ways providing both models and at times more specific culturally appropriate guidance on language. In this model, language socialization is seen as a part of the process of human development.

4.4.1 Community of practice

Given the fact that identity is so complex, it is important to consider a framework for studying learning that takes the complexity of identity into account, yet allows for an examination of the learning process. Watson-Gegeo (2004) suggests that a language socialization paradigm is best suited for studying how people develop language. Watson-Gegeo also argued that a *Community of Practice* framework (Lave & Wenger, 1991; Wenger 1998; Wenger, McDermott, & Snyder, 2002) is central to a language socialization paradigm in providing a means to relate development to access and participation that is situated within a particular sociohistorical context. In particular, a Community of Practice framework emphasizes that development, including language development, proceeds from *legitimate peripheral participation*. Central to the framework is the development of relationship between core and peripheral members of a community of practice, which is conceptualized as a locally constituted participant structure (see Chapter 5) in which people engage in some activity type, and in which members learn from each other in a sustained, ongoing way.

The core members are experienced old-timers and the peripheral members are inexperienced newcomers relative to the practice. When the peripheral newcomers join the community of practice, they can be sequestered or legitimized. When newcomers are sequestered, they remain on the periphery and typically fail to develop mastery in the practice. However, when newcomer, peripheral members are accepted as legitimate members of the community of practice, they are typically asked to perform increasingly complex tasks. Legitimate peripheral members are socialized and nurtured by core members through legitimate peripheral participation, which allows them to eventually gain core membership.

To examine language socialization within a community of practice framework, it is necessary to look at the micro-interactional level of ongoing practical activity. This means that we have to come to understand what people do. Part of knowing how to do something is knowing how to use the language that is instrumental in the doing. Therefore, part of learning how to engage in activity or practice is learning the organization of linguistic behavior that allows social actors to get things done when they come together to do an activity (Jones & Thornborrow, 2004). Communicative repertoires and communicative expertise, then, are developed as people participate within communities of practice.

Each of us participates in communities of practice in our daily lives. To illustrate this point, we will turn briefly to the story of Jack Kerouac, the writer of the novel, *On the Road*, and other works. Kerouac was born in the United States to French Canadian parents who had immigrated to Lowell, Massachusetts. At the time of Kerouac's birth in 1922, Lowell had the fourth largest Québécois (Quebec French) speaking population. In addition, many U.S. East Coast French Canadians spoke Joual, a dialect associated with the French-speaking working class in Montreal. Joual differs from other varieties of French phonologically, morphologically, and syntactically. It also differs from French in its extensive use of English loanwords. Because Kerouac was raised in Lowell, the home of many working-class French-speaking people who emigrated from Quebec, it is not unlikely that he spoke Joual as his first language. In any case, it is clear that he spoke some variety of French as his first language. He did not begin learning English until he entered school around the age of six.

In a manuscript that Jack Kerouac wrote in French, *La Nuit est ma Femme*, he constructs his identity as French Canadian. He states, "I am French Canadian, brought to the world in New England. When I am angry I often swear in French. When I dream I often dream in French. When I cry I always cry in French" (Anctil, 2007). He describes his "identity discomfort" in this manuscript. As he describes it, this identity discomfort seems to be rooted in the fact that he, as a multilingual person, was pegged into a monolingual world where evidently the assumption is one person=one language. As Kerouac lamented, "I never had a language to myself. French patois up to six, and after that the English of the neighborhood boys. And after that, the grand forms, the great expressions of the poet, the philosopher, the prophet. With all that today I am all mixed up in my gum [head]" (Anctil, 2007). Kerouac was schooled in Standard American English from the age of six because it was the language of the elite. Though Kerouac is most well-known for his writing in English, his choice to also write in French demonstrates his need to maintain his French Canadian identity.

Kerouac's example illustrates the societal forces that influence the language variety that individuals develop. First, people typically develop the language that is spoken by their families if that language is positively supported in larger local surroundings. So family and local context play a social role in which languages develop. Second, the languages of the larger social contexts, such as the national languages that are supported by the institutions of education, play a role in language development. As Kerouac's writing illustrates, however, these societal forces can lead to a kind of identity discomfort, when group affiliations are at odds with one another. Kerouac moved between multiple groups, which were associated with different language varieties. The development of his identity, then, was tied to his multilingual development. But this doesn't mean that multilingual development in itself creates discomfort. Part of what matters is how social groups value multilingual development. For example, although the United States is made up of many different language groups, and therefore, many multilingual groups, there are cultural pressures towards monolingualism in English (Lippi-Green, 1997a). The same can often be said, of course, for Great Britain and other countries that have English as a language that holds primary status. Part of Kerouac's discomfort was based in a society that often rejects multilingualism as a legitimate way of being.

Multilingual people, like Kerouac, may become involved in many different communities of practice throughout their lives. Indeed the same is true for monolingual individuals. Participation within communities of practice allows for the development of new language varieties, whether registers, dialects, or languages. Importantly, communities of practice are defined by their members' joint participation in goal-oriented activities, and there is a core-peripheral hierarchical structure within the community of practice.

Let's consider the possible communities of practice that a 10-year-old multilingual might participate in. Assume that our 10-year-old multilingual is Mexican American, the son of Mexican immigrants in Southern California. We'll call him Juan. In Juan's family, they attend a Catholic church every Sunday that holds services and doctrina classes for children in Spanish. Juan's doctrina classes constitute one community of practice. These doctrina classes are considered to be a community of practice because the group is jointly engaged in goal-oriented activities, and there is a hierarchical core-peripheral structure to the group. There are core members, the laypeople and priests who teach the class. Among the children, there are individuals who are closer to core membership due to their knowledge of Catholic liturgy, and children who are closer to the periphery possibly due to the fact that they are newer to Catholic liturgy. The language, Spanish, that is appropriate for use in this church environment, is determined by the core members, but it is also influenced by peripheral members. Membership in the community of practice is largely determined by use of the language of the community of practice.

Juan also attends the local public elementary school where he is in a fifth-grade class, and he is designated an English Language Development student.

All classroom activities take place in an academic variety of English. Indeed, public education in Spanish would be unlikely for Juan since bilingual education for students like Juan who have been designated as English Language Development students is illegal in California. This fifth-grade classroom also constitutes a community of practice in the same ways that the doctrina class does. However, the classroom community of practice typically contains one core member, the teacher, who as the core member has the power to decide which activities and ways of using language are appropriate for the peripheral students.

Juan also lives in a neighborhood with many children of Mexican immigrants. These neighborhood children are also involved in multiple communities of practice. In particular, Juan is involved in one with the group of boys who play pick-up basketball in the park. This group of boys is generally hierarchically arranged with the oldest boys at the core and the younger boys at the periphery, with the youngest boys the most peripheral. Within this group, the boys engage in code-switching between Spanish and English. They also use some lexical items, phonological features, and grammatical features from both Chicano English and African American English because in this community they play with African American children who are proficient in African American English. In order to be fully accepted as members of this community of practice, the younger boys must comply with both the rules of basketball and the rules for language use as set up by the older boys.

These communities of practice that Juan is involved with are not static, however. As peripheral members replace core members, the rules of engagement change. Although the children are unlikely to replace teachers as core members, certainly the younger boys will eventually become the older boys and become more adept at both pick-up basketball and the language. As this happens, the ways of playing the game and of using the language of the group will vary as the membership changes. But it's also important to notice that Juan is in different positions relative to each of these communities of practice. While he is toward the core of the church group, he is more toward the periphery in the school community of practice, and since his basketball group age ranges about six to ten and since he is quite adept at basketball, he is at the core of this community of practice. One more thing to notice, however, is that age does not necessarily guarantee core membership. Consider, for example, what would happen if Juan's teacher came to play pick-up basketball. She still might hold some authority as an adult in the situation, but she would not be a member of the community of practice.

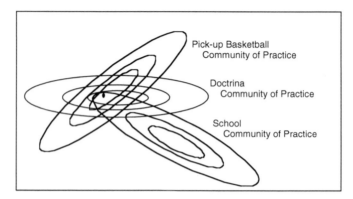

Pick-up Basketball
Community of Practice

Doctrina
Community of Practice

School
Community of Practice

Figure 4.1 Three of Juan's Communities of Practice

It is this ability to examine groups as dynamic, in flux, and hierarchical that makes Community of Practice such an important framework for the study of language development. This framework also provides for examinations of how hierarchal structures within groups affect language socialization. Figure 4.1 graphically demonstrates how Juan's communities of practice come together to help constitute his unique linguistic identity.

Up to this point in this chapter, we have discussed individual language development. In this discussion, we have demonstrated that individual language development is intricately connected to participation in social groups. We explored two types of social groups within which we might conceptualize language development, the speech community, and the community of practice. As we continue, we will consider what happens when social groups interact with each other and how such interaction affects the development of language at the societal level.

In this section we have more closely examined the notion of Community of Practice that related to the larger framework of Language Socialization. A Community of Practice model provides more flexibility for talking about language development within and among different groups than the notion of Speech Community did. The notion of Speech community introduces the idea of different communities, but does not provide as clear a method to discuss how socialization processes work within particular groups. A Community of Practice model partially solves this difficulty by providing a mechanism—different types of participation and interaction with more experienced group members—to account for how socialization processes can occur. It is important to also notice that different individuals can carry different levels of expertise within the various communities of practice they interact with. In this way, different aspects of identity can be instantiated relative to different communities.

4.5 Developing multilingualism/ multicompetence

From a monolingual perspective, Kerouac was "all mixed up." From a multilingual perspective, Kerouac was a user of multiple languages, able to switch between different languages and different language varieties. Recently, scholars in linguistics have offered the notion of multicompetence (Cook, 1991; Hall, Cheng, & Carlson, 2006; Pavlenko, 2003) to help better understand the multilingual experience. In this way of looking at language acquisition, there is the recognition that languages are not homogeneous. In other words, the English that is spoken by one person in one region will not be identical to the English that is spoken by another person in another region. This approach also argues that when people speak more than one language, the languages affect one another. Multicompetence highlights the abilities of multilingual individuals to negotiate in more than one language rather than comparing them negatively to monolingual speakers of any one language. Cook (1999) stated that second language (L2) users are "successful multicompetent speakers, not failed native speakers" (p. 204), placing emphasis on what the L2 user has gained rather than what the L2 user has not attained.

The need to examine the L2 user as multicompetent rather than as a deficient first language (L1) user has produced a large and growing body of scholarship that has demonstrated the need to study second language development in multilingual contexts where multicompetence is the norm (Belz, 2002; Canagarajah, 2007; Cook, 1991, 1999; Kachru Y., 1994; Kramsch, 2000). Several scholars have argued that native speaker language use is not the only legitimate model of competent language use (Bhatt, 2002; Firth & Wagner, 1997; Pavlenko, 2002; Seidlhofer, 2001, 2004; Widdowson, 2003) with many writers arguing that we should be looking at bilingual and multilingual speakers as the models for second language users. This work challenges the dominant ideology that standard language, as spoken by educated elite native speakers, is the ultimate goal of attainment for the L2 user. Rakesh Mohan Bhatt (2002) argued that the native-nonnative dichotomy serves to reproduce the prevailing ideology that native speakers are uniquely legitimate, expert users of the language, whereas nonnative speakers are learners. The body of research concerned with multicompetence has been instrumental in reframing definitions of legitimate language, demonstrating that multicompetent speakers use their language resources in ways that serve their communicative needs, from engaging in multilingual language play (Belz, 2002) to producing culturally significant literature in the L2 (Kachru B., 1986, 1994).

However, as Hall, Cheng, and Carlson (2006) assert, Cook's conceptualization of multicompetence assumes that languages are monolithic and static. Their work, therefore, expands the conceptualization of multicompetence by arguing that people who speak *one* language can also be multicompetent in that they control various registers and styles and in that they are able to gain new language knowledge when they move into new contexts of language use.

If you are a second language user, chances are that you consider yourself to be a more proficient user of your first language than people who are second language users of that language. This viewpoint comes out of a common, but socially constructed, binary that guides the way we think about language use, namely that people are either native or nonnative speakers of a language. Joanna Radwanska-Williams (2008) analyzes this binary by considering the logical presupposition in the term native speaker. She argues that when the term is broken down into its logical presuppositions, there are logical conflicts among them. She points out that these conflicts create a situation in which the term only makes sense if it is evaluated as a metaphor. She then argues that if we accept that it is a metaphor, we must question the social uses and purposes of this metaphor. She argues that one of the main uses of the term is that it sustains a dichotomy between the terms "native speakers" and "nonnative speaker," and that the distinction between the two terms "sustains social discrimination against 'non-native speakers' and NNS [nonnative speaker] educators" (p. 139). In a sense, then, maintaining this binary is a way to maintain a situation in which quite often the native speakers represent a privileged class, while the nonnative speakers are considered to be underdeveloped native speakers.

From a multicompetence perspective, this native-nonnative binary is considered to be false. Instead, multilinguals have at their disposal multiple languages, which are used for different purposes in their daily lives. They may be first language users of one or more of their languages, and they may be second language users of other languages. It is possible that certain multilinguals feel more competent speaking their second language than their first language. For instance, we have met many academics who received their academic training in a second language. It is not uncommon to hear them say that they feel more comfortable talking and writing about their academic area in their second language than in their various first languages.

There are plenty of second language users who are celebrated for their eloquent ways with words in the second language. Kerouac is a good example. Other examples include Samuel Beckett, whose first language was English and second language in which he wrote was French, and Ayn Rand, whose first language was Russian and second language in which she wrote was English.

From a multicompetence perspective, being a second language user is not limiting. As Cook (1991) argued, second language users are not failed native speakers. They have, on the other hand, gained a new repertoire for language use beyond their first language. The first and second language become part of the person's way of constructing identity. As we experience aspects of our lives, we interact with other people and become socialized to participate in various activities and to use the language that goes along with such participation. We develop language in conjunction with our embodied experience in the world as we conduct the day-to-day activities that make up our lives.

As people move into new contexts of language use, they become socialized to use the language of that context. Second language development could, then, include not only adding another language to one's repertoire but also another dialect or even register.

In many multilingual societies throughout the world, second language use becomes part of the ecological composition of language use. There are many places where second language use is a natural part of the way that people use language in their daily lives. Consider again, the extract from a Coca Cola advertisement (Bhatt, 2008, p. 191) we looked at in Chapter 3 and repeated here for your convenience.

> Example 4.3
> Just add Santa Claus
> And you'll never know
> Summers hit New Delhi.
> Fun 'n' food presents its summer long Snow Theme
> *Life ho to aisi!* (Life should be like this!)
> Coca Cola

In this advertisement, Hindi (Life ho to aisi!), mixes the global language, English, a second language for many Hindi speakers, with the local language, Hindi. Second language English use (and in some cases, second language Hindi use), become part of a person's identity. In most of the world, in fact, it is common to see second language use as an integral part of daily life. Most people in the world are multilingual.

4.6 Doing Sociolinguistic: A Thought Exploration

Is using a second language part of your daily life? Can you think of places where second language use is a natural part of daily life? How is the second language used? How is it related to other languages that people speak in the place you are thinking of?

In this section, we looked at concepts related to individuals' developing competence in a language other than their first language. We showed how labels such as "native speaker" and "nonnative speaker" not only do not represent the language development of many speakers, but also can be used to construct an individual learning a second language as deficient in relation to monolingual speakers. We have also discussed how these terms are inherently metaphoric and can also be used by some groups to create power over other groups. We have also introduced a concept that represents second language development in a more positive, linguistically viable, way. This is the notion of multicompetence. When viewed as emerging multicompetent speakers, those developing a new language can be viewed positively for the language development they have achieved as well as compared more appropriately to multilingual speakers.

4.6 Literacy development

Another aspect of language development that is both societal and individual is the development of literacy. When individuals develop literacy, it affects their identities enormously. This is especially the case when they become literate in a variety that is not the variety used in the home. However, even when the language of literacy is quite similar to the language used in the home, becoming literate brings people into a new social order.

Jan Blommaert (2005) demonstrates the tension that occurs when local literacy practices are superceded by imported literacy practices. We certainly see this with English worldwide. Academics often must publish in English worldwide. Hanauer and Englander (in press), for example, have examined how multilingual individuals in other countries struggle to meet academic standards of writing scientific journal articles in English. Their work has demonstrated how people's academic careers in Mexico, for instance, can be in jeopardy if they fail to master academic writing in English. Though these same academics may have been socialized into Mexican literacy practices through their educational experience, their academic careers are dependent upon their ability to accept and become socialized to engage with imported literacy practices.

In this modern, technological age, electronic literacy is increasingly pervasive. Therefore, not only do we learn how to read and write, but we also learn how to e-mail, chat, tweet, blog, and enter virtual lives. This technology transforms literacy practices enormously. Novels can be co-written on blogs. News, music, videos, and art are spread through Twitter and Facebook. The mass media becomes less important to our ability to gather information in the digital age. Benedict Andersen (1983) claimed that the development of the modern nation state was made possible through the mass media and mass literacy. As people gain the ability to control how information is spread and what information is important, the mass media becomes less influential. These new technologies transform the way we use language. Not only do new lexical items develop, such as LOL, OMG, and IMO, but punctuation also changes, the rules for engagement change, indeed the standards for effective rhetoric change. These technological advancements represent the new frontier in global language development. We'll see how it develops.

4.7 Doing Sociolinguistics: A Thought Exploration

How do you think new literacy technologies affect our understanding of the social order? Does it change our understanding of other language groups, for example, that we can so easily access news and information about them?

In this section, we have briefly looked at the notion of literacy, with a particular emphasis on the consequences of what can happen when the literacy practices of one group are superceded by the literacy practices and demands of another culture. In addition we have discussed modern technologies and their potential to affect literacy practices, particular understandings of political states, and global language development.

4.7 Doing sociolinguistics: research activities

1: Analyzing Conversations to Discover your Language Use in Different Groups

Ask your friends if you can record some of the conversations that you have when you are together. Then analyze the conversation to identify the kinds of language use that you do with different groups of friends.

a. You can choose to analyze after transcribing portions of the conversation.
b. Or you can do a more informal analysis by listening repeatedly to the conversations.

2: Keeping a Group Membership Log

Keep a group membership log for one day in which you write down every group that you interact with. Make sure that you keep notes about the kinds of language forms you use in your interaction with that group that either help identify you as a member of the group or make it clear that you are not a member of the group.

3: Interviewing with an Second Language User

Think about people you know who use a second language. This may be a family member, friend, or classmate and interview them about their experiences using a second language. If possible consider audio recording (and possibly transcribe) the interview.

4: Exploring Child Socialization

Audio Record (and possibly transcribe) a conversation that includes at least one child. You could choose to record

a. (with their parents' permission) a group of children,
b. yourself with a child in your family,
c. or a parent and his/her child.

Take a look at the features within the conversation that demonstrate language socialization processes.

5: Considering Technology and Socialization

Keep a log of your own interactions with technology for a 24-hour period. Consider the implications of the types of interactions that you participate in. For example, do you use Facebook? Do you send multiple texts or twitter? How have these technologies affected the forms of language that are specific to the particular technology you are considering? You could also consider the types of information you get from different technologies. What socializing affects do these different types of information have for you?

4.8 Suggested further reading

Bailey, B. (2001). The language of multiple identities among Dominican Americans. *Journal of Linguistic Anthropology, 10*(2), 190–223.

Canagarajah, S. (2007). Lingua Franca English, multilingual communities, and language acquisition. *The Modern Language Journal, 91*(Focal Issue), 923–939.

Cook, V. (1991). The poverty-of-the-stimulus argument and multicompetence. *Second Language Research, 7*(2), 103–117.

Firth, A., & Wagner, J. (1997). On Discourse, communication, and (some) fundamental concepts in SLA research. *The Modern Language Journal, 81*(3), 285–300.

Hall, J. K., Cheng, A., & Carlson, M. T. (2006). Reconceptualizing multicompetence as a theory of language knowledge. *Applied Linguistics, 27*(2), 220–240.

Lave, J., & Wenger, E. (1991). *Situated learning: Legitimate peripheral participation*. Cambridge: Cambridge University Press.

Lippi-Green, R. (1997). *English with an accent: Language, ideology, and discrimination in the United States*. London: Routledge.

Pavlenko, A. (2002). "We have room for but one language here": Language and national identity in the US at the turn of the 20th century. *Multilingua, 21*, 163–196.

Pavlenko, A. (2003). "I never knew I was a bilingual": Reimagining teacher identities in TESOL. *Journal of Language, Identity, and Education, 2*(4), 251–268.

Schieffelin, B., & Ochs, E. (1986). Language socialization. *Annual Review of Anthropology, 15*, 163–191.

Vygotsky, L. S. (1978). Interaction between learning and development. In M. Cole, V. John-Steiner, S. Scribner, & E. Souberman (Eds.), *Mind in society: The development of higher psychological processes* (pp. 79–91). Cambridge, MA: Harvard University Press.

Watson-Gegeo, K. A. (2004). Mind, language, and epistemology: Toward a language socialization paradigm for SLA. *The Modern Language Journal, 88*, 331–350.

5 Language and Social Interaction

In this chapter we will explore micro-interactional approaches to sociolinguistics and identity. The "micro" element of micro-interactional means that we will be looking at interactions that happen between individuals within their local social frameworks. In looking at language at this level, we will consider how participants orient themselves to one another and to the topics they are discussing. We will look at ways in which they maintain or do not maintain social notions such as politeness. Many such notions, of course, vary by culture, so we will also be examining intercultural communication. We will also look at a theory that argues that language is action, Speech Act Theory. Finally, we will talk about conversational interaction as a locally managed system.

5.1 Local constructions of identity

Sociolinguists tend to understand the social world, not as something huge and homogeneous, but as something very complex that is constituted through face-to-face interaction. At the same time, it is important to recognize that all face-to-face interactions are embedded within larger sociocultural and sociohistorical contexts. Therefore, analysis of both the interactional context and the broader sociocultural and sociohistorical contexts in which they are embedded becomes important to an understanding of identity construction in face-to-face interactions.

It is also important to consider that there are many facets of identity that might be indexed within a single interaction because identity is multifaceted. Our identities include our national identities, ethnic identities, gender identities, and professional identities, to name a few. However, we don't necessarily construct all of these aspects of our identities in every portion of every interaction. The aspects of identity that are indexed in any particular situation are both relative to the interaction and to the broader social context. The identities that are indexed within a particular interaction, then, are contingent on the purposes of the interaction and how it unfolds as well as on how the interaction is embedded within the broader context.

Let's take a look at an example of a fairly heated exchange that shows how an interaction can be affected by both its immediate context and by the important historical events that preceded it. Example 5.1 represent an exchange that occurred on the last day of the Iberio-American summit that took place in Santiago, Chile in November of 2007. This summit was attended by leaders from Latin America, Spain, and Portugal including Juan Carlos I, the King of Spain; Spanish Prime Minister José Luis Rodríguez Zapatero; and Venezuelan President Hugo Chávez. In the immediate context of interaction, moments before the following exchange began, Chávez had referred to former Spanish Prime Minister José Maria Aznar as a "fascist." Spain's current prime minister, Zapatero, takes issue with Chávez's label of Aznar. To do this, Zapatero invokes the cultural expectation of respect for elected officials.

In considering this exchange and the broader context surrounding it, we should consider the important historical events that preceded it. In 2002, five years before this exchange, there was a coup d'etat in Venezuela, which resulted in the temporary ousting of the Chávez government. Chávez had accused Aznar of being a supporter of this coup d'etat. Indeed, there had been rumors of Aznar's role in the coup, though Aznar consistently denied his involvement. Chávez's indignation in this segment must be considered in light of the fact that he thought Aznar had supported the coup.

It is also important to note that Chávez, himself, at the time of this exchange, was a controversial figure on the world stage. He was the leader of an oil rich country, Venezuela, which meant that the world nations potentially needed his support. Furthermore, Chávez's far leftist politics and the fact that he allied himself with nations considered to be threatening to Spain, like Cuba and Iran, made him a distrusted figure to the Spanish government that Prime Minister Zapatero represented and to other governments worldwide.

Keeping the broader context in mind, let's look at how particular identities are indexed within this exchange that position both Chávez and Zapatero in terms of their political affiliations and ideologies. There is also an interesting interjection by the King of Spain, Juan Carlos I, in which he essentially asks Chávez to "shut up" (Toklaw, 2007).

Example 5.1

1.	Zapatero:	No se yo no estoy cerca de las ideas de Aznar pero el ex Presidente Aznar fue elegido por los Españoles y exigo
		I am not close to the ideas of Aznar but the former Prime Minister Aznar was elected by the Spaniards and I demand
2.	Chávez:	pero
		but
3.	Zapatero:	y exigo
		And I demand
4.	Chávez:	dígale a él que respete
		Tell him to respect
5.	Zapatero:	exigo
		I demand
6.	Chávez:	la dignidad
		the dignity
7.	Zapatero:	exigo
		I demand
8.	Chávez:	de nuestro
		of our
9.	Zapatero:	exigo
		I demand
10.	Man:	y tu
		and you
11.	Chávez:	pueblo
		people.
12.	Zapatero:	ese respeto por una razon nada mas
		This respect for no more than one reason
13.	Chávez:	dígale usted lo mismo
		you tell him these same words
14.	Zapatero:	por supuesto
		of course
15.	Chávez:	a el presidente
		The Prime Minister
16.	Zapatero:	por supuesto
		of course
17.	Chávez:	dígale lo mismo . . . que anden respetando a Venezuela en todos partes . . . yo tengo derecho a defender

		tell him these same words . . . that they should respect
		Venezuelans everywhere . . . I have the right to defend them
18.	Juan Carlos:	porque no te callas
		why don't you shut up
19.	Zapatero:	Presidente Hugo Chávez
		President Hugo Chávez
20.	Woman:	Por favor no los dialagos
		please do not engage in dialogue
21.	Zapatero:	Presidente Hugo Chávez
		President Hugo Chávez
22.	Chávez:	Podra ser español el presidente Aznar pero es una fascista y
		eso es una falta de respeto
		Prime Minister Aznar may well be a Spaniard but he is a
		fascist and this is an act of disrespect

In turn 1 of this exchange, Zapatero distances himself from Aznar's right-wing politics by literally claiming to not be close to them. In this move, he asserts his own identity as a politician to the left of Aznar. In the same turn, Zapatero asserts an ideology in which a Prime Minister elected by the Spanish people deserves a certain amount of authority and respect. This authority and respect seems to come from the fact that the Prime Minister is a symbol of the will of the Spanish people. He says, "*exigo*" (I demand). His choice of words, using his position's ability to demand, indexes his own role as an elected Prime Minister of Spain who has the ability to demand respect on behalf of the Spanish people.

In turns 2 through 11, Chávez also indexes his own identity as an elected President of Venezuela and implies that Aznar's support of the 2002 coup disrespected the dignity of the Venezuelan *pueblo* (people). His identity as an elected official and therefore as symbolic of the will of the people is invoked here.

In turn 17, Chávez demands respect for Venezuelans. Then in turn 18, King Juan Carlos I responds to him saying, "*porque no te callas*" (Why don't you shut up?). As the Spanish monarch, King Juan Carlos I is constitutionally obliged to represent Spain in international relations. Therefore, his use of these harsh words to President Chávez constructs Chávez as illegitimate as a leader and not worthy of the usual diplomacy afforded leaders of nations. In turns 19 and 21, Zapatero counters this by addressing Chávez as "*Presidente Hugo Chávez*," indexing Chávez's identity as the legitimate president of Venezuela.

At this point, Chávez refocuses his argument away from one that could be seen to address Spaniards to one that focuses his critiques toward the politics of fascism. In turn 22, Chávez argues that he is not concerned with Aznar's identity as a Spaniard, he is concerned with Aznar's identity as a fascist. He defines fascism itself as an act of disrespect. In this way, Chávez ascribes an identity to Aznar, one of being a fascist, and then proceeds to associate that identity with acts of disrespect.

We can see from the exchange between Chávez, Zapatero, and King Juan Carlos I that particular identities are indexed in the interaction. These identities are relevant both to the broader context and to the ongoing interaction. The participants in the interaction have other aspects of identity that might be indexed. However, the aspects of identity that are indexed are relevant to the argument at hand and to the broader context within which the interaction is embedded.

We can see from this interaction that identities do not simply reside within the individual but that they are socially constructed in the process of interaction. Not only do we construct our own identities in interaction, but we also construct the identities of others in interaction. And that includes those, like Aznar, who are not physically present in the interaction.

5.1 Doing Sociolinguists: Thought Exploration

In this short analysis, we have not, of course, been able to look at everything that is going on in this exchange. Go back to the exchange and do some of your own analysis. What else do you see happening that affects how people's identities are being constructed?

At this point, we will turn to some of the theoretical approaches that have influenced the way that sociolinguists understand language use in human interaction. We will also relate these frameworks to current understandings of the construction of identity as an interactional act.

5.1.1 Face-to-face interaction

In the 1960s and 1970s, three new and unique perspectives on language developed at about the same time. The *Ethnography of Communication* was developed by Dell Hymes, an anthropologist. We discussed Hymes' work in Chapter 4, and we will discuss it further in this chapter and in Chapter 8. Another perspective was developed by Harvey Sacks, a sociologist. His work was the catalyst for *Conversation Analysis*, which we will discuss later in this chapter and in Chapter 8. Yet another perspective was developed by Erving Goffman, a sociologist. All three of these perspectives have contributed enormously to our understanding of language in face-to-face interaction, but because we can only write about one at a time, at this point we will turn to Goffman's approaches. Goffman's work is highly influential in modern under- standings of the construction of identity through face-to-face interaction.

It may seem pretty obvious what we mean by the term face-to-face inter- action. As the term indicates, face-to-face interaction refers to people engaged in mutual interaction while all interactants are physically present, or possibly, virtually physically present. This kind of interaction is different from inter- action done through written correspondence, for example. It should be noted, however, that many other types of human interactions fall under the category of face-to-face interaction. Performance is a type of face-to-face interaction. Courtroom exchanges are a type of face-to-face interaction. Dinner table con- versations are a type of face-to-face interaction. What these all have in com- mon, of course, is that the participants of the interaction are present, physically or virtually, when interacting with one another; so we can see that there are many different situations that count as instances of face-to-face interaction.

In considering face-to-face interaction, Goffman focused on what people are concerned with as we talk to other people. We are, of course, concerned with the messages we are communicating, but we are also concerned with our clothing, how our hair looks, what odor we emit, and many other physical aspects of self. In some conversations, we are also concerned with making sure that we "fit in" or with helping to ensure that others fit in. On the other hand, at times we are concerned with ensuring that people recognize boundaries. We may make moves to demonstrate our alignments with some people and topics and our non-alignments with other people and topics. We also change the way we interact depending on who is in the room and what our role is in the interaction. This interactional work occurs largely through language.

5.2 Doing Sociolinguists: Thought Exploration

Think about any conversation that you have recently had with a friend or classmate. Consider some of the conversational moves you made to align yourself with this friend or classmate or, perhaps, some of the moves that you might have made to create distance between yourselves. Now consider what this same conversation would have been like if another person had been present. How do you think would it have been different?

In this section we have discussed the idea that in face-to-face interactions the interactants are physically, or virtually, co-present. As people interact in such situations they pay attention to conversational factors that allow them to align themselves and their co-participants in particular ways depending on the interactional situation they find themselves in.

5.1.2 Frame

Another element of face-to-face interactions is the way that the participants in the interaction define the interactional situation in which they are involved. We might, for example, define a situation as being serious or non-serious, cooperative or confrontational, formal or informal, monologic or dialogic. Goffman (1974) conceptualized these possible definitions we might have about an interaction as the *frame* of the interaction. Let's consider how the notion of frame can be used in relation the exchanges that took place in Example 5.1 presented earlier between Zapatero, Juan Carlos I, and Chávez. In this sequence of exchanges, trouble arises when the expected frame is not followed. The frame for these types of political summit meetings is one in which relatively polite, monologue-type turns occur. Interactants are not expected to engage one another in more pointed dialogues. This expectation is breached in the interaction between Juan Carlos I and Chávez, as evidenced by the moderator's move in line 20 when she says "Por favor no los dialagos" (*please do not engage in dialogue*). Clearly, the moderator's frame for the event was one in which the participants were supposed to engage in monologue rather than dialogue.

It is not only international summits that have frames, of course. What we would typically think of as more simple matters, such as how we are addressed, can evoke particular interactional frames. When we receive phone calls in our office, we expect callers with whom we have close relationships to address us by our first names as they greet us. This evokes a casual frame for us, allowing us to take an appropriately casual, personal line in the interaction. However, if one of us answers our office phone and someone calls us and addresses us as Dr. Deckert or Dr. Vickers, this address indexes a less casual, more formal frame, and we can draw a conclusion that this person must be someone, a student perhaps, who is expecting us to take a professional line in the ensuing interaction. These types of shared expectations are so real that someone creating a breach in expectations in the wrong circumstances can be seen as rude or inexperienced. On the other hand, a breach in expectations in the right circumstances can be humorous. It can be quite humorous when a person with whom we have a close relationship greets us as "Professor" on the phone. We begin to take a professional line. However, when the interactant reveals himself or herself as someone with whom we have a close relationship, our frame for the interaction shifts to casual.

5.3 Doing Sociolinguistics: Thought Exploration

Can you think of a time you thought you were in one type of interaction and your co-participant thought you were in another type of interaction? For example, suppose your friend invites you over for a visit and you come to find out that your friend is actually selling you a product. Consider a similar experience. How did you find out you were engaged in two different frames? And how did you work it out?

In this section we have discussed the interactional features that allow people to know that they are engaged in a certain type of frame.

5.1.3 Participation frameworks

Not only can we define interactional situations as being framed in particular ways, but we also have certain expectations for people's roles and alignments within those interactions. We expect certain participation frameworks to go along with particular interaction types.

In considering interactions at a very basic level, we can see them as dyadic, involving a speaker and a hearer. However, Erving Goffman (1981) shows that even this basic level of interaction is rarely truly dyadic. He demonstrated how even a seemingly dyadic interaction can involve multiple parties. The speaker role itself, for example, can actually involve several different components. These components, which represent the *production format,* include the *animator,* the *author* and the *principal.* The animator is the person who utters the words. However, the words that are uttered may not be authored by the animator, and they may not reflect the beliefs of the animator. Consider, for example, times when we tell stories about prior events. Quite often in telling these types of stories, we tell about what someone else has said. Clearly, the words are coming out of our mouths when we tell the story. We are the animators of the words, but we are not the authors of words. The author of the words is the person who originally created the ideas that were expressed and chose the words used to express them. Goffman defined a principal as "someone whose position is established by the words that are spoken, someone whose beliefs have been told, someone who is committed to what the words say" (p. 144). The principal is "a person active in some particular social identity or role" (p. 145).

We can think of situations in which both the author and the principal are separate from the animator. Political speech writing provides one example. Often a writer is hired to write a speech for a politician. In such cases, the politician is the animator and the principal, but not the author, or at least not fully the author.

Deckert (2006, 2010a) uses these distinctions in her discussions of children who are participating in interviews with adults. In these interviews, adults are asking children about events in which alleged sexual abuse has occurred. Obviously, it is incredibly important that interviewers are not themselves the authors or even co-authors of the accounts that are generated by the interviews. Yet part of the role of an interviewer is to ask specific questions to help determine whether particular events have occurred in particular ways. These questions and their responses do generate details of an event that might not be generated without the questions. It is important to notice, however, that there is a difference between someone asking a question, in this sense, animating the potential for the authoring of an idea, and the actual answer or authoring of the information. In this way, we can talk about how interviews represent co-animated, but not necessarily co-authored accounts. Consider Example 5.2 in which Nicole, all names are pseudonyms, is being interviewed by Jackie. Since Nicole is multicompetent in both English and Spanish and since she felt more comfortable talking about intimate issues in Spanish, Iliana acted as the interpreter in this event. The legal identity of a victim must be constructed in relation to legal definitions of child molestation. In 5.2, Nicole has said that her father has touched her cosa (*thing*) (2006, p. 191).

Example 5.2

T: 14	Jackie (Social Worker)	Iliana (Interpreter)	Nicole (10;0)
462	Okay. How many times did he touch your cosa ?		
463		¿Cuantas veces te ha tocado tu parte, tu cosa? *How many times has he touched your part, your thing?*	

464	About-?		
465		Como.	
466			Como cuatro veces. *About four times*
467		About four times.	
468	About four times? Okay. What did he touch your cosa with?		
469		¿Con que te tocaba? *What did he touch you with?*	
470			Con las manos. *With his hands*
471		With his hands. (papers rustling)	

The legal definition of this particular crime stipulates the particular body parts that must be touched in particular ways for this crime to have been established. The action of "touching" has already been established at this point in the interview process as has been the body part that has been touched. But what must be established in this account is the instruments of the touching. Typically, of course, when children use the word "touch" they mean with the hands. So if this were a typical narrative, the question we see in turn 468, "What did he touch your cosa with?" would be unnecessary. Notice that the purpose of this question is to clarify Nicole's authored information and not to author new information. When Nicole answers, "Con las manos" in line 470, the two of them have succeeded in co-animating this element of this account. But only Nicole has authored information. Another example of this interplay of animator and author occurs in lines 462–468 when Jackie asks how many times the touching occurred. "Under other circumstances in which Nicole could tell this story to an adult—to her mother, for example—it might be enough for the adult to simply become aware that such events had occurred. The need to know how many times they occurred might be a secondary consideration. With the legal requirements of this interview, however, the question of how many times an event occurred is related to the number of legal charges that can be brought" (Deckert, 2006, p. 191). Again, notice that the act of asking the question of how many times something has happened does not itself author information since it has already been established in the interview that this has occurred more than once, but it does provide the authorship of the information "como cuatro veces" (about four times), allowing this narrative to more explicitly author information that satisfies the legal need to know how many charges can be brought.

The animating of ideas authored by others also happens in other areas of lives. When we advocate for others, for example. Lawyers do this for their clients when they state their clients' representations of situations. Parents do this for children when they tell other people about their children's likes and dislikes, fears and desires. Though it may not be possible to purely be a principal since we are filtering others' needs and beliefs through our own cognitive framework, there are instances when we purport to be speaking for another.

Goffman also showed how the notion of the *hearer* can be complex. He claimed that "hearer" is too simplistic and that it actually involves several possibilities. First, hearers may be classed as *ratified hearers* or as *unratified hearers*. A ratified hearer is one who is directly and consciously addressed by the speaker.

There are also, of course, people who are not consciously being directly addressed by the speaker. These unratified bystanders may themselves be divided into two different roles. These roles include *overhearer* and *eavesdropper*. Most often the ratified interactants are aware of an overhearer's presence. We can all probably think of conversations we have had in which there were hearers who were not the person who was being directly addressed at a given moment. In conversations between three people, for example, we can recognize moments when one person is more directly addressing one listener rather than another. An overhearer might be present during a conversation at a party, for instance, when two people engage on a particular topic and another person or people stand together as the two talk. These roles can continuously shift in the process of the interaction as different people may become ratified at different times during the interaction.

An eavesdropper, on the other hand, is a hearer who is not recognized as a hearer by the ratified participants. We may encounter eavesdroppers when we eat at a restaurant and engage in conversation with our dinner partner. Unbeknownst to us, someone from a nearby table may be listening in. Even you may have even been an eavesdropper at some point in your life, perhaps even an unwilling one. These possibilities are addressed in Bell (1984) who provides an even more complex analysis of overhearers. He suggests that there are *acquainted overhearers,* those that a speaker knows personally for whom a speaker may specifically design an utterance, and *unacquatined overhearers.*

This more complex view of the hearer allows for an analysis of the ways in which outside forces exert control over the interaction. If there is the possibility of an eavesdropper, we are likely to engage in different sorts of interactions than if we assume we are in a completely private situation. Basically, we construct particular identities even for people who could be listening, not only those who are listening. Also consider the awkwardness created when someone is talking very loudly on a cell phone in a public place. We can use the notion of eavesdropper to explain part of our discomfort. In many places there are social mores about eavesdropping. When someone talks loudly in a public place, they are, most likely unconsciously, forcing others into the roles of eavesdroppers rather than ratified hearers. To put it another way, they have placed us into a position within a participation framework without our choosing that may make us feel as if we are breaking a social more.

5.4 Doing Sociolinguistics: Thought Exploration

Think about a time that you were somehow aware that your conversation was being overhead. Did you find that the awareness of an overhearer affected how you carried on your conversation? Do you think that you constructed your presentation of some aspect of your own identity in some way? Did you feel compelled, for example, to be more formal with your interactant? Did you choose to entertain the overhearer? What possible options do you think exist?

In this section we have looked at efforts to reveal the complexity of definitions of speaker and hearer. We have also discussed how these more complicated definitions allow for more complex understandings of local constructions of identity.

5.1.4 Footing

As we interact, we display aspects of identity. Goffman's notions of footing provide one way to address these issues. They provide ways of talking about shifts in aspects of identity we index within a particular interaction. We've discussed Goffman's notion of frame and how it relates to interactional participants' definitions of the situation in which they are involved as serious or non-serious, or cooperative or confrontational, among other things. But understanding the type and nature of a particular interaction as cooperative, for example, is not exactly the same as understanding our role or the positions we take relative to others within that type of situation. This is what Goffman would call our *footing*.

Goffman (1981) defined footing as "the alignment we take up to ourselves and others as expressed in the way we manage the reception or production of an utterance" (p. 128). Footing, then, is in line with how we understand the frame of interaction that we are involved in, but in addition, it considers interactant's roles and their positioning of their roles relative to others.

In the process of complex interactions, our footing may shift. A footing shift causes a change in the frame of the interaction. In other words, a change in footing coincides with a shift to a different type of interactional situation. Hutchby (1999) provides an example of a change in footing in the opening of a talk radio call-in show. In example 5.3, we see the change in footing described by Hutchby also coincides with a change in the participation framework (p. 49).

Example 5.3
1. Host: Joan is calling from Clapham now. Good morning.
2. Caller: Good morning Brian

In this very short example of an interaction, there are a number of shifts in footing. In the first sentence of line 1, "Joan is calling from Clapham now," the audience is ratified and directly addressed by the host. But when the host shifts footing to directly address the caller, by saying "Good morning" to her, the audience remains ratified, but audience members are no longer being directly addressed. Basically, in this one turn, they go from ratified and directly addressed to ratified and indirectly addressed. The caller, on the other hand, goes from unratified and not addressed, since typically people who call in must turn their radios down, to ratified and directly addressed as the host greets her.

The change in footing also coincides with a change in the frame of the interaction. At first, the interaction involves a monologue by the radio show host as the audience listens in. Once the caller is addressed, however, the interaction becomes dialogic.

5.5 Doing Sociolinguistics: Thought Exploration

How does your footing change when you are talking among your peers in the classroom before instruction begins and then the professor walks in and begins the lesson?

In this section, we have talked about how footing shifts as the frame for the interaction shifts. A change in footing involves a change in our alignment with respect to the interaction.

5.1.5 Participant structures

Building on Goffman's notion of participation framework, Philips (1972, 1983) developed the construct of *participant structure*. This construct discerns the different ways that participants organize themselves as they engage in interactional events. She studied school children on the Warms Springs Indian Reservation in Oregon, and found that the Native American children on the reservation preferred certain participant structures. They seemed not to prefer a classroom participant structure in which individual students were called on and were expected to demonstrate knowledge in front of their peers. In fact, this kind of individual showmanship was considered to be quite rude among the Native Americans on the Warm Springs Reservation. Therefore, if judged from an outsider's cultural expectations of classroom students, these Native American children often appeared to be quite reticent to interact in the classroom and disengaged from the lessons.

However, Philips demonstrated that while participating in group work that included collaborative teamwork to complete a task, these students were active participants and seemed quite engaged in the task at hand. A participant structure in which they worked collaboratively with their peers was the most common participant structure on the reservation. The focus within this kind of participant structure is on group, collaborative accomplishment rather than on individual accomplishment. Philips found that this type of collaborative participant structure was far more common among both adults and children in the Warms Springs community. When the participant structure in the school did not match these Native American children's ways of typically organizing themselves and managing their behavior, the children disengaged. When the participant structure in the school conformed to these children's ways of organizing themselves and managing their behavior, they engaged.

Philips demonstrated that in different cultural contexts there are preferences for different participant structures. When people are asked to participate in an unfamiliar participant structure, knowing how to do that can be difficult and uncomfortable. Moreover, if the interaction within the participant structure seems to be counter to norms for interaction within the participants' cultural group, people may be unwilling to engage in interaction within that participant structure.

5.6 Doing Sociolinguistics: Thought Exploration

Consider your own classroom experiences. How do your understandings of participant structures correlate or not correlate with your previous life experiences both outside and inside the classroom? If you are thinking of becoming a teacher, how do you think your understandings of participant structures may be similar to or dissimilar from your future potential students? Do you think gender or generational changes may affect this?

In this section, we have seen that people have culturally based participation structures. Though these participation structures are not always obvious, they have important effects on the ways that people engage in various activities.

5.1.6 Face

Goffman (1967) developed the construct of *face* work to provide a means for discussing people's alignments in face-to-face interaction. The idea is that as we interact, we try to construct a particular identity relative to the interaction. Goffman defines face as "the positive social value a person effectively claims for himself by the line others assume he has taken during a particular contact" (p. 5). If an interactant consistently takes a particular line, that interactant can be said to maintain face. As we interact with others, we engage in face work not only on our own behalf but on behalf of the other interactants. In general, if we are feeling positively toward them, we try not to take a line that would somehow threaten the face of our fellow participants. Face work, then, is an interactional achievement in which all interactants work to maintain each other's faces. Goffman claims that people who are adept at engaging in face work are those who others label as having tact or social skill.

However, there are situations in which face work breaks down, and a threat to face occurs. This happens when an interacant's actions cause a threat to the interactant's own face or to another interactant's face. When there is a threat to face, Goffman argues that interactants engage in *face saving practices*. The goal of face work is to minimize the occurrence of face threats and if face threats do occur, to minimize their impact. Even seemingly simple instances of social interaction can involve a face threat.

In Example 5.4, United States Secretary of State, Hillary Clinton, took questions from a Congolese student during a public question-answer session while she was on a diplomatic trip to Congo in 2009 (Skynews, 2009).

Example 5.4

Student   We've all heard about the Chinese contracts in this country (2.5 seconds) their interferences (1 second) from the World Bank against this contract (1 second) what does Mr. Clinton think through the mouth of Mrs. Clinton and what does Mr. Mi Mutumbo think on this situation thank you very much

(5.5 seconds pass while the student's question is translated)

Hillary Clinton Wait you want me to tell you what my husband thinks? (1 second) my husband is not the Secretary of State . . . I am (0.5 second) so you ask my opinion I will tell you my opinion . . . I'm not going to be channeling my husband.

In this example, the line the U.S. Secretary of State is taking is one in which she is answering questions from an audience of Congolese students. By asking Mrs. Clinton to provide the opinions of two men rather than her own, the Congolese student has produced a threat to both the social position Secretary of State Clinton assumes she holds in the situation, that of a powerful political leader rather than the wife of a powerful political leader, and the line she is enacting, that of the U.S. Secretary of State answering questions. Mrs. Clinton's rather blunt response indicates her understanding of the severity of the face threat that has just occurred. Her response involves face saving that very clearly maintains the consistency of the line she has taken as Secretary of State. However, she does nothing to mitigate the faux pas that the student and the translator made. This lack of mitigation on the student's behalf, her lack of making a face saving move for her interactant, was the basis of heavy critique of Mrs. Clinton in the media. Her reaction was portrayed in the media as an outburst. The basis of this critique seems to be that her reply to the student was "out of line" in terms of her role as the head diplomat of the United States, who it would seem holds the social responsibility of displaying the tact and social skills to save face for her interactant.

As this example demonstrates, face work is intimately tied to social roles as well as to the line that people take in relation to the social situation. As Goffman makes clear, we do not always engage in smooth social interactions. We can fail to maintain the consistency of the line that we and our interactants are trying to take by a failure on the part of one or all of the interactants to manage the face work necessary to maintain this line.

5.7 Doing Sociolinguistics: Thought Exploration

In your experience there have probably been times when you were engaged in face threatening situations. Consider one of these times. What was the interaction like? What made it feel face threatening? How did you resolve it if you did?

In this section we have discussed the importance of face work in interaction. Face work is crucial to our ability to maintain our social identities as we are constructing them in any interaction. When face work breaks down, these identities can become threatened.

5.1.7 Politeness

The common understanding of the word "politeness" includes notions of "please" and "thank you" and maintaining other social graces. As we have seen in other chapters in this book, words that have common meanings are used in quite specific ways in language studies that look at the social elements of language. This word, *politeness*, is no exception. Sociolinguists have developed a notion of politeness that allows explanation of the way that people protect their own and take care of others' identity needs.

Politeness Theory was pioneered by Brown and Levinson (1987) to explain how people manage identity needs across cultures. In theorizing about the management of identity needs, Brown and Levinson heavily utilized Goffman's notion of face. They claimed that in doing politeness, we have both negative face needs and positive face needs.

Negative face refers to our need not to be impeded and our need to maintain social distance. One example might be answering the door to a salesperson. This kind of interaction is by its very nature a threat to negative face, if we assume that the salesperson is impeding our ability to maintain whatever line it is that we take when we are at home. The salesperson is impeding our ability to control our time by requesting that we listen to an offer. Knowing this, a good salesperson might engage in interactional strategies by making the request in a way that mitigates the negative face threat. They might say, for instance, "I'm very sorry to bother you" or "Could I take a moment of your time?" These utterances contain negative politeness strategies that work to mitigate the threat to negative face.

At the same time, this same situation represents a potential positive face threat for the salesperson. *Positive face* needs include the need to be accepted and to affiliate with others. Certainly, successfully maintaining the line of a salesperson requires people's acceptance. In the encounter with the door-to-door salesperson, the potential customer's refusal to purchase the product could be seen as a positive face threat since it rejects what the salesperson is pedaling. Therefore, when people refuse the product offer, they engage in interactional strategies to mitigate the threat to positive face. For instance, the potential customer might say, "this is a nice product, but I already have one" or "I'm not interested, but good luck to you." These mitigation strategies index the salesperson's positive face needs. The act of refusing the product is a threat to positive face, but the mitigation lessens this threat.

Brown and Levinson claim that the basic notion that people attend to negative and positive face both for themselves and for the people they are interacting with is universal. Some scholars have taken issue with this claim of universality. For instance, Wierzbicka (1985, 1992) has critiqued Brown and Levinson's claim that their Politeness Theory is universal. Much of the critique of the universality claim has been rooted in distinctions between East and West. Chen (2010) labels the universality stance as the *Similar Position* and the claim that there are major differences in East and West pragmatics as the *Different Position*. Those scholars who take the Different Position claim that Brown and Levinson's Politeness Theory is about Western language use and that this theory cannot readily explain Eastern language use. Chen (2010) summarizes the Different Position by citing scholars of Japanese politeness. For instance, Ide (1989) and Matsumoto (1989) claim that Japanese politeness is based on discernment, which is characterized by a "sense of place or role in a given situation according to social convention" (Matsumoto, 1989, p. 230). Western politeness, conversely, is based on volition, which is characterized by individual face needs. Similarly, Mao (1994) takes a Different Position in explaining Chinese politeness. According to Mao, Western face is based in static, individualistic notions of negative and positive politeness. Chinese politeness, on the other hand, is, according to Mao, based in notions of context and community. As Mao (1994, p. 460) asserts, Chinese face "identifies a Chinese desire to secure public acknowledgement of one's prestige or reputation."

Chen (2010) makes the claim that his own work (Chen, 2005) is the sole voice from the field of Chinese pragmatics that supports the Similar Position. Chen argues that it is important to go beyond the surface forms of politeness in the East and the West to uncover their underlying motivations. For Chen, it is, presumably, the underlying motivations that are similar.

Chen's argument makes sense, especially if we revisit Goffman's notion of face, upon which Brown and Levinson based their Politeness Theory. If we examine the critiques of Brown and Levinson's universality claim made by those scholars who take the Different Position, they typically focus on the idea that the positive and negative face needs are individualistic and devoid of notions of community, context, and social roles. However, implicit in Brown and Levinson's (1987) Politeness Theory is the relationship between line and face that is built into Goffman's theory of face work. Goffman's argument is precisely that face work is dependent on the line we take in social interaction. Within the context of that line, we engage in positive and negative face work to maintain that line and to maintain the lines of those around us. The way we go about face work in different social contexts results in *different surface phenomena* as Chen (2010) terms it. However, the underlying motivation to engage in face work for the purpose of maintaining a line may remain universal.

5.8 Doing Sociolinguistics: Thought Exploration

Think about how you do politeness differently depending on who you are talking to and where you are. Consider the idea of inviting someone over for dinner. How would the invitation differ in terms of politeness if you were asking a romantic interest or if you were asking your boss?

In this section we have explored notions of politeness. We have addressed the fact that this notion is intimately tied to the notion of face and social identity. We have also addressed the fact that many people have asserted that politeness varies across cultures using the argument that people in different cultures align themselves in divergent ways with respect to notions of individual or group orientations. However, although there are different surface phenomena, the

basic notion that politeness is tied to the line we take in particular social interactions is consistent across cultures. So politeness is done differently across
cultures, but it is done in some structured way in all cultures.

So far in this chapter we have looked at some of the processes related to
how speakers and their interactants negotiate various complex aspects of
interaction. In particular, we have addressed the notion that individuals orient
themselves to various conversational frames and that shifts in frame can
affect the various footings that an individual takes. We have discussed the
idea that notions such as "speaker" and "hearer" are not simple ones. We can
create our own words, voice the words of others, and perform a variety of
authorship, animator, and principal roles. In our roles as listener we can be
authorized or unauthorized, known or unknown, or maintain a variety of
other relationships to the conversations we are a part of or observe.

We have looked at the notions of face and politeness and the intricate
interconnections between these ideas, and addressed the different ways that
these can play out in various cultures. In the following section of this chapter
we will continue our exploration of communication in various cultures by
exploring how individuals from different cultures face challenges in communicating with one another.

5.2 Intercultural communication

The literature on intercultural communication often focuses on communication breakdown in institutional settings. *Communication breakdown* can be
defined as any failure to communicate in face-to-face interaction. Communication breakdown can, for example, result in two people getting bad impressions of each other based on their interpretation of each other's communicative
styles. In a potential worst case scenario, communication breaks down to such
a degree that the two interactants simply walk away from the interaction, probably puzzled and possibly angered, without any successful communication
happening at all. We will see examples of communication breakdown later in
this section.

Considering that so much research on intercultural communication has
taken place within so called institutional settings, let's define what we mean
by *institutional setting*. Agar (1985) attempts to define the institution, but
admits that the definition is open to debate. According to Agar, an institution
is "a socially legitimated expertise together with those persons authorized to

implement it" (p. 164). This definition implies that many client-institutional representative encounters would constitute an institutional setting. Importantly, as Gumperz and Roberts (1991) assert, much of modern life consists of institutional encounters as both the public and private sectors become increasingly beaurocratized. Therefore, interactions with institutions constitute a large part of modern human life and of modern human communication. In multi-ethnic societies, many of these institutional encounters involve instances of intercultural communication.

In their studies of intercultural communication in institutional settings, scholars have concentrated particularly on certain speech events, such as the social service interview and the job interview. The *speech event* is an important unit of analysis that was developed within the Ethnography of Communication. Hymes (1974) clarifies the difference between the *speech act*, the *speech event*, and the *speech situation* by providing examples as follows: "a party (speech situation), a conversation during a party (speech event), a joke within a conversation (speech act)" (p. 56). Other types of speech events include a doctor's appointment, a school counseling session, a job interview, and retail sales transaction. There are many different speech events that we all participate in on a daily basis.

5.9 Doing Sociolinguistics: Thought Exploration

What speech events can you think of that you have participated in during the last few days or that you regularly participate in?

John Gumperz was an early pioneer in the work on intercultural communication. According to Gumperz, people from different cultures may have different interpretive frames within the same speech event. The interpretive frame surrounds the speech event in a Gumperzian analysis. The *interpretive frame* is rooted in Goffman's concept of frame; it is the way that we understand the interaction that we are involved in. So people from different cultures may have different inherent understandings of how particular speech events progress. Within cultures, interactants use various types of cues to move through and maintain their interactions within speech events. These *contextualization cues* (Gumperz, 1982) signal that we are involved in a particular type of speech event. Contextualization cues are at work in the production of speech. In particular, they operate at the level of prosody, paralinguistic signs, code choice, and choice of lexical form or formulaic expressions to help constitute the interpretive frame.

When people who come from different backgrounds interact with each other, there is potential confusion and tension. This is because for each interactant, differing contextualization cues can lead to divergent interpretive frames for the speech event at hand. Gumperz, Jupp, & Roberts (1979) studied interactions between customers and cashiers in a British bank. The following constructed pair examples are based on their observations of interactions between Indian customers and British cashiers (Gumperz et al., 1979, pp. 21–24). Example 5.5 relates to interactions between two British people; communication seems to run smoothly.

Example 5.5 British-British
Customer: good morning . . . I want to deposit some money please
Cashier: certainly sir you'll need a deposit form
Customer: thank you very much . . . oh no . . . this is the wrong one my account's in Wembley
Cashier: oh I see . . . in that case you'll need a Giro form sir . . . there you are
Customer: thank you
Cashier: you're welcome

Although there is a little misunderstanding about the form that the customer needs, the two easily repair the misunderstanding and continue with a cordial interaction. However, compare this to the interaction to Example 5.6 between the Indian customer and the British cashier (Gumperz et al., 1979).

Example 5.6 Indian-British Bank scene
Customer: excuse me
Cashier: yes sir
Customer: I want to deposit some money
Cashier: oh I see . . . ok . . . you'll need a deposit form then
Customer: yes . . . NO NO this is the wrong one
Cashier: oh you need a Giro form then
Customer: yes Giro form
Cashier: why didn't you say so the first time
Customer: sorry I didn't know

Here we see the misunderstanding about the same form as in the British-British interaction. It seems that the British cashier becomes irritated with the Indian customer. In the end, the Indian customer apologizes to the British cashier. The point of contention seems to be the customer's way of informing the cashier that he had received the wrong form, "NO NO this is the wrong one." In British English, "NO NO" said in such an emphatic way is associated with a contextualization cue that indicates scolding as when parents scold their children. The Indian customer's use of "NO NO," then, indicates to the cashier that the customer is blaming him/her for the mistake. However, in Indian English, there is no contextualization cue that leads to an interpretation of scolding in the emphatic use of "NO NO." It simply works to indicate that something has gone wrong. As this example demonstrates, different ways of doing contextualization in different cultures can lead to differing interpretations, and these differing interpretations may lead to different consequences for the interaction, including communication breakdown.

The scholarship on intercultural communication has typically been concerned with those troubled moments in interaction that result in communication breakdown. However, it is important to consider that intercultural communication may also result in more positive accommodations. Vickers (2004) considers such instances when intercultural communication is relatively smooth. Even in such smooth situations some people's interpretive frames become more represented than the frames of others due to power differentials that exist among interactants. In Chapters 6 and 7, we will further discuss the relationship between intercultural communication and power.

5.10 Doing Sociolinguistics: Thought Exploration

Think of some of your own intercultural encounters. How did you manage them? Were there instances of communication breakdown? What strategies did you use to try to repair the breakdown?

In this section, we have looked at what happens when people from different cultural and language groups come to an interaction using different contextualization cues that invoke different interpretive frames for the interaction. Divergent ways of doing contextualization can cause different interpretations that can lead to communication breakdown.

5.3 Talk and action

In the 1960s, the philosopher, J. L. Austin (1975) argued that language was not simply about truth value or information. He argued that we actually *do things* with words. He argued that in "issuing an utterance," we perform an action. This framework, further developed by John R. Searle (1990a, 1990b), is known as *Speech Act Theory*, and it has been quite influential in sociolinguistics. These theorists defined the minimal unit of communication as the utterance. Speech Act Theory provides a framework for the analysis of utterances like requests, commands, and assertions, among others as *performative speech acts*. The idea is that by stating the utterance, the speaker actually does an action. A classic example is the "I now pronounce you man and wife" in a marriage ceremony. The result of the performance of this utterance in the right circumstances is that the two people are officially married.

Speech Act Theory conceptualizes utterances at three distinct but inter-related levels. These levels include the locutionary act, the illocutionary act, and the perlocutionary act. The *loctionary act* refers to the uttering of specific words. The *illocutionary act* refers to the speaker's intended meaning in making the utterance. The *perlocutionary act* refers to the effect of the act on the hearer, or the hearer's interpretation of the act. Let's look at Example 5.7 to illustrate an analysis of a speech act using the three different levels of analysis. In this example, Sarah and Thomas are involved in a conversation.

Example 5.7
1. Sarah: It's warm in here.
2. Thomas: I'm sorry, dear. I'll call about fixing the air conditioner tomorrow.
3. Sarah: Oh no dear. I like it warm. In fact, I just turned on the heater.

Sarah's utterance, "it's warm in here," has a literal meaning. That literal meaning is an assertion about the temperature. As a locutionary act, Sarah's utterance is an assertion. Thomas, however, seems to interpret the utterance as a request, and assumes that he should do something about the temperature. The perlocutionary act, therefore, is one of a request. In Turn 3, however, Sarah makes clear that her intention was not to make a request, but simply to make an assertion. Thus, Sarah's illocutionary act is an assertion.

Both Austin and Searle demonstrated that speech acts can be direct and indirect. Sarah's utterance is a direct assertion, but Thomas interpreted it as an indirect request. Indirect speech acts are quite common. We may utter a question, such as "Do you have the time?" as a request for someone to tell us the time. The illocutionary act is the equivalent of "Can you tell me the time?" We may utter an assertion, such as, "I see your bed isn't made," as an order. The illocutionary act is the equivalent of the order, "Make your bed!"

The notion of performativity has been further developed by Judith Butler's (1993, 1997) work in regard to identity construction. Butler's performativity is coherent with a conceptualization of reality as a social construction. As people interact with one another, they perform this reality. In other words, this socially constructed reality is continually performed by individuals through their use of language as well as their use of the body. People *do* language and people *do* their bodies in Butler's performative terms.

As we go about constructing identity, then, we engage in identity acts. Such identity acts could be "gender acts" as discussed by Butler. Waugh (2010) demonstrates how interactants do "identity acts" in constructing a particular social reality. Throughout Waugh's paper, Karim, a person of Tunisian decent who has lived large portions of his life in both France and the United States, attempts to construct a transnational, tricultural identity in which he is Tunisian, French, and American. In Example 5.8, Karim asserts that he speaks English and French (Waugh 2010, p. 117).

Example 5.8
Maher: Ouais, je-sais ouais, toi tu-parles le ['Yeah, I-know yeah, you-speak']
Sylvie: y-a ça aussi [There-s that too']
Maher: français ['French']
Karim: et l'anglais! ['and English!']
Maher: anglais ['English']

Waugh explains that English does not have the symbolic capital in France that it does in other parts of the world. In fact, in France, English is seen as a threat to the French language. Therefore, rather than only asserting his symbolic capital as an English speaker, Karim is asserting his identity as both French and American. Through this identity act, he constructs a social reality in which he is a member of both groups. To perform this identity act, then, he indexes the social conventions of a French identity in some aspects of the conversation and an American identity in other aspects of the conversation.

5.11 Doing Sociolinguistics: Thought Exploration

Consider instances when your interactant misinterpreted the illocutionary force of your utterance. How did it affect the interaction? How did you make your meaning clear if you were able to?

In this section we have discussed talk as action, the notion that as we use language we perform acts. The ways that we engage in acts in language are dependent on and help construct our social identities.

5.4 Conversational interaction

Scholars who have studied conversational interaction have worked within a conceptualization of talk as action. Harvey Sacks was the early pioneer in the study of conversational interaction. In a series of lectures (Sacks, 1992), he outlines a theory in which our conversational contributions create membership categories. In one of his classic examples taken from a book of stories that children have told, titled *Children Tell Stories*, he refers to a story a young child told in which she says, "The baby cried, the mommy picked it up." Sacks argues that there are certain actions that we connect with particular categories. The act of picking up a crying baby when performed by a woman is connected to the category of "mother." Sacks argues that the little girl interpreted the woman as the child's mother because she had performed this act of picking up a crying baby. The words themselves both construct the reality of the event and reflect membership categories that have previously been constructed in the cultural reality. There could, of course, be an alternate reality. It is possible that the woman was the baby's aunt, babysitter, or friend. Perhaps the woman was a stranger to the baby, a police officer, kidnapper, or concerned citizen. There are many alternate possibilities, but the reality constructed by the child telling the story of the event was that the woman was the baby's mother. This contribution becomes the reality for the observer's interlocutors, unless it is disputed.

Sacks (1984) argued that conversation provides a rich source of data for those who are interested in sociological perspectives. His work led to the development of a theoretical framework, *Conversation Analysis* (CA), to look at the intricacies of naturally occurring conversation. CA has been quite influential in the field of sociolinguistics.

The development of CA was influenced by the work of both Goffman (1959, 1967, 1974, 1981b) and Garfinkel's (1967) *Studies in Ethnomethodology*. Meaning is seen as something that is created through face-to-face interaction in the work of both Goffman and Garfinkel. However, Goffman places primary importance on the gesture/symbol in meaning making while Garfinkel concentrates on the internal mind and how we make meaning in our interactions as we go along.

In Goffman's work, society creates our roles, and we carry out these roles in face-to-face interaction. Following in the tradition of symbolic interaction, Goffman expands Mead's (1934) work to develop a concept of *role construction*. Goffman claims that members of society step in to pre-existing roles, and symbols are manipulated in an effort to achieve impression management. This falls within Mead's concept of the society creating the individual and within Mead's idea that gesture assignment creates new objects. "The framework bears upon dynamic issues created by the motivation to sustain a definition of the situation that has been projected before others" (Goffman 1959, p. 239). For Goffman, communication and the manipulation of symbols create a certain impression which either succeeds or fails in achieving the construction of some pre-existing role.

In Garfinkel's work on *Ethnomethodology*, conversely, meaning is created in the process of interaction. Garfinkel (1967) argues that situations "in their actually and intended logical structures are essentially vague" (p. 96). He adds that these structures are modified and created in the contexts in which they are enacted, and that this is partially how meaning is produced in conversations. He argues with Schutz (1970) that individuals have common sense knowledge of social structures that they use when interpreting ongoing speech. In other words, in the process of face-to-face interaction, interactants rely on their background knowledge to make sense of the interaction. However, interactants also make sense of the interaction in an ad hoc manner as they go along. As Goodwin and Heritage (1990) explain, "intersubjective understandings are actively achieved as the outcome of concrete interactive processes" (p. 286). Moreover, the social context influences the interaction, but also, according to an Ethnomethodological perspective, social context can be defined or redefined by the interaction. Ultimately, the study of language in face-to-face interaction is central to the work of Garfinkel and CA.

Conversation Analysts have demonstrated the sequential structure of conversation in face-to-face interaction. They have informed us of the need to go beyond the sentence level to understand how meaning is achieved through language in discussing the organization of conversation. The Conversation Analysts purport that conversation is a *local management system* as well as an *interactionally managed system* within which there is a definite structure followed by conversants. Central to CA is the concept of the *Adjacency Pair* (Sacks, Schegloff, & Jefferson, 1974). The concept of the Adjacency Pair is a basic pair sequence to CA in which one utterance achieves meaning only in relation to what comes before or after it. Furthermore, as Goodwin and Heritage (1990) state, the adjacency pair "describes a procedure through which participants constrain one another, and hold one another accountable, to produce coherent and intelligible courses of action" (p. 288). However, a CA analysis conceptualizes all turns at talk within a conversation as being interrelated and contingent upon one another. So utterances take on meaning in large part through the way that they are uptaken, or understood in the conversation. In this way, CA allows for an analysis of individuals' understanding of meaning. We can see, for example, how a hearer interprets the meaning of a speaker by the way in which the hearer responds.

CA has been employed to identify and study various types of conversational discourse, including but not limited to talk about troubles (Jefferson, 1981, 1984), service encounters (Bailey, 1997), and arguments among children (Goodwin, 1990) as well as talk unique to various institutional settings, including the medical setting (Heath, 1992), the courtroom (Atkinson, 1992), the classroom (McHoul, 1978), the media (Heritage, 1985), and the government agency (Gumperz, 1982). CA is a rich framework for the description of conversational interaction in that it allows the examination of the organization of conversation, the construction of meaning in conversation, as well as differentiation among types of talk in various social settings.

Conversation Analysts bring with them an important and unique definition of context that is often different from other fields of study that look at language and its social uses. In this CA definition, context is determined and defined within the conversation itself.

This does not mean, however, that CA analysts are unable to address larger social issues. By looking at multiple examples of a particular aspect of conversation or conversation type, CA analysts have been able to draw conclusions about the nature of conversation as well as the social patterns that exist in language, which individuals can index as one of the tools they use to construct aspects of identity.

Consider an example from Gail Jefferson (2002, p. 1346). In this example, she is looking at how people often use the word "no" to show agreement with a conversational partner's point. In Example 5.9, Jefferson reports that "Co-workers Maggie and Sorrell went to a wedding reception where Maggie had some sort of momentary blackout and felt ill. Next morning she phones Sorrell at work to say that she will not be coming to work, is going to the doctor" (p. 1346).

Example 5.9
```
1   Maggie:       .hh because I(c) (.) you know I told Mother what'd ha:ppened
                  yesterday
2                 there at the party,
3   Sorrell:      [°Yeah.°]
4   Maggie:       [a::] n d uh,.hhhhh (0.2) uh you know she asked me if it was
5       (-)       because I'd had too much to dri:nk and I said no=
6   Sorrell: (-)  =[N o:::::.]
7   Maggie:       =[because at the t]i:me I'd only ha:d,h you know that
                  drink'n
8                 aha:lf when we were going through the receiving line.
9   Sorrell:      Ri:ght.
```

From a CA perspective, this example is analyzable in at least two ways. In the first perspective, CA allows for an analysis of the structure of the conversation. In the second perspective, we can analyze how individuals construct identity within the framework of a particular conversation.

From the first perspective, Jefferson is pointing out that Sorrell's long "no" (the colons show that the vowel was significantly lengthened) in line 6, shows a sense of "'I'm on your side.' 'Of course you didn't. How could anyone think such a thing'" (p. 1346). So what Jefferson's analysis adds to our understanding of conversation is that a language element like "no" that is typically assumed to demonstrate dissent, can actually in particular uses for particular users demonstrate agreement. Specifically, Jefferson found a difference in the ways that British speakers of English and American speakers of English would use this type of "no." She found that British listeners used this form of "no" as a "continuer," a kind of back channeling, to show that they are actively listening. For some Americans, however, the use of "no" in this fashion shows a type of agreement with the speaker that would mark a listener's affiliation with the speaker. In one sense, then, the different uses of the form of "no" index a listener's identity as either a British English or American English speaker and as someone who is listening supportively or acting affiliatively, respectively. In both cases the appropriate use marks the listener as a person with community appropriate language competence.

From the second perspective, we can see that Maggie is very careful in her interaction with Sorrell to construct her own identity as someone who is a responsible worker. In her phone call to Sorrell telling her that she will not be coming in to work because she is going to the doctor, she makes it clear that this is not due to a simple case of hangover, but to something that could be more serious. In lines 4–8 she briefly narrates a conversation with her mother in which she assured her mother that her blackout had nothing to do with her drinking as she had only had a drink and a half. In orienting toward an identity as a person who is suffering from an illness rather than as someone who is simply suffering a hangover, and possibly drinks too much, she is constructing herself as both a responsible drinker and a responsible worker. In supplying the affiliative "no," her co-worker, Sorrell, provides support for these constructions essentially co-constructing Maggie as a sick individual and not an irresponsible individual with a drinking problem.

CA, then, allows for analysis of turns of talk that are interrelated and contingent upon one another. CA views conversation as a system that is locally constructed as well as a system that is interactionally managed. It allows for an analysis of meaning making that is derived within the context of the conversation itself. It provides for an analysis of the structural features of the conversation. In addition, CA allows for a close analysis of how individuals construct identity because we can examine the contributions speakers make in the process of conversational interaction.

5.12 Doing Sociolinguistics: Thought Exploration

Think about whether or not you can draw conclusions about conversation without collecting some type of data. When conversation analysts do work they record and transcribe their data. Why is this necessary? Why, for instance, couldn't we just "think about" our own conversations and draw conclusions about what precisely happened in the conversation?

In this section of the chapter, we have explored how Conversation Analysis has contributed to our understanding of conversational structure and identity construction. The type of fine-grained analyses that Conversation Analysis offers allows insight into the micro-interactions that contribute larger societal constructs including identity.

5.5 Doing sociolinguistics: research activities

1: Exploring the Footing Shifts in an Interview

Watch an interview and pay particular attention to the footing shifts.

a. How do their alignments shift?
b. What seems to instigate the shifts?
c. How do the footing shifts contribute to participants' identities?

2–4 Analyzing Recorded Conversations.

Record approximately 10–15 minutes of informal conversation between you and your friends or your family. Look at the conversational features. Keeping in mind the fact that conversations are locally managed phenomena, consider features of this locally managed system that you might discover such as overlaps, pauses, and segments that may be said particularly loudly.

2. As you listen to the recording of your conversation, what sorts of features do you notice? What kinds of features surprise you?
3. One of the things that you will find is that in typical, informal conversations, there are times that people overlap one another.

a. When overlap appears in the conversation you recorded, what is it like?
b. Does it seem like interruption or are there times when it shows cooperation?

4. You will also find that there are times when pauses occur.

a. When do people pause in your conversation?
b. Do all of these pauses seem the same to you?
c. What might be the significance of these various types of pauses?

5.6 Suggested further reading

Austin, J. L. (1975). *How to do things with words* (2nd ed.). Cambridge, MA: Harvard University Press.

Brown, P., & Levinson, S. C. (1987). *Politeness: Some universals in language usage* (2nd ed.). Cambridge, MA: Cambridge University Press.

Butler, J. (1993). *Bodies that matter*. New York: Routledge.

Goffman, E. (1974). *Frame analysis: An essay on the organization of experience*. Boston: Northeastern University Press.

Goffman, E. (1981). *Forms of talk*. Philadelphia: University of Pennsylvania.

Goodwin, C., & Heritage, J. (1990). Conversation analysis. *Annual Review of Anthropology, 19*, 283–307.

Gumperz, J. J. (1982). *Discourse strategies*. Cambridge: Cambridge University.

Philips, S. U. (1983). *The invisible culture: Communication in classroom and community on the Warm Springs Reservation*. Prospect Heights, IL: Waveland Press.

Sacks, H. (1984). Notes on methodology. In J. M. Atkinson & J. Heritage (Eds.), *Structures of social action: Studies in conversation analysis* (pp. 21–27). Cambridge: Cambridge University Press.

Sacks, H., Schegloff, E. A., & Jefferson, G. (1974). A simplest systematics for the organization of turn-taking for conversation. *Language, 50*, 696–735.

Searle, J. R. (1990). What is a speech act? In A. P. Martinich (Ed.), *The philosophy of language* (2nd ed., pp. 115–125). New York, NY: Oxford University Press.

6 Language, Power, and Micro-interactions

Key Terms: *language ideology; referential indexicals; deictic expressions; evidentials; anaphoric reference; person deixis; honorifics; hegemony; ratification; resistance; institutional discourse; gatekeeping encounters; interpreter; mediated interaction; language crimes*

This chapter explores conceptions of language, ideology, power, and identity at the local, micro-interactional level. Examples of these local contexts include notions of family, for example, as well as notions of how identities are constructed in relation to family, educational, legal, medical, and workplace settings. Ideology is naturalized. This means that it is taken for granted and often unnoticed, in practice and lived relations. It is also enacted in discourse, and revealed quite explicitly in metalinguistic discourse.

To begin, we should articulate what sociolinguists mean when they use the term *language ideology*. Language ideology can be understood as the "representations, whether explicit or implicit, that construe the intersection of language and human beings in a social world" (Schieffelin, Woolard, & Kroskrity, 1998, p. 3). Scholars who study language ideology, then, are interested in how social interactions are shaped by the language ideologies at work in the social world (Woolard, 1998). Of course human beings in a social world experience a wide variety of situations, so it is important to understand how language ideologies affect linguistic interactions in many different areas. Ultimately, relating ideas of identity construction to larger language ideologies within the social world can provide a rich picture of the way that individuals engage in linguistic interaction.

Examining human beings in their social worlds carries with it the need to examine the power structures and power relationships that are inherent within those social worlds. A focus on language ideology allows insights into the roles power plays in the construction of identity.

6.1 Indexicality

An American television commercial in the 1990s for *Polaner All Fruit*, displays an example of a language ideology in action. The setting is a formal dining one. People are seated around a formal table, they are dressed formally, and their gestures and movements index a formal social interaction. In the course of dining, the diners politely ask one another to "Please pass the All Fruit," the subject of the commercial. In the midst of this formality, a man asks in a Southern accent, "Wudja please pass the jelly?" This utterance causes a communal gasp at the table, and one woman swoons. In interpreting the commercial, listeners must be able to index certain cultural understandings. The structure of the request seems polite enough and follows the conventions of dining etiquette, requesting that others pass items rather than reaching for them. It places the request in a question form beginning with the modal *would*, and it uses the word *please*; both mitigate the negative face threat inherent in imposing on others. The problem is the use of the word "jelly." The reaction to this word clearly indexed something shameful, something lesser than *All Fruit*. Evidently, common jelly did not belong at this correct table. Audiences of this commercial must perform this social interpretation of the language event to come to this conclusion. It is interesting, too, to note that the producers of the commercial chose to give the man who made the social *faux pas* a Southern American accent. Lippi-Green (1997b) argues that entertainment producers often use accent to index aspects of a character's identity. In this case, this man's southern accent was used to represent a lack of sophistication and intelligence that matched his apparently unsophisticated request. In one way this commercial indexes cultural understandings about a particular accent, including the biases that accompany these understandings. In addition, it also reconstructs those notions about this particular accent. As we can see, indexicality is important to the way that we make meaning, in both the processes of interpretation and construction.

The notion of indexicality is crucial to an understanding of the relationship between language and ideology on the one hand and language and identity on the other hand. Broadly defined, indexicality is a "property of speech through which cultural contexts such as social identities (e.g., gender) and social activities (e.g. a gossip session) are constituted in particular stances and acts" (Ochs, 1992, p. 335).

To begin our discussion of indexicality, we will turn to the notion of *referential indexicals* (Fillmore, 1997; Hanks, 2009). These are also known widely as *deictic expressions*. These expressions include ways that we reference *persons*, as seen in the English pronoun system; *places* as seen in the English words *this* and *that*; *time*, as seen in words like *now* and *then*; and elements of *discourse*. Languages worldwide contain deictic expressions, and deictic systems are quite diverse cross-linguistically. What deictic expressions have in common is that to be understood they must be grounded, or *anchored*, as Fillmore (1997) would express it, in a particular context. Consider, for example, what Fillmore would call "a worst possible case" for an unanchored expression. He writes that he imagines finding a bottle afloat in the middle of the ocean, and the bottle contains the following message, "Meet me here at noon tomorrow with a stick about this big" (1997, p. 60). Notice that because we cannot anchor the expression in relation to person, time, place, or discourse in any way, we have absolutely no idea whom we are supposed to meet when or where, and we have no idea of the size of the stick we should bring, or even, the reason for bringing it. It is these types of knowledge that we get from indexicals when they are grounded in given contexts.

Hanks (2009) argues that one of the basic functions of referential indexicals is to individuate. As Hanks (2009, p. 10) states:

> If I say "this podium," I individuate the object before me; "This pen" (holding up), I individuate the object in my hand, "Sit over there." (pointing), I individuate a place. In each case the deictic token-cum-gesture picks out the object I am talking about, apart from all other possible objects, by situating it in the immediate surround.

At a basic level, deixis refers to indexing within the immediate context. Let's go back to the example words *here* and *there*. As noted, without their spatial context, it is impossible to know what they refer to. The speaker is a point of reference that grounds understandings of these words. So *here* is the area relatively close to the speaker, and *there* is some area relatively far away from the speaker. The same goes for the deictic expressions *this* and *that*. However, if speakers additionally *point* at the pen in front of them, and say "this," then we know exactly which object is indexed. In the same way, if speakers point at the pen in front of an addressee and say "that," we know exactly which object is indexed. From the perspective of spatial deixis, we can say that *this* indexes an entity that is relatively close to the speaker. *That*, on the other hand, indexes an entity that is relatively distant from the speaker.

As Hanks (2009, p. 12) asserts, however, the question for deixis reaches beyond the spatial location of the referent to the identification of the referent in relation to the speaker and addressee. It becomes more complex than simply indexing relative distance. The semantics of deixis, for example, varies from language to language. Hanks (2009, p. 14) provides an example of Yucatec deictics to show this point. Hanks' analysis is more complex than will be represented here, but this example is instructive. Hanks identifies three deictics that are part of what he terms the "ostensive evidential series (héel)." Evidentials in language index speakers' understandings of the knowledge they are providing. In Yucatec, there are three distinct morphological endings that speakers can attach to héel (a', o', be') to distinguish their different perceptual modalities. They are used to indicate whether the understanding is the result of a sense of touch, sight, or sound with each of these having implications:

hé'e(l-) a'	'here is it (tactual)'
hé'e(l-) o'	'there it is (visual)'
hé'e- be'	'there it is (audible)'

In Example 6.1, from Hanks (2009, p. 14), he provides the following examples to demonstrate the uses of these deictics:

Example 6.1
1. hé' le kib a'
   OSTEV art candle TACTUAL
   'Here's the candle (presenting)'
2. hé' síná'an o'
   OSTEV scorpion VISUAL
   'There's a scorpion (look out!)'
3. hé' inw-alak peek be'
   OSTEV my dog PERIPHERAL
   'There's my dog (listen)'

In these examples, the deictic expressions do more than refer to an object in terms of its spatial relationship to the speaker. Though space is certainly involved, the reference is more complicated. First, the choice of deictic seems to be dependent not just on the spatial perspective of the speaker. Rather, the choice is based on the relationship between the type of knowledge the speaker has, the addressee, and the referent. So considerations are whether something is in tactical range, visual range, or listening range. Therefore, for speakers of Yucatec, perceptions of physicality and space are involved in the choice and interpretation of deictic expressions.

Discourse deictics are used to refer to something that came previously in the discourse. These deictics both refer to the item that came before and essentially represent it in the new point in the discourse. We can say that they are used *anaphorically*. If we take the examples of *this* and *that*, we can find discourse examples in which both are used anaphorically. In the following excerpt from *Scientific American*, "Looking for Life in the Multi-verse," Jenkins and Perez use the deictic *this* to anaphorically refer back to a previous statement.

> Einstein's general theory of relativity requires that all forms of energy exert gravity. If *this* energy is positive, it causes spacetime to expand at an exponentially accelerating rate.

In the example, *this energy* refers back to the "energy" as it was contextual-ized in the previous phrase, "all forms of energy exert gravity." Using the deictic *this* makes the prior utterance conceptually proximal to the audience. If the authors had chosen to use *that energy*, the effect would be to make the prior utterance conceptually distal. In discourse, then, these deictics are used in a metaphoric spatial way, but they do more than simply refer proximally or distally. The choice actually constructs the concept as proximal or distal in our minds.

6.1 Doing Sociolinguistics: Thought Exploration

Chose a paragraph or two in this book where you can find the use of words "this" and "that" in the prose of the text. Think about the uses of these spatial deictics. Consider how they function to construct meaning in the text.

In this section, we have discussed indexicality as a basic mechanism for conveying social relations through language. We have seen that indexicality can be used to refer to particular referents in space, time, and discourse, constructing them as proximal or distal.

6.1.1 Indexicality and micro-interactions

If we broaden our contextual perspective from the immediate to the larger social context, we can see the indexing of social level concepts. For instance, the English indexical, *that*, can index more than simply spatial or discourse distance. It can index social distance and notions of otherness. During the 2008 United States presidential campaign, Sen. John McCain was accused by the Obama campaign of accentuating Sen. Barack Obama's "otherness." Example 6.2 (tpmtv, 2008) provides an excerpt from a debate between McCain and Obama, in which McCain said the following:

> Example 6.2
>
> McCain: By the way my friends . . . I know you grow a little weary of this back and forth..there was an energy bill on the floor of the senate loaded down with goodies..billions for the oil companies..and it was sponsored by..Bush and Cheney . . . you know who voted for it? . . . you might never know..*that one* (pointing with his index finger by moving his arm across his chest at Obama while still directing his gaze toward the audience) . . . you know who voted against it?..me

It seems unlikely that the use of the pointing reference and the deictic expression "that one" to refer to Obama was used simply to index physical distance from Obama. The two sat next to each other and were the only two on the stage. A more likely analysis seems to be that McCain was attempting to index social, and, more specifically political, distance from Obama by referring to him as "that one." It's important to notice that McCain referred to Obama as "that one" as opposed to "that senator" or even "that man." The utterance as a whole places Obama in a socially distant category that does not index his respected role as a senator or even as a man. The expression conjures images of selecting some object, as in "I'll take that one."

As this example demonstrates, referential indexicals can index aspects of an utterance beyond the immediate context. McCain used the referential indexical, *that*, to position himself socially in relation to Obama. He used *that* to disaffiliate from Obama and to construct an identity for Obama as other.

Pronouns also constitute a deictic category often termed *person deixis*. We cannot know who *you* refers to or who *he* refers to, for example, without the ability to index the immediate physical or discourse context. Our use of pronouns points to the context in order to attribute meaning to the pronoun.

In the following example, the pronoun *they* is used anaphorically, meaning that within the context of the discourse it indexes a prior referent.

> Example 6.3
> A: *Mary and Sam* play the piano well
> B: *they* have taken lessons for many years

They and *Mary and Sam* are co-referents. We know that "they" in B's utterance refers to the same entities as the "Mary and Sam" in A's utterance. We could also imagine a situation where A and B are in the same room listening to Mary and Sam play the piano. In this case, A could say "they play the piano very well," and the referent of *they* would be obvious from the immediate context. Pronouns derive their meaning from the discourse context or from the immediate physical/spatial context.

As we saw with McCain's use of the deictic "that one," pronoun use can also index social notions that are much more complex and interesting. Not only can we index the immediate and discourse context through our pronoun usage, we can also index ideological affiliations and construct identity through our choice of pronouns.

In Waugh (2010), she examines the face-to-face interactions of Karim, a French citizen of Tunisian ethnicity who had spent part of his childhood in France and part of his childhood in the United States. At the time that Waugh collected the recording, Karim had just finished his freshman year at an elite Ivy League U.S. university and was on vacation in France.

His face-to-face interactions as he talks to two French people demonstrate how he uses pronouns to shift national affiliations. In the following example (Waugh, 2010, p. 122), Karim explains in French that U.S. driving conditions are calmer (than French driving conditions), which makes it easier to drive long distances in the United States.

> Example 6.4
> Karim: Aux Etats-Unis c'est beaucoup plus calme. Alors c'est facile, on-est pas
> fatigué après avoir fait six heures six heures de route
> *'In the US it's much calmer. So, it's easy, we-aren't*
> *tired after having been six hours six hours on the road.'*

Karim uses the French pronoun *on- (we)* when he says "on-est pas fatigue" (*we are not tired*), identifying himself as part of the "we" that constitutes

American drivers. In this section of the conversation, he constructs his affiliation with Americans.

In a later part of the same conversation, however, we can see Karim shift his pronoun use to shift his national affiliation. In this part of the conversation, the topic has moved to one about gun laws, and Karim's pronoun use indicates that he does not affiliate with Americans (p. 124).

Example 6.5

Karim: Ouais ouais à quatorze ans] dans le Montana. C'est c'est ridicule on-a même pas besoin de permis, t'vois c'est juste on-s'en va, on-achète son arme et on-sort. C'est ridicule! <..> Et après ils-sont étonnés d'avoir des trucs, des tueries comme ça!

Yeah yeah at fourteen years old] in Montana. It's it's ridiculous one-doesn't even need to have a permit, y'see it's just one-goes, one.buys one's gun and one leave(s). It.s ridiculous! <..> And afterwards they.are surprised to have these things, these killings like that one!

Karim uses the third person plural pronoun, *ils- (they)* to refer to Americans in this passage, "Et après ils-sont étonnés" (*And afterwards they.are surprised*). In using "they" rather than "we," he disaffiliates with Americans, and Montanans in particular, based on what he sees as "their" ridiculous stance toward gun ownership.

As Waugh (2010) argues, Karim's choice of pronouns indexes a national identity as an American when he talks about driving in the United States and a national identity other than American when he discusses American gun laws. Since Karim is a French citizen who has lived for many years in the United States, he has access to multiple national identities that he can index in different contexts. Pronouns are one way we can index the social categories within which we place ourselves. They can also index our ideological positions and how we identify ourselves when it comes to specific ways of behaving and thinking.

As we use language, the meaning of what we say goes beyond simple denotation. The words we use, the structure we use, and even the phonological aspects of our formulation of an utterance can index many aspects of our social world and our position within that social world.

There are other linguistic constructions that index particular social categories. Irvine's (1998) discussion of the use of *honorifics* provides an instructive example. "Honorifics are deictic forms of speech signaling social deference, through conventionalized understandings of some aspect(s) of the form mean-ing relationship in language" (Irvine, 1998, p. 52). Social deference may be signaled by a speaker's choice of words or affixes. A very quick example of this would be the choice to address Queen Elizabeth II as "your majesty." So we can see honorifics in word choice, but it can also include entire respect vocabularies. Irvine provides an example from Doke and Vilakazi (1958) to demonstrate the differing lexical forms in the ordinary and respect vocabularies in Zulu. For example, in Zulu "*to be dejected*" is "aluka" in the ordinary vocabulary and "gxaba" in the respect vocabulary; "*house*" is "indlu" in the ordinary vocabulary and "incumba" in the respect vocabulary (Irvine, 1998, p. 54).

ChiBemba, a Bantu language spoken primarily in Zambia, provides an illustration of affixes used to signal levels of honorifics. For example, prefixes provide layers to the following ways of saying "*wife*" (Irvine, 1998, p. 55):

Example 6.6

abakaʃl	honorific
umakaʃ	disrespectful
akakaʃl	insult
itʃikaʃl	insult
ilikaʃl	"a little derogatory"

Whether the honorifics are realized lexically, as words, or morphologically, as affixes, in both Zulu and ChiBemba, Irvine argues that the use of honorifics is tied to language ideologies. The differential usage in these honorific systems indexes a language ideology in which there are refined ways of speaking and non-refined ways of speaking. For speakers, the use of a certain honorific indexes this ideology and constructs the speaker and often the hearer in particular ways.

As the earlier example of the advertisers' choice of a southern regional U.S. accent illustrated, the speech sounds we use can index particular social understandings and construct aspects of our identities. For instance, in a study of high school alignments, Eckert (2000b) found that high school students who considered themselves to be "burnouts" spoke in one way, while high school students who considered themselves to be "jocks" spoke in another way. In particular, she looked at the pronunciation patterns of their vowel sounds. She found, for example, that those high school students who identified as burnouts engaged in the backing of the vowel /e/ more often than did high school students who identify as jocks. This means that in order to construct their affiliation with fellow burnouts, members of this group shifted their pronunciation. This type of variation in vowel sounds, then, has social meaning.

In considering the use of /ay/ raising, however, she discusses a more complex pattern. While burnout girls led everyone in /ay/ raising including burnout boys, jock boys led jock girls in the same raising pattern. We find a greater difference in the /ay/ raising patterns, then, between burnout girls (most of any group) and jock girls (least of any group), and a weaker difference between burnout boys and jock boys.

One explanation that Eckert gives for this is that boys tend to be categorized based on their physical activities, such as whether or not they play football along with their language use. Boys, then, are not as readily identifiable as jocks or burnouts based on the way they sound. Girls, on the other hand, tend to be categorized based on physical attributes, such as appearance, in addition to the ways they sound. Girls who dress, do their hair and makeup in a particular way, and sound like burnouts are likely to be identified as burnouts. Girls who dress, do their hair and makeup in another way, and sound like jocks are likely to be identified as jocks. These examples show that both gender identity and group identity are constructed in these choices. Identity construction in these groups, then, is based on a complex of contrasting choices related to activities, physical appearance, and language use.

In language use, indexicality is transient and dependent on life experience, including an awareness of which particular contrasts exist. In Eckert's (2000b) example, the high school students were aware of and used the contrasts in sounds to construct differing group identities. But this is not always the case for all contrasts. Johnstone and Kiesling (2008), for example, discuss /aw/ monophthongization in Pittsburgh, Pennsylvania. Monophthongization occurs when a vowel sound that is pronounced as a movement between two sounds begins to be pronounced more like a single vowel sound. Typically in standard American English pronunciation, for example, the word *house* is pronounced as /haws/. However, in a non-standard variety of English spoken in Pittsburgh, "house" is often pronounced /ha:s/. Because monophthongized /aw/ is associated with a certain local Pittsburgh dialect, Johnstone and Kiesling assumed that its use would index a Pittsburgh identity for speakers of this dialect. They found that speakers of this dialect in Pittsburgh, however, did not consistently make the association between the form and a Pittsburgh identity. Johnstone and Kiesling proposed that because attention is not drawn to the phonological variant among those who use the variant, it is not noticeable to them as different. Though there may be a correlation between being a local Pittsburgher and the use of monophthongized /aw/, this does not mean that Pittsburghers uniformly take note of this phonological variant and attach indexical meaning to it as a badge of Pittsburgh identity.

In their analysis of Esther, one of the participants in their study, Johnstone and Kiesling (2008, p. 25) state:

> But nothing in Esther's environment calls attention to these correlations or invests them with meaning. Thus Esther does not perceive the difference between monophthongal and diphthongal variants of (aw), and this variable carries no higher-order indexical meaning for her.

There were, however, individuals who were aware of the distinction. Johnstone and Kiesling (2008) note that another participant in their study, Lydia, could hear the distinction. Rather than interpreting this distinction as one that indexes a Pittsburg identity, however, she interpreted it as a marker of "incorrectness." For Lydia, the use of particular forms indexes correctness, while the use of other forms indexes incorrectness. Lydia's interpretation is rooted in an ideology in which some uses of language are "correct" and others are "incorrect." In other words, Lydia attaches particular values to each language. We will further discuss the process of attaching differential values to languages in Chapter 7.

6.2 Doing Sociolinguistics: Thought Exploration

Think about phonological, grammatical, or lexical features that function as indexicals in your social world. Consider how these indexicals construct particular meanings and identities.

In this section, we have discussed how indexicals, including deictics and particular language sounds, become referential in terms of demonstrating social relationships. We have also talked about the fact that language users are not necessarily aware of what particular features of language index for others, and finally, that for some, these types of differences index value.

6.2 Family

Family life sets the stage for an ongoing local negotiation and prioritization of particular values, including notions of different types of correctness. Typically, in family structures, parents are in powerful positions relative to their children in terms of their ability to define and enforce what is considered correct and incorrect. For example, Wingard (2007) demonstrates that parents have the power to dictate children's use of time as they socialize children "to a hierarchy of activities" (p. 87). This power asymmetry can be seen in language by the fact that parents tend to use directives, while children tend to make requests. The following example from Wingard (2007, p. 86) demonstrates the kinds of requests that children make and the kinds of directives that parents give:

Example 6.7
1.   Aurora: Mommy?
2.   Mother: °Yeah?
3.   Aurora: Can I resume playing?
4.   Mother: Resu::me?
5.   Aurora: Mm hm continu::e?
6.   Mother: ((*laughs*))
      . . . Unrelated lines omitted . . .
      ((*talk is related to mother feeding the cat and Aurora drinking juice*))
24.   Mother: Okay what else do you need to do, Aurora?
25.   You need to- before you do any kind of
26.   video game you need to- uh-
27.   go over your piano stuff. (.5) remember?
28.   Aurora: ((*drinking juice*))
29.   Aurora: ((*speaking into cup*)) Wait a sec, ((*still drinking*)) (4.0)
30.   ((*puts down cup, gets up*)) Okay I'll go over my piano.

The power differential between Aurora and Mother can be seen by the fact that Aurora, the child, must ask for permission to resume playing in line 3. The mother, on the other hand, is in the powerful position that allows her to give Aurora directives as seen in lines 24–26.

Families, of course, can have many different kinds of configurations. They range from extended families living together to single parent families. In this continuum, there are other configurations, including childless couples, same sex partners with or without children, and other family arrangements. Within these various family configurations, power issues extend beyond the parent-child relationship. Kendall (2008), for example, discusses how power relations play out between a husband, wife, and child. Though the main focus of this article is to demonstrate how family members enact different identities, such as host, language monitor, and caretaker as indicated in the double parenthesis in Example 6.8, it can also be argued that in particular interactions, power relations can be an important component in terms of how these identities are achieved. In Example 6.8, Kendall (2008, p. 561) demonstrates how Elaine's attempt to act as a language monitor is undermined by her husband, Mark.

Example 6.8

1	Mark:	You want another bowl? ((host))
2	Beth:	Ew.
3	Mark:	Hm?
4	Beth:	No! They're disgusting.
5	Elaine:	Excuse me. ((language monitor))
6	Beth:	Sorry!
7	Elaine:	Just say 'no thanks'.
8	Beth:	No thanks!
9	((6 seconds))	
10	Mark: →	‹chuckling, whispered› Disgusting.›
11	Beth:	‹scoffs›
12	Elaine:	Go take your vitamin. ((Caretaker))

In lines 5 and 7, Elaine enacts her role as the family language monitor, correcting Beth's phrasing and directing her in what to say. However, in line 10, Mark, rather than ratifying Elaine's language monitor contribution in lines 5 and 7, aligns with Beth. In this case, Elaine's power to decide what is correct had been accepted by Beth, as seen in her directed apology and polite refusal "no thanks" in lines 6 and 8. However, as Kendall (2008, p. 561) states, "Mark's humor undercuts Elaine's parental authority."

In power relationships, resistance to dominant people is often enacted by those who are in subordinate positions. The enactment of resistance, in this sense, both reveals the presence of power and enacts agency (Abu-Lughod, 1990).

Although parents with young children are in powerful positions relative to their children, children can still show agency and perform resistance. As Ochs and Kremler-Sadlik (2007) demonstrate, parents work to socialize their children to participate in activities in ways that they follow particular rules of morality. In this way, morality is a family practice, and parents are in control of the family understanding of moral actions. This control is revealed in practice in the way that parents speak for their children (Kremer-Sadlik & Kim, 2007), and in the way that they "monitor their children's moral displays" (Ochs & Kremler-Sadlik, 2007, p. 6).

However, not surprisingly, children may at times show resistance to the way that their parents talk for them and monitor their moral displays. The following example from Hutchby and O'Reilly (2010, pp. 59–60), reveals how parents speak for their children in family therapy sessions and how children resist this. In Example 6.9, Mum and Alex, the stepfather, say that Steve threw something across the floor. In line 3, we can see Steve's resistance to his parents' account.

Example 6.9
```
1   Mum:   And'e got'is hair off with that and >chucked it< on the
2          flo::or >and I says< we[ll once ↓yo-
3   Steve:                      [NO I HAVEn't I dropped *it on the↑flo:
4   Alex:  <YOU [threw it> across the livin' ro:om befo:re n↑ow
5   Mum:         [N- <YOU CHUCKED IT>.hh I was↑ there and seen ya
6          >and I says< once you break that <you ARE NOT'avin'
7          another one> because they're not ↓cheap they are a lot of
8          money.
```

Though parents generally have the authority to make claims on behalf of their children and to have the final word when it comes to the construction of truth, as seen in this example, children do resist at times. Of course there are other forms of resistance that children display as well.

6.3 Doing Sociolinguistics: Thought Exploration

How do you think people typically think about power and authority within family life? Who do we typically think of as having power and authority? How do these people enact power and authority as they interact with their family members? How do you see this local enactment of power and authority reflecting ideological notions of who is considered powerful in society?

In this section, we examined how power and authority are enacted in various ways in family life. Particular family members enact roles of authority, while other family members remain subordinate. Moreover, the power positions between family members are negotiated and contested.

6.3 Service encounters

Service encounters are interesting from this perspective of language and power because they require a negotiation of power in which the service provider must accommodate to the customer. Institutional speech events also involve situations in which the institutional representative is dependent upon the client for economic well-being. Such situations provide interesting examples of the institutional representative's accommodation strategies to meet the needs of the client. One such speech event is the service encounter in the privately-run business. Pan (2000) describes the different face work strategies involved in state-run versus privately-run businesses in China. In the state-run business, "interaction between the clerk and her unacquainted customers is characterized by minimal verbal exchange, lack of face strategies and being task-oriented" (p. 32). In contrast, in the privately-run business, in which the clerk is dependent upon the sale, the salesperson uses "a large amount of politeness strategies to attend to the positive face of the customer" (p. 49).

In the United States, service encounters have inherent power balances and expectations, with customer satisfaction as one of the ultimate goals of the service provider, particularly when their continued patronage is wanted. In his seminal work on service encounters, Bailey (1997) discusses the inter-actions in privately run convenience stores in Los Angeles between Korean immigrant clerks and African American customers. Bailey describes the African American politeness strategy in such encounters as "involvement" and the Korean immigrant politeness strategy as "restraint." In Korean-Korean service encounters, restraint is practiced between both customer and clerk. As Bailey suggests, the Korean-Korean service encounters consist of the socially minimal service encounter "(a) greetings or openings, (b) negotiation of the business exchange, and (c) closing of the encounter" (p. 332). On the other hand, the African American customers assert solidarity with the clerk in the service encounter. Bailey describes how the Korean clerk in the privately-run business accommodates to the style of the African American customer. In one such service encounter, the African American customer states "I haven't seen you for a while" (p. 333), and the Korean clerk responds "hehe Where have you been" (p. 333). The African American customer "asserts solidarity with the cashier" (p. 333), and the cashier accommodates to the African American customer's assertion of solidarity by asking a personal question to allow the customer to tell his story.

Bailey argues that though the Korean clerks attempt to use the involvement strategy to accommodate to the African American involvement style in service encounters, there is still tension between Korean clerks and African American customers. Specifically, the African American customers perceive the Korean clerks as distant and racist, and the Korean clerks do not understand why the African American customers "suddenly accuse them of being racist" (p. 352). Though the accommodation strategy on the part of the Korean clerks often allows smooth relations with the African American customers, other times, the different politeness strategies lead to complementary schismogenesis (Bateson, 1972), meaning that the more the Korean clerk engages in a distancing politeness strategy, the more the African American customer engages in an involvement politeness strategy and vice versa. The accumulation of these instances of communication breakdown result in these two groups having bad feelings toward one another.

6.4 Doing Sociolinguistics: Thought Exploration

Consider service encounters that you have been involved in as either the customer or the clerk. Are there times that such encounters have been more difficult to negotiate? What happened? Did you leave the encounter with bad feelings toward your interactant? What social factors in the interaction can you see had an effect in the interactions that led to these feelings?

In this section, we have discussed service encounters as enactments of power relations. In these encounters, the service providers generally try to accommodate to the needs of the customer when they are dependent on the customer for their ability to earn money, but even these forms of accommodation do not guarantee that participants' intents in social interactions will be more clearly understood.

6.4 Bureaucracy and institutional settings

Bureaucratic settings are interesting not only because of the ways that language is used within the particular bureaucratic settings, but also because of the ways that this institutional discourse reproduces social and national ideologies (Agar, 1985).

We typically think of bureaucratic settings as associated with institutions, such as social service agencies, educational institutions, medical facilities, and legal facilities; and we think of the interactions within them as exemplified by institutional representatives interacting with noninstitutional individuals.

Anderson (2006) provides a compelling argument that nations are imagined communities held together by a sense of sameness that is largely constructed through the idea that being part of a nation presumes using the national language—French people speak French, English people speak English, Spanish people speak Spanish. However, it is important to consider that this sense of sameness goes beyond the question of which language code an individual participates in; it also includes assumptions about a sense of sameness related to ways of using that language.

Bureaucratic settings not only function in relation to the social and cultural practices of speakers of a particular language or languages, but the linguistic practices within bureaucratic settings serve to reproduce and reconstruct the worldview of the individual nation state. In other words, bureaucratic settings are sites in which the hegemony of the state and other powerful interests is reproduced at the local level. Gramsci (1971) defined *hegemony* as a set of processes by which powerful interests gain and maintain the consent of the populous. This includes control over the worldview that people have and use as they live their lives. This control is particularly evident in the interactions that occur within bureaucratic settings, such as school, doctor's offices, and legal settings. In this section, we will focus on educational, legal, and medical settings. We will demonstrate how these bureaucratic settings reproduce macro-level ideologies and how these settings are sites in which ideologies about language use develop in turn affecting processes of interaction at the micro-level.

In a review of language in bureaucratic settings, Philips (2006) argues that these settings are often sites where communications take place between people who are in asymmetrical power relations. This is generally the case, for example, with teachers and students, lawyers and witnesses, and doctors and patients. Due to the asymmetry involved in interactions in bureaucratic set-tings, the ideological positions of those people in the more powerful positions become the positions that are used to frame the interactions. Philips uses Sack's (1992) notion of *ratification* to discuss one process by which a more powerful person's worldview frames the interaction. This type of analysis looks at how one individual's ideas and conversational moves will be ratified, or validated and picked up in the ongoing interaction, to the point that his or her worldview or understanding of the event, frames the interaction at the same time that the interlocutor's ideas and conversational moves are generally either not present or unratified to the point that the interlocutor's worldview is left invisible or is marginalized.

According to Philips' (2006) argument, this asymmetry forms the basis for social inequality. Social inequality, then, can be seen as constructed in individual, ongoing interactions. The interactional processes behind such unequal power relationships will be discussed in more detail in Chapter 7; but in this chapter, we will address how these asymmetrical relationships affect our understanding of micro-interactions.

In this section we have seen how power is enacted at the micro-interactional level in bureaucratic settings; and this micro-interactional work reproduces ideological power structures at the macro-societal level.

6.4.1 Gatekeeping

An area of institutional discourse that has been well investigated involves the analysis of the types of speech events in which an institutional representative communicates with an individual who needs the institution's services. Since the individual is dependent upon the institutional representative to fulfill a need, most often that individual will be in a less powerful position than the institutional representative. In many cases, for example, the institutional representative essentially has the authority to control the discourse, quite often by being the one who controls the questions. This means that clients cannot choose the topic and must find a way to represent themselves through the institutional representative's choice of topic. Such power-laden encounters are often called *gatekeeping encounters* (Erickson & Shultz, 1982).

In a gatekeeping encounter, institutional representatives must fit client frames into institutional frames as efficiently as possible (Agar, 1985; Trinch, 2003). Gatekeeping encounters do not allow much room for negotiation or consideration of the client's needs outside of these institutional frames. The need to match institutional frames and client frames efficiently seems to be fertile ground for communication problems because the client and the institutional representative may be working from different assumptions about the purpose of the encounter. As such, clients who come from cultures other than the institutional representative's may encounter even more severe communication problems. For these clients from a different culture than the institutional representative, not only may the institutional frame and the client's frame not match; but, the basic frames for interpersonal communication may not match.

One example of a speech event in which the differing power relations are played out is the social service interview. Gumperz and Roberts (1991) discuss social service interviews noting that "there is a hierarchical role relationship" and focusing on ". . . the differential distribution of power between counselors . . . who by virtue of their knowledge of the institutional discursive practices, have access to institutional resources and exert control over the encounter" (p. 54). Thus, the institutional representative is in a higher power position than the client. This does not mean that the client is entirely powerless. The client in the social service interview is using the governmental organization to have a service provided. In one sense, the client is entitled to the service provided by the institution, making it important for the institutional representative to find a way to fit the client frame into the institutional frame. When interpretive frames are not shared, as may be the case with service providers and clients from different cultural backgrounds, the difficulties in fitting client frames into institutional ones can be particularly challenging to the point of potential breakdown.

Gatekeeping job interviews provide an example of how a cross-cultural difference in the assumptions behind the meaning of contextualization cues can lead to miscommunication in job interviews (Roberts & Sayers, 1998). A contextualization cue, as defined by Gumperz (1982), is constituted by "constellations of surface features by which speakers signal and listeners interpret what the activity is, how semantic content is to be understood, and how each sentence relates to what proceeds or follows" (p. 131).

Roberts and Sayers describe a job interview between a British interviewer and a South Asian interviewee seen in Example 6.10 (from p. 34). The interviewer asks, "how's your maths?," with the frame "eliciting the quality of the applicant's maths." The interviewee pauses after the question because he does not understand the content of the question, but the interviewer takes the pause to mean that the applicant's maths are "not so good, eh?." The applicant replies "no" which is taken as agreement that his maths aren't good, when he probably meant to disagree with the statement considering the fact that he had a high level of expertise in math.

Example 6.10
Interviewer: how's your maths?
Applicant: (silence)
Interviewer: not so good eh?
Applicant: no

In this situation, the interviewee is deemed to be a poor candidate for the job, mainly because the interviewer felt that he lacked mathematics skills due to his misinterpretation of the applicant's silence.

In another example of how interpretive frames can shape individuals' abilities to communicate, Trinch (2003) describes differences in the interpretive frames that Latinas bring to legal clinics when they are seeking help in relation to domestic abuse. She argues that while what "clients say aids service providers in shaping the way services are provided, the actions that can be taken to help them, the content and form of the information disclosed, and the types of continued support, if any, service providers believe can be given" (p. 60), there are culturally different definitions of what might constitute "need". She points out that "research conducted on battered women suggests that women from different ethnic, racial, and socio-economic backgrounds define domestic violence differently" (p. 7). These differing definitions and women's narrative styles in talking about violence might not fit in with the institutional requirements and definitions of violence. This means that the women's stories are affected by their interactions with the various types of institutions that they encounter in trying to get help. As Trinch notes, "the system is designed not to be receptive to change, but rather to alter those narrative representations that challenge it" (p. 57). Essentially this means that "Latina's narratives of domestic violence undergo a process of institutionalization" (p. 57) in which they are affected by the particular needs and definitions of the institution. Example 6.11 from Trinch (2003, p. 157) shows an interaction in which the two interlocutors have different definitions of violence where P is the paralegal interviewer and C is the client.

Example 6.11

1. P: [He called you where? At your house?

2. C: At my cousin's house yes.

3. P: At your cousin's house.

4. C.   Where I'm living at. And um, I told him that it was over. I didn't want anything to do with him no more. He kept telling me, "Well I'm the baby's daddy. I need to see him." "So how do you expect to see the baby, if you don't give me no money?" He told me, "Well, that's your problem," 'cause I don't call him back you know, when he calls me.

5. P: Mhmm

6. C: And he started getting mad' cause I kept telling him that it was over, and it was over. So finally he told me that he was gonna go over that night. And I said, "Come over and I'll call the cops on you." And he said,

"you won't have to um I'm gonna take the cops with me. I'm gonna see my son and I'm gonna take him away from you." And I told him, "They won't let you take him." He lives in a boarding home where a bunch of crazy people are at.

7. P: Mhmm

8. C: And supposedly, he's supposed to be working there also. Uh . . .

9. P: Did he make any specific threats to hurt you?

As Trinch points out, this exchange demonstrates differing definitions of threats of harm. The client is clearly narrating what she perceives to be a threat of harm—her baby's father's threat to come with the police, see her baby, and take him away as narrated in turn 6. The paralegal's question in turn 9, however, "Did he make any threats to hurt you?" can only be interpreted as one in which the paralegal did not perceive the threat to take the baby as a threat of harm. The institutional definition of harm as it is framed by the paralegal clearly is one in which this client's narrative does not count as a viable threat, and the paralegal does not ratify it as such. Trinch points out this can be due to the institution's connection to the state's stance, which views both parents as viable caretakers.

This example, then, also demonstrates one quality of many gatekeeping activities and that is that they exist within institutions that are often integrated into larger institutional systems (p. 60). We can see the paralegal's definition of "harm" as representative of the clinic's integration into the larger legal institutional system's stance toward parenthood, for example.

Trinch notes that this "linguistic divide" that separates the ways that victims and institutions define acts of violence leads to negations between service providers and clients which, while having the potential to narrow the gap, "leave the victims meaning, and their means of representing themselves and their experiences at risk in several ways" (p. 3).

6.5 Doing Sociolinguistics: Thought Exploration

Consider how gatekeeping encounters have affected your life. What types of events have you participated in that you might identify as gatekeeping events? How did the institutional representative interact with you? Did you experience any constructions of power?

In this section, we've talked about how gatekeeping interactions represent processes in which unequal power relations affect the quality of the ongoing interaction. These gatekeeping processes represent interactions in which we can see how these ongoing interactions are affected not simply by the power of the representative of the institutions themselves but also by institutional definitions and by the fact that many gatekeeping processes represent events within institutions that are often embedded in and affected by even larger institutions.

6.4.2 Education

The educational setting is one in which gatekeeping encounters are quite prevalent. Clearly, teachers and professors have significant power when it comes to the grades students receive and whether or not they pass classes. However, gatekeeping happens in other aspects of the educational setting as well. Much of the research in educational settings has demonstrated that differences in communicative background can affect the process of the educational gatekeeping encounter. However, as we will demonstrate, it is typically the person in the powerless position, the student, who is denied access or whose access is restricted when miscommunication happens in an educational gatekeeping encounter.

The academic advising session is one type of gatekeeping encounter in the educational setting. In their seminal work on gatekeeping, Erickson and Shultz (1982) studied academic advising sessions between white community college counselors and African American community college students. These data demonstrate that gatekeeping can result simply because of different communicative styles. As the counselor works to conduct the interview with the student as per the institutional role, subtle differences in verbal and non-verbal listening responses as well as verbal and nonverbal listening response relevant moments between the African American student and white counselor cause the counselor to think that the student does not understand the counselor's previous utterance. Thus, the counselor proceeds with hyper-explanation in attempting to be comprehensible to the student. As a result, both counselor and student leave the institutional encounter with negative impressions of each other. For instance, after one such interview in which the counselor hyper-explained after missing the student's listening cues, the student commented, "This guy seems like he was trying to knock me down, in a way you know. Trying to say no . . . I don't think you can handle anything besides P.E." [physical education] (p. 137). The counselor, on the other hand, did not realize that he had insulted the student. Small differences the verbal and non-verbal ways of turning the interactional responsibility over to the other participant in the interaction caused a negative reaction in terms of the counselor's intentions toward the student even though the counselor attempted to address what he perceived as the students' lack of understanding. The cumulative result of such encounters, however, is that students are consistently placed into certain kinds of courses, essentially keeping the gate in terms of access to certain classes.

In some instances, the student with the different cultural norms might make an attempt to accommodate to perceived cultural norms. In a study of graduate academic advising sessions, Bardovi-Harlig and Hartford (1996) describe interactions between lower status second language graduate students and their higher status academic advisors. In the interactions, many graduate students seem to use fewer politeness markers than they would have in their first language in the American academic advising session. They use fewer politeness markers under the assumption that English speakers are not as polite, and they try to accommodate to this presumed less polite style. However, their advisors "are often surprised when students from groups they expect to be polite seem to be rude, stubborn, or aggressive" (p. 186). Therefore, the students' accommodation strategy in the advising interview with the higher status interlocutor backfires, causing the advisor to develop a bad impression of the student. This bad impression can keep the gate for graduate students as they need their academic mentors' support in entering the profession for which they are being trained in graduate school.

It may also be the case that the institutional representative is the one from a cultural group other than the dominant one, and the student is from the dominant cultural group. Tyler (1995) examines a tutoring session between a Korean tutor and an American student. Her study demonstrates that it is not only the form of language used but also the differing ways of managing discourse and the differing cultural assumptions that contribute to breakdown. Interestingly, however, the Korean tutor attempts to accommodate the American student by using Korean politeness strategies. For instance, in one conversation, the two discuss a computer programming problem that involves some knowledge of bowling. The American student asks the Korean tutor if he knows anything about bowling; in an attempt to be polite, the Korean tutor, who has bowled quite frequently, responds that he knows "a little bit" about bowling. The phrase "a little bit" causes the American student to consider herself as having more expertise in the sport of bowling. She then becomes quite offended when the Korean tutor continually corrects her when she states information about bowling that pertains to the problem at hand. The Korean tutor does not understand why the American student refuses to accept his advice and seems to become irritated in the course of the conversation. In this case the gate was not kept intentionally but in practice; the inability of the student and the tutor to communicate smoothly affected the student's access to an educational opportunity.

6.6 Doing Sociolinguistics: Thought Exploration

Think back to an important moment in your academic career that you see as a gate-keeping experience. What typified that event as a gatekeeping one? How did you experience the power relations in that activity? Were there any social or language aspects to that event that you recall as instantiating power imbalances?

In this section we have discussed how communicative expectations can have important consequences in educational encounters. Even though the denial of access is sometimes unintentional, it is the powerless person who feels the effect of that denial. Studies from the educational setting have demonstrated that people in powerful positions control what are considered appropriate and effective ways of interacting and using language, to which the powerless people must accommodate lest they are denied access.

6.4.3 Medical settings

The medical setting is another context in which gatekeeping power becomes quite obvious. Clearly, medical providers have the power to control medical tests and prescribe medicines. Patients must pass through the gate in order to gain access to healthcare, and that gate can be examined through analysis of clinical interactions.

Gaining entry into the healthcare system may be a difficult issue for some people. The first issue here may be whether or not healthcare services are available in a language that can be understood. Antia and Bertin (2004), for instance, report that in a nation like Nigeria, where about 400 languages are spoken, language concordance between physician and patients and nurses and patients is not always possible. Moreover, professional interpretation services are not always available when the medical provider and patient do not speak the same language. Not surprisingly, physicians cite communication difficulty as a reason why they find many of their clinical interactions with patients to be professionally dissatisfying. This communication difficulty also seems to be a reason that patients become disenchanted with healthcare in Nigeria. Though Antia and Bertin's research is based on a survey of medical professionals, it points to the inequalities in healthcare that arise because care within the micro-interactions of the medical consultations cannot be properly implemented. Nigerian patients who speak a language that is not represented within the healthcare setting are essentially denied full access to care.

The same can be said for patients who speak languages other than English in the United States. There has been an abundance of research among medical scholars and policymakers in the United States that demonstrates that lack of access to healthcare in a language that one can understand is a major contributor to health disparities in the United States (see, for example, Carmona, 2007). We will discuss issues of language hierarchy, which will help in explaining why certain languages are represented in certain contexts further in Chapter 7.

Even though there are federal laws in the United States that restrict federal funding in medical facilities that do not provide equal language access, Martinez (2008) suggests that such laws are ineffective. The day-to-day micro-interactions that take place within the medical consultations themselves ". . . reflect and reify the local linguistic order" (p. 361) with English at the top of the hierarchy. This is true even when medical providers speak the language of their patients, Spanish in the case of Martinez (2008), because often these providers are not trained to use Spanish professionally within medical consultations.

Even when professional interpreters are used in the medical setting, gatekeeping can happen in other ways. Davidson (2001), for instance, has demonstrated that hospital interpreters do not always translate exactly what either the medical provider or the patient say. Therefore, the interpreter becomes the ultimate gatekeeper in terms of filtering the information that is conveyed between the provider and patient.

Vickers' ongoing ethnographic study of a clinic within the United States in which providers are trained to use Spanish for medical purposes examines interactions where the gate is more open. Let's look at an example from these data in which Maria, a medical assistant in the United States who was trained as a physician in Guatemala, takes Ramon's medical history. Ramon came to the clinic because he was suffering from a rash on his neck. In this example, M is Maria, the medical assistant, and R is Ramon, the patient.

Example 6.12

<T=02:22.00>	
1. M: oh sí.. ¿qué	M: oh yes . . . what's going on
2. te pasa hoy?	with you today?
3. R: este:..me sale	R: um:..it shows up
4. como:..esto ((he shows	like:..this ((he shows
5. her his neck)) no sé	her his neck)) I don't know
6. como llamarle . . . siempre	what to call it . . . always
7. cuando me pongo	when I collect
8. ajuntar botes . . .	cans . . .
9. me sale esta alergia	this allergy shows up
10. M: ((speaking softly)) oh:	M: ((speaking softly)) oh:
11. okay. ¿te da comezón?	okay. does it itch?
12. R: sí bastante.	R: yes a lot.
13. M: ¿te arde?	M: does it burn?
14. R: sí (0.6)	R: yes (0.6)
15. M: ¿te siente caliente?	M: is it warm?
16. R: no: caliente pero sí me	R: not warm but yes it burns
17. arde con ganas de	and makes me want to
18. rascarme	scratch myself
19. M: ¿solo en ese	M: it only shows up in this
20. lugar te sale?	place
21. R: todo aquí también.	R: all around here too
22. M: ¿pero en el pecho no te sale	M: but it doesn't show up on your chest
23. [ni] en la espalda	[or] on your back?
24. R: [no] . . . solamente	R: [no] . . . only
25. apenas me está	barely it's been showing
26. saliendo aquí también	up here too
27. M: oh okay ¿Cuánto tiempo	M: oh okay ¿how long
28. tiene de estar así?	has it been like this?
29. R: ah tres días	R: ah three day
30. M: oh okay	M: oh okay
31. R: los primeros días fue	R: the first days it was not
32. muy poco y no me da	a lot and it didn't
33. mucho comezón.	itch a lot.
34. M: m:hm (1.5) ((typing))	M: m:hm (1.5) ((typing))
35. R: aquí esto me pica más	R: here this has more pain
36. M: oh okay yeah: (1.0) tres	M: oh okay yeah: (1.0) three
37. dias tiene de estar [con eso]	days you've been [like this]
38. R: [sí:]	[yes]
39. <T=00:03:04.5>	
40. ((typing is audible))	((typing is audible))
41. <T=00:03:14.9>	

42. R: había estado usandolo=	R: I have been using it=
43. M: =qué qué te qué había	M: =what what had you
44. comido este día, o qué?..	eaten this day or what? . . .
45. No te recuerda	you don't remember
46. [que lo habias]	[what you had]
47. R: [no me acuerdo]	R: [I don't remember]

We can see in this interaction that Maria, in very nuanced ways, asks specific questions that allow for a diagnosis of Ramon's condition. Maria obviously speaks Spanish for medical purposes very well. However, even in this best case communicative scenario in which the medical personnel and patient can clearly communicate, there are barriers to communication that lead to an inability on Ramon's part to completely pass through the gate. Specifically, in lines 5–6 when Ramon shows Maria his neck and describes the problem, he says "no se como llamarle" (*I don't know what to call it*). Notice that he does not get a name for the condition from Maria, though it is clearly a visible rash. Rather her response is "oh: okay. ¿te da comezón?" (*does it itch?*). Here we can see that Ramon's attempt to gather information is denied. Moreover, in line 42, Ramon says "habia estado usandolo=" (*I've been using it=*), which Maria cuts off with her next question. He was clearly trying to supply information at this point, but that information was never conveyed.

Basically, in the medical consultation, the medical provider controls the information flow. However, there is another layer to this. As Maria talks to the patient, she is also following a patient-history-taking program on the computer that guides her through sets of questions for different types of conditions. This use of the computer for taking patient histories is standard in the medical practice in which Maria works. It is a bureaucratic ritual (Cicourel, 2005) that Maria follows. So in some sense, the computer, as the institutional representative, becomes the dominant interactant, filtering the flow of information. The human-computer interaction (Greatbatch, Luff, Heath & Campion, 1993) mediates the human-human interaction and ensures that Maria sticks to her identity as a bureaucratic representative.

6.7 Doing Sociolinguistics: Thought Exploration

Think about a time you have interacted in medical settings in a first or second language. How did you see those interactions as ritualistic? Did you experience occasions where the language of the medical setting proved difficult to negotiate for any reason? What social or language aspects do you think created those difficulties?

As we have seen in this section, medical settings keep the gate in a variety of ways. Lack of language concordance between the patient and provider generates a situation that is ripe for denial of access to patients. However, even providers' ways of interacting with language concordant patients can result in a lack of access for the patient.

6.5 Sociolinguistics and the law

Individuals who study language use and the law approach the topic in many different ways. Some provide evidence for the legal status of particular languages; some examine legal documents for the social constructions that can be found; some examine interactions in legal settings; some examine legal cases; some examine how experts in particular areas become expert witnesses in legal cases.

The study of language use and the law can have broad social effects. For example, Geneva Smitherman, along with a group of other linguists, collected sociolinguistic data and presented evidence for the defendants in the 1977 U.S. civil rights case, Martin Luther King Junior Elementary School Children et al. v. Ann Arbor School District Board. Their work affected the way that the local school educated a group of local African American children. It also affected social understandings of African American English and the legal status of African American English within the United States, which resulted in more equal educational opportunities for children who use this variety of English.

In this case, parents of children living on Green Street in Ann Arbor, Michigan, a street that represented a predominantly African American community, had deep concerns for the success of their children in the elementary school that they attended, which had a predominantly white student and teacher population. The parents noticed that some of the children had been classified as mentally handicapped or learning disabled or tracked to lower grade levels, and that some had been misreported as having hearing difficulties, among other complaints. They filed a case against the Ann Arbor School District Board citing these complaints and arguing that these actions had been taken "without regard to plaintiffs' racial and linguistic backgrounds" as quoted in Labov (1982, p. 168).

In his decision relative to the defendants' motion to dismiss, the judge dismissed all causes of action except the complaint related to the claim that the school had "failed to overcome language barriers." This decision was based on the plaintiffs' claim that the children spoke "a vernacular known as 'Black English'" that was different enough from the language spoken at the school to qualify under the language barrier violation. As Labov notes, "The 'King School Case' was thus transformed into the 'Black English' case" (p. 170). This language is also referred to as African American Vernacular English (AAVE).

Once this focus on understandings of AAVE became the legal focus of the complaint, Geneva Smitherman, director of the Center for Black Studies at Wayne State University in Detroit, responded for the defense. First, she began recording the everyday speech of the children who lived on Green Street and collected excerpts from these data as evidence for presentation in court. These tapes provided compelling evidence that the language the children spoke in their home community was different from the language of the elementary school. When these tapes were used in court, they also provided an example of the difference in the ways that the children spoke fluently at home, but were affected by the formal setting and standard language of the courtroom, which repressed their spontaneous flow of language (Labov, 1982, p. 196), and demonstrated that language choice could have affected interactions in the classroom as well. Second, Smitherman headed up a team of researchers who provided linguistic evidence that AAVE was a full language and not the "restricted code" assumed by some of the educators of the day.

The case was decided in 1979 with the judge finding in favor of the plaintiffs. Judge Joiner gave the school board 30 days to create a plan in which they would specify exactly how they were going to help their teachers identify and provide AAVE speaking students with appropriate assistance in reading standard English. The school board did not appeal the decision (Labov, p. 193). The Ann Arbor case exemplifies the role of linguists in establishing the legal status of particular languages.

Other linguists have examined language in relation to legal witnesses. They have looked at the stances that witnesses take relative to their understandings of events (Conley & O'Barr, 1990), how juries view testimony styles of witnesses (Di Paolo & Green, 1990; O'Barr, 1982), how particular types of questions affect witnesses (Danet, 1980; Philips, 1982), and how the descriptive use of language in a question can affect the testimony of eyewitnesses (Loftus, 1979), for example.

Researchers, such as Philips (1985, 1998), have considered the language of judges. Philips (1985), for example, provides a detailed examination of the strategies judges use to try to make proceedings more comprehensible. When judges accept guilty pleas from criminal defendants, judges have a responsibility to determine whether the defendants are knowingly and voluntarily waiving their constitutional rights. While Plea Agreements include a written listing of those rights, Philips notes that in the Pima County Arizona Supreme Court, where she did her research, not only did judges routinely ask defendants whether they had understood their rights, but they also provided the defendants with a verbal restatement of those rights. Philips examined the strategies judges used to clarify the rights in their restatements. These strategies involved simplification techniques that clarified legal culture. In that sense, judges treated defendants as "culture learners" (Philips, 1985, p. 435), which is consistent with the inherent cultural assumption that court proceedings are very different from other typical communicative environments.

Researchers looking at language use in both the law and in public discourse have studied social and cultural categories of identity such as landowner (Mertz, 1988), or those related to notions of legal citizenship (Coutin & Chock, 1995), race (Dominguez, 1986), legitimacy (Lazarus-Black, 1994), or nationality (Eades, Fraser, Siegel, McNamara, & Baker, 2003).

More specific aspects of identity have also been considered. Greg Matoesian (1993; 2001), for example, studied the ongoing interaction within a courtroom to determine how an attorney's use of questions can construct the identities of witnesses in rape crimes. He shows how defense attorneys and prosecuting attorneys attempt to construct the identities of witnesses of rape as either "willing participants" or "victims" respectively, and how each side attempts to produce separate cohesive narratives of the rape event in constructing these differing identities.

In a similar examination of how identities are constructed in the ongoing interaction of question-and-answer sequences, Deckert (2010a) examines the language processes of question-and-answer sequences in the forensic interviews with children that result when accusations of child sexual abuse have been made. In this analysis, she not only looks at how children both participate in co-animations of events that construct them as victims, but also at how they show resistance to certain types of agency in their narratives of the events themselves. In particular, they show agentive resistance to the actions of the events themselves possibly indicating that children are aware of the social consequences of the identities in question.

In this section we have looked at the fact that language and the law can be examined from multiple perspectives. Legal situations have the potential to effect change in people's lives. Therefore, research in this area provides an opportunity for both clearer understandings of the micro-interactional aspects of legal events and for the potential to effect social change.

6.5.1 Law and multicompetent language users

It seems obvious that second language speakers of English may have greater difficulties than other speakers of English in the legal setting and that they would require interpreters. In the United States, it was not until 1978 that Congress passed a law that provides for the consecutive interpretation of bilingual proceedings and of proceedings involving hearing impaired persons in federal courts (28 USC. US Code Title 28: Judiciary and Judicial Procedure, January 2003). Individual states have since passed various laws providing for interpreters in state-level courts (Berk-Seligson, 1990). These laws, however, also construct particular identities for groups of people. Consider, for example, how the following text from US Code Title 28 constructs members of the deaf community:

> (a) The Director of the Administrative Office of the United States Courts shall establish a program to facilitate the use of certified and otherwise qualified interpreters in judicial proceedings instituted by the United States.

> (b) (1) The Director shall prescribe, determine, and certify the qualifications of persons who may serve as certified interpreters, when the Director considers certification of interpreters to be merited, for the hearing impaired (whether or not also speech impaired) and persons who speak only or primarily a language other than the English language, in judicial proceedings instituted by the United States.

It is important to notice that while this code does provide for interpreters for the deaf community, it also indexes their need for interpreters as different from those who need interpreters due to their second language needs. Essentially, this code constructs members of the deaf community within a medical framework of disability rather than as second language speakers. As Regan (2001) notes in his discussion of this medial perspective, "Although certainly well meaning, such an approach is profoundly paternalistic, and is clearly grounded in an understanding of deafness as a disability" (p. 168).

Despite the impetus for their inclusion, interpreters have introduced new variables into the courtroom situation. Berk-Selingson's research has found that "the presence of the foreign language court interpreter does indeed alter the normal flow of events in the courtroom" (1990, p. 156). An initial way that interpreters change the flow of events is that judges and attorneys draw attention to them. This often occurs even during the *voir dire*, as potential jury members are questioned regarding their qualifications for jury membership. During this event, they are introduced to the interpreters and asked whether they have any objections to the presence of interpreters. A second occasion where interpreters draw attention is when they are sworn in. Interpreters are required by law to take an oath in open court that they will interpret to the best of their ability and as accurately as possible.

Berk-Selingson points out that ideally an interpreter "should not exist as a distinct verbal participant in her own right during the course of a judicial proceeding" (1990, p. 156). Yet this is not always the case. Judges and attorneys often directly address the interpreter rather than the witness or defendant. Interpreters may need to address an attorney to clarify a word or a question. With varying levels of coerciveness, interpreters may halt examinations to explain grammatical constructions that differ from one language to another, such as the use of negation in Spanish. They may stop to explain an apparent inadequacy of a witness's answer or witnesses may even make comments to the interpreter on the side. In an even more potentially influential and coercive role, interpreters may command witnesses to speak or to be silent. For example, if witnesses are not responding quickly, interpreters may give them commands to answer. If an attorney has objected to a question, interpreters may silence witnesses with verbal commands, which often include non-verbal gestures.

Berk-Seligson (2000) also looked at the role of interpreters in pretrial events, including police questioning of suspects. One of the things that she examines in this work is the question of who acts as the interpreter. She found that it is often the case that family members and friends of the suspect take on these roles. A second possibility is that a police officer who self-identifies as bilingual will become the interpreter. Obviously, these often untrained interpreters can affect the interactions of these crucial events.

In this section, we have seen that the use of the interpreter in legal settings clearly carries significant consequences. Sociolinguistic research in this area provides rich social data that clarifies the social responsibility that the interpreter carries and emphasizes the need for further examination of the roles untrained interpreters play in many pretrial legal events.

6.5.2 Forensic linguistics

One area that forensic linguists have examined is the definition of particular language crimes. J. L. Austin proposed the idea that under certain conditions, "the issuing of an utterance is the performing of an action" (1975, p. 6). It is possible then for an act to be accomplished through speech and not just through physical action. Certain types of language use, for example, can constitute crimes (Shuy, 1993; Olsson, 2009). Verbal slander and libel are examples of this as are uses of language that would incite others to certain types of actions that could cause physical harm. In the United States, for example, speech that incites others to violence is not covered by the U.S. First Amendment right to free speech. In relation to the law, decisions often center around whether certain conversational acts, such as requests, can be considered illegal acts. As Shuy points out, one can request certain things quite legally, but a request to have someone kill a spouse may, under certain conditions, be a crime (1993, p. 1). In some cases, the issue for both the linguists and the representatives of the law becomes one of defining the conditions that differentiate a legal offer from the criminal act of offering a bribe, for example. After studying the evidence from many bribe situations, Shuy determined the event structure of a bribe. A successful bribe, he argues, contains four essential conversational elements, or phases: a statement of a problem, a proposal, completion of the agreement, and an extension of the offer of further assistance. He argues that for a bribe to be a complete speech event, the first three of the four phases must be completed (Shuy, 1993).

Another area of speech acts that has stirred more recent controversy is the area of hate speech. Although the issue has a history extending back to the 1920s, the U.S. Supreme Courts' overturning of many of the campus speech codes of the 1980s and 1990s proves how difficult it can actually be to define a verbal action as criminal (Butler, 1997; Hower, 1997; Walker, 1994). As these examples indicate, issues relating to language crimes are often not clear cut and issues of both politics and power can come into play.

The language of covert FBI tape recordings has also been an issue that sociolinguists have considered. Shuy (1987) examined the language of covert FBI tape recordings and found that they deviate from normal conversations in hidden power differentials between the agents who control and camouflage settings and agendas as well as create conversational significance by coaching other participants prior to meetings.

In his "brief history of forensic linguistics," John Olsson (2008, pp. 4–8) notes that in the United Kingdom, many cases examined by forensic linguists were related to "questioning the authenticity of police statements" (p. 5). He points out notable cases, such as appealing the convictions of "Derek

Bentley (posthumously pardoned), the Birmingham Six, the Guilford Four, the Bridgewater Three, and so on" (p. 5).

In this section we have looked at examples that reveal how forensic linguists not only provide analyses of various types of language, but also have the potential to serve the larger social good in very concrete ways. Forensic linguistics, then, provides a rich area for the study of sociolinguistics.

6.6 Doing sociolinguistics: research activities

1. Ask two friends to write descriptions of their houses. Ask them to carefully describe the spatial layout of the rooms inside the house. Then examine their written description paying attention to their use of deictic expressions. How do they use the deictic expressions? How do these uses help convey the sense of space in the house? How do they reflect ideological notions about what houses typically contain?

2. Record a few minutes of family conversation. Listen to the recording repeatedly, and transcribe sections you might want to consider more carefully. Analyze how power is instantiated in different family roles. Is the family role consistently correlated with enactments of power? Do you see examples of people supporting or undercutting the authority of others?

3. Chose a television show that relates to either a medical or legal situation. Consider your own experiences in either of these situations, Provide an analysis of how you see the writers' understandings and portrayals of power relationships in types of incidents that you experienced. Do you see the writers instantiating the same types of power differentials? Do you see the same types of communication challenges?

6.7 Suggested further readings

Anderson, B. (2006). *Imagined communities: Reflections on the origin and spread of nationalism.* New York: Verso.

Bailey, B. (1997). Communication of respect in interethnic service encounters. *Language in Society,* 26(3), 327–365.

Berk-Seligson, S. (1990). Bilingual court proceedings: The role of the court interpreter. In J. N. Levi & A. G. Walker (Eds.), *Language in the judicial process* (Vol. 5, pp. 155–201). New York: Plenum.

Davidson, B. (2001). Questions in cross-linguistic medical encounters: The role of the hospital interpreter. *Anthropological Quarterly,* 74(4), 170–178.

Eckert, P. (2000). *Jocks and Burnouts: Social categories and identity in the high school.* New York: Teacher's College Press.

Erickson, F., & Shultz, J. (1982). *The counselor as gatekeeper: Social interaction in interviews.* New York: Academic Press.

Fillmore, C. (1997). *Lectures on deixis.* Stanford: Center for the Study of Language and Information.

Gramsci, A. (1971). State and civil society. In A. Gramsci (Ed.), *Selections from the prison notebooks* (pp. 206–276). New York: International Press.

Lippi-Green, R. (1997). *English with an accent: Language, ideology, and discrimination in the United States.* New York: Routledge.

Matoesian, G. M. (1993). *Reproducing rape: Domination through talk in the courtroom.* Chicago: The University of Chicago Press.

Ochs, E. (1992). Indexing Gender. In A. Duranti & C. Goodwin (Eds.), *Rethinking context: Language as an interactive phenomenon* (pp. 335–358). Cambridge: Cambridge University Press.

Olsson, J. (2008). *Forensic linguistics* (2nd ed.). London: Continuum International Publishing Group.

Philips, S. U. (2006). Language and social inequality. In A. Duranti (Ed.), *A companion to linguistic anthropology* (pp. 474–495). Malden, MA: Blackwell.

Woolard, K. A. (1998). Introduction: Language ideology as a field of inquiry. In B. B. Schieffelin, K. A. Woolard & P. V. Kroskrity (Eds.), *Language ideologies: Practice and theory* (pp. 3–47). Oxford: Oxford University Press.

Language, Power, and Macro-societal Issues

This chapter explores conceptions of language, ideology, and identity at the macro-societal level. This means that we are looking at how language is used at the societal and cultural levels. This discussion includes an introduction to the relationship between indexicality and language ideologies and hierarchies. Next, the chapter relates language ideologies to language in the public sphere, including language usage in the media and in political discourse. Finally, the chapter considers notions of language ideology and hierarchy to address societal issues related to language policy and planning. The chapter deals with discussions of such societal-level issues of language and social capital, including the notion of linguistic imperialism, and examines how these issues affect individuals as well.

In Chapter 6, we discussed the role that language ideologies play in the construction of power and identity at the local, micro-interactional level and introduced the idea of indexicality and how it operates between the micro- and macro-levels of language and social understandings. Chapter 7 is also concerned with the role of ideology. However, this chapter will focus on how ideology shapes language use at the societal level. In this chapter we will address how language varieties themselves can be indexical and how this can influence language use at the societal level.

7.1 Language hierarchies

The fact that language is indexical is important for the way that we make meaning, but it is also crucial to understanding how language use leads to relationships of domination and subordination. At its root, the tendency to stereotype and to assign social categories to individuals based on their language use is indexical. Not only do language forms index social categories, but in social life, people place these language forms and the social categories into hierarchies so that in using a language, one indexes its place in the hierarchy.

In this way, the use of a particular variety in itself is indexical, and the variety that we use in a given interaction indexes our social categories. Very early work in Sociolinguistics demonstrated that linguistic features are correlated with social categories, such as gender, class, and ethnicity as we discussed in Chapter 3. For instance, Labov's correlations of "r" and "r-less" sounds in department stores illuminated the social stratification that accompanies language use in real-life contexts. These correlations alone, however, cannot explain how social stratification is tied to people's ways of viewing language and the social world. To understand how language variation plays into worldview, it is necessary to turn to theoretical frameworks that allow richer theorizing about the connection between language use and worldview.

Bourdieu is one theorist whose work has been quite helpful in understanding the relationship between language and worldview. Bourdieu (1977b) provides a reexamination of sociolinguistic data in which he presents the idea that language use is a form of symbolic capital. He relates this symbolic capital to social capital and economic capital. According to Bourdieu, social understandings of prestige varieties provide greater access to social and economic resources for those who use these prestige varieties of language. This differential access to social capital contributes to the formation of a dominant and dominating class. Bourdieu termed this phenomenon *symbolic domination* since one group of people stand as dominant largely because of the symbolic capital that they hold. Since the education system is invested in the prestige variety, it tends to reproduce this symbolic domination. As a result, not only the users of the prestige variety but also users of subordinated varieties come to see the prestige variety as "correct," "good," and "better."

In multilingual contexts, it is often the case that one language takes on symbolic domination. Gal (1987) discusses three multilingual situations in Europe. One of these situations was Romania during the communist era, a time that included Gal's research. It is relatively accurate to say that at that time, at least in Europe, the language that an individual spoke indexed the individual's national identity.

Gal (1987) indicates that the correlation between language and an individual's national identity generally held even when the individual's primary language was not the national language of the country in which the individual lived. For example, in the case of Romania, individuals who spoke German were considered German nationals even though their families had lived in Romania for centuries alongside Romanian speaking people. German speakers, then, were identified as German and Romanian speakers as Romanian. Even though the national language of Romania was Romanian, it was not the language that held the most symbolic capital among the German speakers. As Gal explains, German speakers saw themselves as a historically privileged class compared with the Romanians. For them, the use of German was a form of symbolic capital that indexed a history of social and economic capital in Romania. This could explain why, although they had been embedded in Romania and surrounded by a majority population that spoke Romanian, these German speakers maintained their language.

This situation is very different from the case of Spanish in the United States. Spanish is historically embedded in California. In fact, as Bucholtz, Bermudez, Fung, Edwards, and Vargas (2007) explain, Spanish had been spoken in California for almost 250 years before California became a state in 1850. At the present time, there are many Latino people in California who are bilingual in Spanish and English. However, in California, the use of Spanish does not bring with it the same symbolic capital as English. For this reason, it is not uncommon in California, and in the United States more generally, to see second or third generation Latinos who are monolingual English speakers. In California, the use of Spanish indexes a relative lack of social and economic capital for many people. From a social perspective, the Spanish speaking population tends to be associated with undocumented workers, a class of people within the United States who have minimal access to resources. While this population of Spanish speakers does exist, of course, the cultural representations correlating Spanish speaking in general with this population are very inaccurate ones.

We have heard many personal stories in which people who attended California schools were made to feel ashamed of speaking Spanish. Spanish speakers were told, often by educators, that it was not possible to simultaneously maintain their Spanish language and become full-fledged English users. They became convinced that they would not be able to succeed in the United States if they maintained their Spanish language, and especially if they failed to speak English without a recognizable trace of Spanish accent.

In the late 1990s, Proposition 227 was passed in California. This proposition initiated a law declaring that Spanish-speaking children could not be educated bilingually until they demonstrated proficiency in English. This clearly illustrates the hierarchy. It is written into the law that learning English is the priority. Only if children already speak English can they then learn in Spanish.

Additionally, we have heard many stories from Californian parents of their children being mistakenly placed into English Language Learner programs, though their children speak English as their dominant language. This mistaken placement stems from the earliest forms that parents fill out when they enroll their children in kindergarten in a California public school. One seemingly innocent question on the form concerns languages that are spoken in the home. If a parent includes anything other than English, their children are automatically categorized as English Language Learners. So in some districts, bilingual children who are fluent in English are categorized English Language Learners. Parents have reported that in order to become recategorized as mainstream learners, these children must pass rigorous English tests that would be difficult for any English-speaking child to pass. Though this information is anecdotal, it is interesting that multiple parents have reported similar anecdotes regarding their bilingual children's experiences in the public school system. Perhaps this is an area that deserves further research. Children who are designated as English Language Learners often report having a very difficult time overcoming that categorization and resulting status. In addition, parents have reported feeling that these students are tracked into English classes that require less rigor and fewer challenges than their peers, providing them with less-advanced educations. These perceptions reflect an understanding that English clearly occupies a higher position on the hierarchy than Spanish does in California.

Hierarchical distinctions between languages become actively reproduced through the use of language in public spaces. Hill (1998) discusses how public space is used to construct powerful groups as normative and subordinate groups, which Hill terms "racialized populations" as "disorderly." Hill (1993, 1995, 1998) provides a strong argument on the outward expressions of racism in the use of Spanish in public space in the United States. She calls this use of Spanish, "mock Spanish." As an example, she notes the tendency for developers in the Southwestern United States to use Spanish street names, though these Spanish street names are often ungrammatical and nonsensical. For instance, one street name that we came across in Orange County, California is "Verde Lomas Circle"—Verde, *green*, Lomas, *hills*, and circle. This street name would then translate into English as Green Hills Circle. However, in

Spanish, the adjective must agree with the noun in gender and number. In this example, the noun, *lomas*, is plural, while its adjective, *verde*, is singular. That is ungrammatical in Spanish. Moreover, the adjective in Spanish is typically in the position immediately after the noun except in very semantically specific contexts. In this example, the more typical Spanish construction would be "Lomas Verdes," and needless to say, it would not include the English word "circle." Hill's argument is that developers use these Spanish names to add a certain southwest ambience. However, the Spanish that is used is embedded in English structures. Hill claims that such ungrammatical uses of Spanish in public spaces in the United States index the low value placed on Spanish, almost as though it is not worthy of its own grammar. If street names were in ungrammatical English, people in the United States would find it distasteful. However, it is acceptable for street names to be ungrammatical in Spanish.

Hill argues that this relationship between English and Spanish in the United States indexes the relationship between typically White English-speaking people and typically Hispanic Spanish-speaking people. Spanish-speaking people are constructed as the racialized other, while White English-speaking people are constructed as the norm. The use of mock Spanish, then, appropriates Spanish for use in white public space.

The sign represented in Figure 7.1 is an example of the types of signs found in California on the roads leading to border crossings with Mexico. Signs can be analyzed as part of the *linguistic landscapes* that surround us (Cenoz & Gorter, 2006; Landry & Bourhis, 1997). Linguistic landscapes include, "The language of public road signs, advertising billboards, street names, place names, commercial shop signs, and public signs on government buildings" (Landry & Bourhis, 1997, p. 25). Taken together the signs of any area, can serve at least two functions, "an informational function and a symbolic function" (p. 25).

The sign in Figure 7.1 represents illegal immigrants fleeing across the border to the United States. Once again, we see the relationship between English and Spanish in the United States represented in this linguistic land-scape. The English word "caution" provides a message to English-speaking drivers that they should watch out for people running across the roadway. The Spanish portion of the sign, however, says "prohibido" (*prohibited*). The choice of "caution" written in English and "prohibido" written in Spanish constructs English speakers as the individuals who are doing the legal driving and must maintain appropriate care, and Spanish speakers as those who are walking or running and must be informed that it is prohibited to cross

Figure 7.1 Linguistic Landscape of Border Crossing. Division of Work & Industry, National Museum of American History, Behring Center, Smithsonian Institution

the road in this particular area. This sign, then, provides an especially clear demonstration of language hierarchy as it is performed in this linguistic landscape.

As the linguistic history of California indicates, attitudes toward dominant and subordinate language are not static relationships. In addition, attitudes toward the dominant and subordinate languages represent a complex inter-action of social values related to various communities and social groups. It cannot be taken for granted, for example, that all individuals find value in the knowledge and performance of the dominant language. Community and group membership is marked in part by language use, and the maintenance of membership in good standing in a group dictates that group-appropriate language be used. Woolard (1985), for example, talks about the community pressures exerted by various groups. She notes, for example, that adolescents in Barcelona reported to her that "Castilian speakers ridicule their peers who attempt to speak Catalan" (p. 744). She references a similar example from Gal (1979, p. 106) where Gal tells of a woman who spoke to her in standard Hungarian during her interviews and was later ridiculed by her fellow villagers for choosing the standard over the local Hungarian form. Woolard describes this type of ridicule as one form of "effective *negative sanctions*" that can be at play in relation to language choices in non-standard

community domains providing pressure "toward a solidary community linguistic norm" (p. 744).

In order to gain full membership within a local context, then, a person
must be able to engage in language use that conforms to the rules of linguistic
conduct within that group. That does not necessarily mean that everyone
within a particular group must use exactly the same language variety. It does,
however, mean that everyone within the group must conform to certain
expectations for linguistic behavior in the norms that define the group.

The complex sets of linguistic norms that occur in reference to standard
and local varieties of a language can also be discussed using notions of prestige. Speakers who use the standard form of a language are employing *overt
prestige*, while speakers who use their local variety, particularly for the purposes of solidarity, can be said to be employing *covert prestige*. In looking
again at Gal's example of the woman ridiculed by her fellow villagers for using
standard Hungarian while being interviewed by Gal, we can say that part of
what they were ridiculing her for was her attempt to employ overt prestige.

7.1 Doing Sociolinguistics: Thought Exploration

Consider signs in your environment. Do you see them as neutral? Do you see them as
reflecting ideological notions about language or other societal issues?

In this section, we discussed the nature of language hierarchy through
the illustrations of German in Romania and Spanish in the United States. We
have looked at how language hierarchies are displayed in linguistic landscapes.
We have also considered how individuals value community solidarity whether
this is with the dominant language for those language users or the local
language for those language users.

7.1.1 Language hierarchies and government policies

In some cases, official government policies contribute to one language
becoming dominant. Low, Sarkar, and Winer (2009) discuss the case of
Quebec, where educational policies implemented by the government in the
1970s made French the dominant language of Quebec among young people.
This official French is not just any French, but a specific standard that is
monitored by the government. Low et al. discuss the situation in Quebec in

terms of Blommaert's (2005) *orders of indexicality*. Blommaert defines these as operating within "a stratified polycentric system in which people orient to a variety of (hierarchically ordered) systematically produced indexicalities (p. 402). In the case of Quebec, Low et al. (2009) claim that the government has imposed an order of indexicality that regulates hierarchical orders that had developed naturally and historically.

In particular, Low et al. look specifically at the Montreal Hip Hop scene to understand how Quebec's language policy has influenced language use among this group. Though the group conforms to French as the dominant language of use, this is not the standard, official French endorsed by the government. They employ non-standard varieties of French, including world Frenches, such as the French of Haiti and Senegal. Moreover, Montreal Hip Hop also contains English. Low et al. argue that the language of the Montreal Hip Hoppers rejects the orders of indexicality prevalent within Quebec. Instead, they engage in language use that indexes their own multi-lingualism and multiculturalism. They work within and subvert the orders of indexicality within Quebec and engage in language use that reflects their own world views.

Notions of standard languages and their dominance can be seen as rooted in the historical formation of the nation state. Anderson (2006) attributed the rise of both the nation state and standard language to the rise of mass media. As people began to read en masse and listen to the radio en masse, a standard language for these media was formed. That standard language was, of course, the language of the groups who were doing the writing and speaking in the media. This standard language created imagined communities in which people imagined group cohesion based on sharing the same language. In contrast, those language varieties not used in the mass media began to be interpreted as having lower social value.

7.2 Doing Sociolinguistics: Thought Exploration

Think about the language of the mass media and the language that you may speak within your community or identity group. Are they identical? If so, how do you see that in connection with ideas of overt prestige? If not, how do you see the challenges of negotiating language in your different community experiences and your negotiations between covert and overt prestige?

In this section, we have considered how conceptions of power in language are intricately related to the positions within a social hierarchy that each language occupies, and have discussed how these hierarchies are related to historical factors, such as government policies and the rise of the mass media.

7.2 Language in the public sphere

The public sphere continues to have an influence on the way that people use language, the way that people perceive the languages around them, and the way that people interact through language. Language in the public sphere is language as it is used in situations in which many people have access to that language. In this definition, most language use is public. An example of language in the public sphere would be a news broadcast of a political speech. Language in the public sphere is not necessarily oral; it can also be written. Published works of fiction and poetry would be language in the public sphere. Blogs, websites, and Facebook posts, to name a few examples, would also be examples of language in the public sphere even though they may reach much narrower audiences. The size of the audience, then, is not what defines the public sphere, rather it is the fact that the language use is shaped for other people to have access to it that defines the public sphere.

7.2.1 Critical perspectives on language in the public sphere

Scholars who take a critical perspective on the study of language take overtly political stances to demonstrate how language use indexes societal-level issues. This perspective is often termed *Critical Discourse Analysis*. This type of analysis can be used to address questions of language and identity or language and ideology. A critical discourse analysis is achieved by looking closely at linguistic features (Fairclough, 1989), such as vocabulary, grammar, and textual structures, and analyzing how these features construct meaning and how that meaning constructs power. So, for example, they might consider the value of particular vocabulary words and how they relate to other words. They might also closely analyze the grammatical choices and the significance of these choices in terms of the construction of meaning. Finally, structures of either oral or written texts may be examined. They might be attuned to ways that some participants control others or how texts are organized. For example, van Dijk (2006) demonstrates that public figures manipulate language in particular ways in order to construct political situations. Example 7.1 (from van Dijk, 2006, p. 378) is an excerpt from Tony Blair's address to the British people regarding the war in Iraq.

Example 7.1

1   The country and the Parliament reflect each other. This is a
2   debate that, as time has gone on, has become less bitter but no
3   less grave. So why does it matter so much? Because the
4   outcome of this issue will now determine more than the fate of
5   the Iraqi regime and more than the future of the Iraqi people who
6   have been brutalized by Saddam for so long, important though
7   those issues are. It will determine the way in which Britain and
8   the world confront the central security threat of the 21st century,
9   the development of the United Nations, the relationship between
10 Europe and the United States, the relations within the
11 European Union and the way in which the United States
12 engages with the rest of the world. So it could hardly be more
13 important. It will determine the pattern of international politics
14 for the next generation.

van Dijk argues that Blair's linguistic choices within this text index his worldview. van Dijk further argues that Tony Blair uses particular words and structures to persuade the British people to accept his worldview. In particular, this address employs an "us" versus "them" dichotomy. Blair's "Britain and the world" in lines 7 and 8 indexes a worldview in which Britain is a part, essentially constructing an "us." Furthermore, this "us" becomes associated with legitimized political institutions, such as "the United Nations" in line 9 and "the European Union" in lines 10 and 11. On the other hand, he characterizes Saddam's Iraqi regime as "them." "They" are characterized in line 8 as "the central threat of the 21st century." So Blair is able to establish categories that paint a picture of legitimized political affiliations (us) against the threat of Hussein (them).

Blair also uses highly expressive and hyperbolic lexical items to refer to Hussein's Iraqi regime. For instance, in line lines 5 and 6, he indicates that his alliance must protect "the Iraqi people who have been brutalized by Saddam." The word "brutalized" reflects an extreme action. Note too the use of the first name of the Iraqi leader. Rather than choosing to address him using his full name and political title, this form of address delegitimizes Hussein as the respected leader of Iraq.

The textual structure is also important to Blair's ability to convey a worldview. For instance, in line 3, Blair asks the question, "So why does it matter so much?" Embedded in the meaning of this question is the presupposition that it does matter "so much." By creating this element as a question that reflects one that his audience is presumably asking at this point, he sets up his response as one that directly addresses the expressed concerns of the British people in relation to the reasons that it matters so much. In this way, the audience is framed as co-constructors of the answer because they are framed as the authors of the question.

7.3 Doing Sociolinguistics: Thought Exploration

For each headline and story segment that follows, consider who is being defined as being responsible for the act, consider who is defined as being affected, consider how the process is defined, and consider how the circumstances are defined. Note that these categorizations are different for each of the headline-report combinations. How might the differences reflect different worldviews? (adapted from Trew, 1979)

from *The Times* June 2, 1975
    RIOTING BLACKS SHOT DEAD BY POLICE AS ANC LEADERS MEET
    Eleven Africans were shot dead and 15 wounded when Rhodesian Police opened fire on a rioting crowd of about 2,000.

from the *Guardian* June 2, 1975
    POLICE SHOOT 11 DEAD IN SALISBURY RIOT
    Riot police shot and killed 11 African demonstrators and wounded 15 others.

In this section, we have seen that language in the public sphere can be defined as language that is made public in some way. We've seen how Critical Discourse Analysis methods can be used to examine language in very detailed ways providing the potential to analyze power in discourse. In particular, we have examined how public language has the potential to be framed in ways that convey particular worldviews and that it can be manipulated to convey a particular worldview. Particular ways of viewing the world can become naturalized as people are told, for instance, what is legitimate, what constitutes a threat, and how positionalities are to be understood.

7.2.2 Media

The media constitute an important site in which language ideologies become naturalized in particular areas. As we mentioned before, Anderson (2006) argued that the media were a central component in the formation of the nation state. It was not until the media began to broadcast and print in standardized languages that people began to see themselves as a community of speakers bound together by the use of that standardized language within a nation state.

The use of a particular language or language variety within the national media reproduces notions of that language as the "official" language. Kulyk (2010), for example, demonstrates that Ukrainians primarily use the Ukrainian language, which is considered to be a symbolic marker of national identity. However, Russian is also considered an acceptable language of use in many social practices. This bilingualism is reflected in the use of both languages in the Ukrainian media. Kulyk argues that this normative use of Russian is an inheritance from the past when the Soviet Union wielded political power in Ukraine. The media's use of Russian, then, serves both the bilingual nature of various social practices and reflects a past political structure.

As discussed earlier in this chapter, in multilingual nations, decisions about what will be broadcast and in what language it will be broadcast reflect and reproduce language hierarchies.

Spitulnik (1998) demonstrates the powerful role that the media plays in shaping language ideologies in her study of Zambian broadcasting. She refers to the situation in Zambia as "the politics of language value." Zambian radio is broadcast in seven Zambian languages and in English. This might at first seem as if it were a broad range of languages, but considering that there are 73 distinct tribes in Zambia with 73 distinct language varieties, the choice of those seven language varieties for broadcasting is neither broad nor neutral. This choice places those seven varieties in a more dominant position relative to the 66 varieties that are not broadcast. Moreover, some of the seven languages are allowed more airtime than others, and some are aired at prime times for listening, while others are not. These decisions then differentiate between the seven.

English, in contrast, is broadcast over two radio services, Radio 2 and Radio 4, while the seven Zambian languages share time on Radio 1. Broadcast topic and language is also an important issue to consider. The types of broadcasts that would be of interest to the educated people in Zambia, such as international news, tend to occur in English. In this case, English becomes the broadcast language that is associated with education and sophistication, making English broadcasts more highly valued than the Radio 1 broadcasts for educated people in Zambia.

According to Spitulnik, these decisions about broadcasting attempt to balance an ideology of linguistic pluralism in which the linguistic diversity of Zambia's 73 tribes is celebrated with an ideology that is encapsulated in the national slogan, "One Zambia, One Nation." The linguistic-pluralism ideology and the one-Zambia-one-nation ideology seem to be in conflict with one another, and, indeed, these two ideologies are the source of continuing conflict within Zambia. Decisions related to language and broadcasting bring that conflict to the fore.

7.4 Doing Sociolinguistics: Thought Exploration

Spitulnik argues that language ideologies are not only about language they are also about

1. the construction and legitimation of power,
2. the production of social relations of sameness and difference, and
3. the creation of social stereotypes about speakers and social groups.

Think about how languages are portrayed in the media. How do Spitulnik's three distinctions provide a useful way of considering the representations of languages?

Not only do linguistic choices in the media contribute to a hierarchical relationship between languages, but such choices can also reinforce stereotypes about people who speak particular varieties within a language. Lippi-Green (1997a) demonstrates how linguistic choices often rely on and construct ideological assumptions about people who speak in particular ways.

In particular, Lippi-Green examines how discrimination against various language varieties is evidenced in children's stories and films. She provides examples of this discrimination as it is enacted in animated characters in the films, *Dumbo* and *The Jungle Book*. Lippi-Green identifies the crows from *Dumbo* and the orangutan, King Louie, from *The Jungle Book*, as speaking African American Vernacular English (AAVE). Lippi-Green argues that these characters exemplify a trend in animated film in which characters who speak AAVE tend to be animals rather than people and tend to ". . . be unemployed or show no purpose in life beyond the making of music and pleasing themselves . . ." (p. 94).

Lippi-Green argues that animated filmmakers use accent and dialect to build characters who embody societal stereotypes about people who speak with accents and minority dialects; many of these embodiments construct very negative aspects of these stereotypes. In other words, these characters do not merely speak with accents and particular dialects; the type of character— animal or human—and the qualities of that character construct negative stereotypes that are correlated with the characters' accents and dialects, constructing the accents and dialects, and consequently the people in real life who speak them, in negative ways. Another crucial point is that the primary target audience of these animated films is children. Therefore, these constructions become particularly influential as children categorize the linguistic world around them.

The use of linguistic features to build characters in film, television, and fiction contributes to the construction of otherness. Consequently, this ideological construction of the other contributes to particular groups being identified as other. The media is in a particularly powerful position with regard to constructing such ideological labels because mass media is so far-reaching. Meek (2006) discusses what she calls "Hollywood Injun English" (HIE). In Meek's analysis, HIE is commonly found in Hollywood movies to portray Native American characters. Meek argues that the HIE portrayals, constituting a kind of mocking of Native American ways of speaking, are surprisingly consistent across Hollywood films.

Meek (2006, p. 35) provides several examples to support her argument. One of these examples is exemplified in the Indian Chief from the 2002 movie, *Peter Pan*. In the excerpt provided in Example 7.2, the Lost Boys talk to the Indian Chief while they are tied to a pole and dangled over a fire, after having been accused of being complicit in Indian Princess, Tiger Lily's, disappearance.

Example 7.2

1.	Boy 1:	Okay, chief, you win this time, now turn us loose.
2.	John:	Turn us loose?
		You mean this is only a game?
3.	Boy 2:	Sure, when we win, we turn them loose.
4.	Boy 3:	When they win, they turn us loose
5.	Boy 4:	(They) turn us loose
6.	Chief:	This time (1) no turn-um loose
7.	Boy 2:	Huh? (laughs) The chief's a great spoofer.
8.	Chief:	Me no spoof-um
		Where you hide Princess Tiger Lily?
9.	Boy 1:	Uh, Tiger Lily?
10.	Boy 2:	We ain't got your old princess.
11.	John:	I've never seen her.
12.	Michael:	Me neither.
13.	Boy 2:	Honest we don't
14.	Chief:	Heap big lie.
		If Tiger Lily no back by sunset burn-um at stake.

Meek argues that the Chief in this example exemplifies HIE in terms of the use of several linguistic features. In turns 8 and 14, there is the lack of tense and aspectual markers in the verb phrase. The Chief's language takes on a telegraphic quality, resembling baby talk in its lack of function words, its pronoun deletion or substitution ("me" instead of "I" in turn 8) and its lack of auxiliary verbs ("Where you hide . . ." in turn 8 rather than, "Where did you hide . . .").

Linguistic features such as these make the Chief's language seem both foreign and simplistic, contributing to his identity as other. The language works in conjunction with other semiotic features, such as the Chief's clothing and hairstyle, to solidify a construction of the Chief as different from the protagonists. As Meek argues, the portrayal of Native Americans using HIE across multiple films leads to societal stereotypes of Native Americans, which significantly contrast with the way modern Native Americans, and previous generations of Native Americans for that matter, construct their identities in the real world.

7.5 Doing Sociolinguistics: Thought Exploration

Think about a movie that you have seen recently. How were characters' uses of language constructed? Were the characters the major protagonists or antagonists? Did you recognize stereotypical characteristics in the development of these characters, or did you find them constructed as multi-aspected individuals?

In this section, we have examined how media practices, including those related to language choices in broadcasts and those related to how characters are portrayed in films and movies, have the potential to contribute both to constructions of language hierarchies and to stereotypes about particular dialects and varieties.

7.2.3 Politics

Language ideologies play an important role in the way that politicians represent groups of people and in the way they represent themselves. In the political realm, language ideologies provide the fodder for the ways that politics are practiced and accomplished. For example, the way that people talk about issues, such as immigration, provides a window into their ideological positions when it comes to immigration. The same would go for any other political process or topic.

Mehan (1997) provides an interesting illustration of the political construction of immigrants in California. In 1994, Californians voted on a ballot initiative, Proposition 187. The goal of this proposition was, among other things, to exclude undocumented immigrants and their children from public school education, from access to free healthcare, and from other state services. While the proposition initially passed, it was later overturned by the federal courts, and Governor Gray Davis halted any potential appeals of the federal court's decision in 1999. Mehan (1997) addressed why this proposition passed in California. In his words, he analyzed the "politics of representation" of proponents and opponents of the proposition to discover how each side framed the affected population. He found, for example, that the proposition framed the debate in a way that set the population in question up as the "enemy" of society.

In order to construct a group as an enemy, members of the group must be constructed as the ideological other. In California, the discussion of the issue became one in which the affected population was constructed as a separate group from Californians, who were framed as taxpayers. As Mehan says, it became an *us* versus *them* dichotomy. According to Mehan, proponents of the proposition referred to the potentially affected group as "illegal immigrants" or "illegal aliens" framing them as "outside of society" and essentially "them." The use of the term *alien* is a particularly striking example of establishing one group of people as "other." On the other hand, opponents of the proposition referred to members of the affected group as "non-resident workers" or "undocumented workers" framing them as productive workers who may soon become "one of us."

Illegal immigrants were constructed as threatening to take jobs from Californians and as overwhelming the social services system, thereby burdening California taxpayers. The advertisements supporting the proposition made the situation seem quite urgent and frightening, as though the state would run out of money if this group continued to use so many of the state's resources and as though taxpaying Californians would be jobless on account of these individuals taking all the jobs. As cited in Mehan (1997, p. 258), Proposition 187 made the following claims:

Example 7.3
[The people of California] have suffered and are suffering economic hardship caused by the presence of illegal aliens in this state.
That they have suffered and are suffering personal injury and damage caused by the presence of illegal aliens in this state.

The linguistic binary of "us" versus "them" set the two groups up in opposition, making the opposition seem natural, inevitable, and urgent. Mehan proposes that these constructions can account for the original passing of the proposition.

The ideology of urgency that prompted Californians to vote for Proposition 187 is not unusual in political persuasion. There are many examples in recent history in which an urgent crisis has been the justification for political action worldwide. Huysmans and Buonfino (2008) use the term "the politics of insecurity" to explain how politicians have framed the relationship between immigration and terrorism in Great Britain; "the history of immigration and asylum policy is permeated by references to the threats of immigration and asylum for social and community cohesion, the welfare state, the sustainability of the labour market, cultural and racial identity, etc." (p. 781). The politics of insecurity allows debates to be framed in such a way that persuasion is based on threats to self-interest.

Chang and Mehan (2008) argue that the Bush administration engaged in the politics of insecurity as it constructed an urgent crisis in Iraq to justify going to war there. As an example of this construction, Chang and Mehan (2008, p. 468) cite Secretary of State Colin Powell's February 5, 2003 presentation to the United Nations:

> Example 7.4
> Some believe, some claim these contacts do not amount to much. They say Saddam Hussien's secular tyranny and Al Qaida's religious tyranny do not mix. I am not comforted by this though. Ambition and hatred are enough to bring Iraq and Al Quaida together, enough so Al Quaida could learn to build more sophisticated bombs and learn to forge documents, and enough so that Al Quaida could turn to Iraq for help in acquiring expertise on weapons of mass destruction.

In this portion of his speech, Powell constructs an urgent and frightening situation; foreign enemies are threatening the American people. He also manages to merge two enemies into one enemy. Again, it is linguistically constructed as "us" (Americans) versus "them" (the Iraq-Al Quaida collaboration). Such constructions become the basis of political policy.

In this section, we have examined how language ideologies related to constructions of groups of people contribute to political arguments and decisions. In particular, we examined how "us" versus "them" dichotomies function in representations of groups of people, and how these representations are used in conjunction with political constructions of urgency to validate particular types of political decisions.

7.3 Language policies and political contexts

Politics also come into play in the ways that languages are used in particular contexts. The political decisions that are made are based in ideological notions of the role of particular languages. Language policies are often explicit in these constructions. For example, in California, as mentioned earlier in this chapter, there is an explicit legal policy against educating students in a language other than English unless they already know English. This policy reproduces the ideological notion that English is the official language in California, even though there is no explicit policy that states that English is actually the official language. In some cases, it is not a single legal policy but an aggregation of policies in multiple institutions that reproduce particular ideological notions. In Sweden, for example, particular language requirements to gain entry into higher education and language qualifications for many elite jobs help to reproduce the ideology that English is the language of the elite (Berg, Hult, & King, 2001). Language policies often reflect the language ideologies at work within particular contexts.

Older understandings of how multilinguals used language, particularly in contexts in which one language is highly valued (H) and another lowly valued (L), argued that multilinguals manipulated H and L varieties in distinct, separate contexts with the H and L languages maintaining their relative value across contexts. However, recent research on multilingual language use complicates this H/L analysis.

Modern research on multilingual communities demonstrates that the H/L distinction is a shifting one, which is dependent on the context of language use. As we discussed in chapter 3, Messing (2007) illustrates the contextual nature of H and L valued varieties in her study of Mexicano-Spanish bilingualism in central Mexico. Among the group of Mexicano-Spanish bilinguals that she studied, Spanish is considered a public language, while Mexicano is considered a private language. In this group, Spanish is highly valued for use in public contexts, such as public meetings and school. However, Spanish is lowly valued and Mexicano is highly valued in private contexts of language use in which all participants are users of Mexicano. For them, Mexicano is highly valued as a private language, but not as a public language. An ideological preference has evolved among this multilingual population for the use of Spanish in public domains and the use of Mexicano in private domains.

It is not uncommon in multilingual societies, in which one language is a colonizing language, for the colonizing language to take on high public value and the indigenous language to take on high private value. This pattern of language value may explain why attempts to introduce Mexicano into school contexts have been met with some resistance by indigenous Mexicano language users.

In this section we looked at how assumptions about highly valued and lowly valued languages and their contexts of use do not always describe complex linguistic situations, including those that have been affected by colonizing languages. Recognition of the complex ways in which speakers use languages, allows us to understand why social policies about language are difficult to implement.

7.3.1 Language policies, political contexts and the workplace

In Chapter 3, we discussed educational language policies. Although choices related to languages of instruction are clearly political ones, we will not repeat the discussion of educational language policies here. In this section, we will discuss the implementation of language policies and their consequences in other macro-societal institutional contexts, particularly those related to the workplace.

Language policies are often implemented in the workplace. This is, perhaps, no more evident than in the international centers that serve as outsourced customer service call centers for Western companies. International call centers represent an enactment of globalization and of English as a global language. Typically in these centers, multilingual people provide customer service to monolingual English speakers. As King (2009) defines them, ". . . call centers involve connecting service-seeking customers from wealthy, English-speaking countries with service providing workers from more multilingual, less economically powerful states or regions" (p. 1).

The fact that these call centers are a growth industry in many countries has affected language policies. In the Philippines, for example, the existence of call centers has had an effect on the way that English education programs are implemented. Frignal (2009) describes call centers in the Philippines "as a key growth industry currently providing jobs and revenues to the country" (p. 64). He adds that "the government and the education sectors appear to be ready to respond to the language needs of call centers" (p. 64) because, as Friginal makes clear, if Filipino workers generally cannot use English in the call centers in a way that American customers find satisfying, the call centers will be moved out of the Philippines. In this way, the Western companies that outsourced the call centers affect language demands in the call centers, and language policy that responds to these demands is implemented due to the economic benefits associated with these centers.

Morgan and Ramanathan (2009) note a similar process at work in India. Call centers demand that a certain type of non-Indian sounding English be spoken. In India, this means that more privileged Indians who are educated in English medium schools have an advantage when it comes to access to call center jobs.

In both of these examples, the onus is on the service provider to make sure that the customer is satisfied with the use of language. However, this relationship between the call center service provider and the customer reflects a language ideology in which some forms of English are more validated than others.

Friginal's (2009) analysis of the call centers in the Philippines also provides an example that illustrates the need for call center agents to appear as non-descript as possible. Example 7.5 provides an excerpt from a call (Friginal, 2009, p. 57) in which the call center agent has tried to mollify a customer who has become agitated as the call center agent tries to collect the caller's records. This excerpt begins after the caller has asked to speak to the call agent's supervisor.

Example 7.5

Agent: Ok sir, uh, I'll be transferring you over to my supervisor right away, ok I just need to know I have the correct information on my end

Caller: I don't want you to, listen, if you're offshore I don't wanna, I wanna talk to an American that's what I wanna know, are you in the United States?

Agent: Yes [agent lied] [long pause] [no response from the caller for more than 5 seconds] sir, all I need is the first and last name and your complete billing address and I'll be transferring you over to my [interruption]

This segment would seem to indicate that the customer believes that customer service implemented from outside of the United States is inherently inferior, and the customer seems rather determined, in fact, to discover where the service is being provided. The caller's statement about wanting to talk to an American, and the direct question, "are you in the United States?" is actually the second attempt by this caller to determine the location of the agent. Earlier in the call, the caller had asked where the agent was located. The agent responded that she could not divulge this information for security purposes. It is interesting that the agent claims to be in the United States, when asked directly about this in the example above, though she was actually in the Philippines. Clearly, the policy in the outsourced call center is to conceal from the customer the fact that the call center is outside of the United States.

Possibly in response to the types of language attitudes displayed by the caller in Example 7.5, the language policy within the call center is to disguise the national background of the call center agents so that callers are unable to detect a difference in the agent's language background. The call center agents, then, must assimilate to the linguistic practices that their western customers prefer. This practice reproduces a language ideology in which western ways of using English are enacted as dominant and better.

7.6 Doing Sociolinguistics: Thought Exploration

Consider your experiences doing business or seeking technical support for a product. In these situations, have you spoken to someone whose use of language differed from your own? How did the communication go? As you think about it now, can you identify aspects of the communication that indexed specific types of training the call representative might have received?

In this section we have looked at a kind of globalized economic phenomenon not uncommon in the world today, that of outsourced customer service call centers. In these centers, linguistic resources are connected to economic benefits, and consequently to language policies that respond to these economic pressures. Language ideologies, then, have real consequence in the daily lives of human beings, becoming the basis of relations of domination and subordination.

7.3.2 Language policies, political contexts and asylum processes

Asylum processes are another area where it can clearly be seen that language ideologies have real consequence in the daily lives of human beings. Blommaert

(2009) demonstrates that language policies and the assumptions about language use inherent in those policies have important implications in the asylum process.

Blommaert provides an example of a refugee, Joseph, who claims to be Rwandan but is rejected for asylum by immigration officials in the United Kingdom largely because his linguistic repertoire did not match what they deemed to be typically Rwandan. Blommaert's analysis of the asylum seeker's story, however, demonstrates the real possibility that the story was a valid account.

Rwandans would typically be expected to speak French and Kinyarwanda, a Bantu language spoken in Rwanda. Joseph did not control either of these languages well enough to satisfy officials that he was Rwandan. According to Joseph's account, the reason for this is that he spoke English at home with his parents until they were both murdered. Even when his parents were alive, he traveled and spent extended periods of time outside of Rwanda. After their deaths, Joseph lived with his uncle and became proficient in Runyankole, a Bantu language spoken in Uganda. Blommaert's analysis demonstrates the feasibility of Joseph's account based on the history and complexity of the region. According to this analysis it was quite possible that Joseph was Rwandan. Based on his linguistic repertoire, however, the immigration officials in the United Kingdom labeled Joseph Ugandan and deported him there, though he claimed never to have set foot in Uganda.

Blommaert's analysis reflects the consequences of applying assumptions about national languages to complex regions and personal situations. Given the turmoil in Rwanda around the year 2000, about when Joseph sought asylum, it is not wholly surprising that there were disruptions in his life that led to an unusual set of migration patterns and linguistic experiences for him. However, the immigration officials stuck to an ideologically based and quite rigid expectation for language use that matched a Rwandan identity with French and Kinyarwanda. The consequences for Joseph were that he was labeled as Ugandan and deported to Uganda, a place he claimed to have no attachment to.

In this section, we briefly examined how notions of national identity are ideologically based in relatively fixed associations between languages and national identities, and we looked at the consequences that this had for the asylum application and the life experiences of one individual.

7.4 Doing sociolinguistics: research activities

1. Create a short survey in which you ask questions about which languages people find the most useful to know. Create 3–5 questions being careful not to simply ask yes/no questions. Survey 8–10 people. Once you have collected your data, try to put the languages into categories. What do your findings reveal in terms of language hierarchy?
2. Collect a series of photographs of signs displayed in your area, or an area that interests you. Analyze the language and/or the visual representations depicted in these signs. What does your analysis reveal about how signs reflect language and social ideologies?
3. Choose a medium (e.g. television, radio, Facebook, Twitter, etc.). Consider how different languages are represented in these media. For example, how much airtime do they get, or when are they broadcast? Is a particular language set as a default language? How does the web design position the languages? Consider how the time or special positionalities reflect language hierarchies.

7.5 Suggested further reading

Blommaert, J. (2009). Language, asylum, and the national order. *Current Anthropology, 50*(415–441).

Bourdieu, P. (1977). *Reproduction in education, society and culture.* London: Sage.

Fairclough, N. (1989). Discourse and power. In C. N. Candlin (Ed.), *Language and power* (2nd ed., pp. 43–108). London: Longman.

Gal, S. (1987). Codeswitching and consciousness in the European periphery. *American Ethnologist, 14*(4), 637–653.

Hill, J. H. (1998). Language, race, and white public space. *American Anthropologist, 100*(3), 680–689.

Lippi-Green, R. (1997). Teaching children how to discriminate: What we learn from the Big Bad Wolf. In R. Lippi-Green (Ed.), *English with an accent: Language, ideology, and discrimination in the United States* (pp. 79–103). New York: Routledge.

Meek, B. A. (2006). And the Injun goes "How!": Representations of American Indian English in white public space. *Language in Society, 35*(1), 93–128.

Mehan, H. (1997). The discourse of the illegal immigration debate: A case study in the politics of representation. *Discourse & Society, 8*(2), 249–270.

van Dijk, T. A. (2006). Discourse and manipulation. *Discourse & Society, 17*(3), 359–383.

Woolard, K. A. (1985). Language variation and cultural hegemony: Toward an integration of sociolinguistic and social theory. *American Ethnologist, 12*(4), 738–748.

8 Sociolinguistics: Methods and Approaches

Key Terms: *participant observation; Observer's Paradox; narrow transcription; broad transcription; corpus; Interactional Sociolinguistics; contextualization cue; narrative structure; Ethnography of Communication; speech community; speech situation; speech event; speech act; Ethnomethodology; Conversation Analysis; turn; preference organization; repair: self and other*

Chapter 8 provides an in-depth examination of many of the practices and empirical approaches fundamental to doing sociolinguistics. Sociolinguistic research is interested in data that come from what people say, write, and do in the real world, with some sociolinguistic work even looking at virtual worlds. People who look at language from a social perspective argue that looking at how people interact naturally and authentically through language yields accurate analyses of language use. This sounds like it should be relatively easy to do. However, collecting sociolinguistic data is not without pitfalls, so it is important to keep some issues in mind. Three important areas to focus on include the following:

1. the ethical protection of participants,
2. the means of observing and recording,
3. the setting and time that the data are collected, and
4. the influence of the observer on the observed.

8.1 Doing Sociolinguistics: Thought Exploration

Consider each of the items on this list. How might each of them be related to collecting data? How might each of these affect the data that is collected?

8.1 Ethical and legal considerations when collecting sociolinguistic data

When we begin the process of collecting data for a sociolinguistics project, we have to think about how we will observe and record the people that we are studying. It is important to consider several elements related to research in general when we begin this process. First we must consider the ethical issues related to dealing with participants. As M. Brewster Smith (2000) has noted "Moral or ethical judgment is a human universal, but systematic treatments of ethical principles obviously vary across religious traditions and schools of philosophical thought" (p. 4). Second, we should consider legal issues related to collecting data.

Language that has already been made public, such as anything you find on television, on the radio, in public sectors of the internet, or in print is generally fair game. One question at issue is whether it is unethical or even illegal to record individuals without their consent. Many people consider this to be unethical; in addition, in many places, it is illegal to audio record everyday participants without their consent. The laws on audio recording people without their knowledge vary by country and often within a country. Within the United States, for example, individual states have different laws regarding this matter. What is at stake here is making sure that we protect the privacy of individuals who are not public figures enacting their public roles. We need to make sure that individuals consent to anything that happens to them without any feeling that they are being coerced. Important concepts to consider are making sure that we respect both persons and their autonomy, and that we are guided by the principle of *beneficence*. "Benificence requires that researchers minimize possible harms and maximize possible benefits from research" (Scott-Jones, 2000, p. 27).

8.1.1 Boards that review research

In order to help researchers make sure that they are protecting their participants, many universities have special boards set up to review research projects that will be published in any way. In this use, the word *published* means to make public. So if you want to present your work at a conference or write a paper that you would like to publish, you will need to consider making sure that you have your work approved by one of these boards that review research, if your university or college has one.

In the United States, for example, Institutional Review Boards (IRBs) were instituted in response to a 1965 exposé providing evidence that unethical research practices were being carried out, including drug trials without the patients' consent. The Tuskeegee syphilis study in which 600 low-income African American men were left untreated for syphilis long after a cure was discovered also emphasized the need for such boards. Because the origins of IRB in the United States began in the context of the protection of the public health, it may seem odd at first that the work done by individuals studying language use should be under the same scrutiny. However, it should be noted that whether a researcher is doing research that affects the physical well being of an individual or something seemingly more benign like doing observations, they have ethical responsibilities to research participants, and this includes their psychological and social well-being. Finding and working closely with the board at your university or college can help ensure that your work has addressed any possible ethical concerns.

Some issues to consider in relation to collecting recorded data include considering who your participants are. As noted, public data of public officials does not need additional consent. But with private individuals, we should ask for consent. This becomes more complex when we consider the situation of individuals who for some reason are not considered capable of giving consent. This includes, for example, children. In the case of children, we would certainly want to get their permission, or assent, for recording them since we would want to respect their personhood. But since they are not typically legally responsible for themselves, we would need to ask for consent from their parents or legal guardians.

A second major issue is one of protecting the anonymity of certain participants. Within legal and ethical guidelines, we should consider the responsibility of protecting the anonymity of individuals whom we might put at risk in some way by recording them. This can, for example, be the case for individuals who are discussing issues that might put them at legal risk due to the subject matter. A second example, here, might be the possibility of putting someone's legal status at risk.

8.2 Doing Sociolinguistics: Research Activity

a. Find out if your institution has a board or committee that reviews research for ethical and legal considerations.
b. Collect any information that you can about the specific processes that this board has established for the review of research including any application forms there might be.

In this section, we have considered some of the ethical and legal considerations related to the protection of people who might participate in sociolinguistic research. We also discussed the importance of familiarizing ourselves with any legal requirements that might apply to the way we carry out research.

8.2 Observations

There is, of course, more than one way to collect data while observing people. First, we can observe without participating in a particular event. Many people consider this a more detached method of gathering data. We can also, however, carry out *participant observations*, meaning that as researchers we are also actively participating in activities with the people we are studying as we collect the data. In either of these cases, events can be recorded, or the researcher keeps careful, detailed notes.

As we will discuss in Section 8.7 on the Ethnography of Communication, the choice between being a detached observer or an interactive observer has consequences for the quality of the data collected. We will also have to decide how we will record the data. We must decide whether we take field notes, copious written notes on our observations, and whether we will audio or video record. All of these possibilities carry with them benefits and drawbacks. Taking copious field notes in the process of observation can mean that we get a great deal of data, but it can also mean that we miss certain aspects of the interaction. For some research goals, it may, therefore, be better to audio or video record. But even this choice comes with cultural considerations. In some situations, participants may not be comfortable being audio or video recorded. For instance, Susan Philips' (1983) ethnography of the Warm Springs Indians in Oregon was conducted through the use of field notes. In this case, she respected the fact that the Warm Springs people were as a culture uncomfortable with any kind of recording made of themselves.

Audio recording means that we get a great deal of very rich data. Since human interaction is incredibly complex, recording does not mean that we get everything. But as Harvey Sacks (1984) has noted, "Tape-recorded materials constituted a 'good enough' record of what happened. Other things, to be sure, happened, but at least what was on the tape had happened" (p. 26). Obviously, for example, part of what an audio recording will miss is the visual aspects of the interaction. Nevertheless, in some situations, audio recording may be preferred over video recording. For instance, in Vickers' current study of interactions between doctors and patients in a low-income clinic in Southern California, audio recording is preferable to video recording because it allows more anonymity. This is desirable in the clinical context because of the sensitive nature of doctor-patient interactions and because of the fact that many of the patients in the low-income clinic may be legally undocumented.

Video recording obviously allows for a rich analysis of both verbal and non-verbal interaction. However, the researcher must carefully think through issues related to video recording, such as the loss of anonymity of participants. Additionally, it is important to remember that video recordings, like audio recordings, are themselves recontextualized versions of the events that took place. By the very nature of video recording, we focus the lens on some aspects of the interaction and not others. A camera lens has one point of view. Therefore, in considering your data collection and in analyzing your data it is important to consider what is missed in video recording.

Many researchers choose to combine data collection methods. For instance, in Vickers' work in a Southern California medical clinic, she conducted participant observation, took field notes, and audio recorded the clinical interactions. This allowed her to observe and record in her field notes the visual aspects of the interaction that would not be visible on the audio recording. Participants' pseudonyms could be taken down in the field notes so that participants could remain anonymous. Researchers, then, may choose to combine methods. They may engage in participant observation, record field notes, and video record to obtain a richer set of data to reach a thick description (Geertz, 1973) of interactions.

The researcher also needs to consider the setting and the time that the data are collected. It makes a difference whether people are in their own homes, in the classroom, in the workplace, or in the police department, for instance. We need to understand how the setting where the data is collected affects the data. Additionally, the time of day is important. People's interaction may be affected according to how tired they are, whether they just ate a big meal, or how busy they are, for instance. We need to take such issues into account when we make decisions about where and when to collect data.

Finally, the fact that research participants are being observed affects the way that they interact. As we mentioned in Chapter 3, in the late 1960s, Labov described the difficulty of doing observations. He noted that linguistic research has the goal of finding out how people actually talk when they are not being observed, but that the problem is that we can only find out how people talk by actually observing them. He called this *the Observer's Paradox*. As researchers, we cannot avoid the Observer's Paradox: our very presence initiates a change in the behavior we are observing, but we can take steps to limit our effects on the data. Labov and Waletzky (1966) decided that if individuals became so engrossed in the story they were telling, part of their awkwardness in talking to researchers would be mitigated. Therefore, they asked their story-tellers to relate stories when they were in danger of being killed or had been in a memorable fight.

A second way, as mentioned above, to collect data that reduces the observer effect is to collect data in the ongoing stream of interactants' conversations. As they become engaged in their interactions, they can reduce their awareness that they are being recorded. Therefore, it is important to collect data for a long enough period of time that it is possible to see the participants' inter-actions in multiple phases of the observational period. Moreover, protecting the participants' anonymity is also important in relation to this element of observation. If participants know that the researcher will make them as anonymous as possible and use a pseudonym in place of their name, they may be less fearful or self-conscious.

8.3 Doing Sociolinguistics: Thought Exploration

Think about the kind of research that you are interested in conducting. What method of data collection would be suitable to answering the research questions you might have?

In this section, we have focused on using observation and recording to collect sociolinguistic data. We have considered why we might make particu-lar data collection choices and some of the consequences of those choices. In considering some of these consequences, we have addressed researchers' responsibilities to protect research participants.

8.3 Transcription

One crucial issue for the sociolinguist is transcription. Philips (1998) points out the importance of transcripts for researchers committed to examining how language users jointly construct meaning in fact-to-face interactions. "Thus, to understand how meaning is produced, it is necessary to examine actual discourse in the form of transcripts of tape recordings of socially occur-ring speech" (p. 11). As Ochs (1979) discussed, transcriptions are a researcher's data, and creating a relevant transcription requires a process that reflects the theoretical goals of the research. Quite often, researchers collect a great deal of data and must select certain parts of that data to scrutinize more carefully in a transcript. A transcript should also contain the levels of detail needed for us to look at language in relation to the questions we are considering.

When we go about making a transcript of audio or video-recorded inter-actions, the first decision we have to make relates to the type of analysis we want to do. If we are examining dialects or changes in language varieties, for example, we might want to have a phonetic transcription of the data. This type of transcription is often called a *narrow transcription* because it keeps a very detailed account of the sounds of particular consonants and vowels. These types of transcripts may employ the International Phonetic Alphabet and take some training to read. A slightly broader type of transcript is represented in the work of many Conversation Analysts. These transcripts show detail, such as pauses, emphasis, and breath sounds, to name a few details. Consider an example from Jefferson (2002, p. 1346). In Example 8.1, she is looking at how people often use the word "no" to show agreement with a conversational partner's point.

Example 8.1

```
1  Maggie:       .hh because I(c) (.) you know I told Mother what'd ha:ppened
2                yesterday there at the party,
3  Sorrell:      [°Yeah.°]
4  Maggie:       [a::] n d uh,.hhhhh (0.2) uh you know she asked me if it was
5      (-)       because I'd had too much to dri:nk and I said no=
6  Sorrell: (-)  =[N o:::::::.]
7  Maggie:       =[because at the t]i:me I'd only ha:d,h you know that drink'n
8                aha:If when we were going through the receiving line.
9  Sorrell:      Ri:ght.
```

In this case, Jefferson is analyzing the use of "no" in certain situations. She is interested in when this use of "no" might overlap cooperatively with another speaker or if it might be emphasized in some way, so she chooses a level of transcription detail that reflects the analysis she is performing. This transcript, then, provides the level of detail that Jefferson needs to examine the various uses of "no". If she had, for example, not transcribed length or overlap, this use of "no" might have gone unnoticed.

However, not all transcriptions must be this detailed. Consider the follow-ing transcript from Vickers' data between two engineering students discussing a project they are working on.

Example 8.2

1. John: so I don't know if we wanna wait for that then I just thought
2.   this this looks like it's five volts too
3. Ben: ah actually no
4. Peter: no three

This is a much broader transcript. It shows some pronunciation detail—the "wanna" in line 1, for example, and notes where there is repetition, such as the "this this" in line 2, but for the most part, this transcript represents a rather *broad transcription*.

In both of these examples, the speakers are represented one after another in a vertical order, and the transcription uses relatively standard orthography. Generally, in transcripts, utterances that are produced later in time come below and are seen as relevant to what came before.

However, we can make other decisions about how to order the interaction on the page. As Ochs (1979) argues, top-bottom ordering makes the top utterance look more important because of a natural bias that favors those things that are on top. Ochs proposes a side-by-side transcription in which the utterances of each speaker are represented in separate columns. This method of transcription can be particularly useful when a researcher is examining the interactional patterns between speakers. Let's look again at the example from Deckert (2006, p. 191) we saw in Chapter 5. In this case, the choice was made to view the participants side by side because Deckert was analyzing what role the interpreter played in the interview and analyzing the potential effects the interpreter had on the exchange.

Example 8.3

T: 14	Jackie (Social Worker)	Iliana (Interpreter)	Nicole (10;0)
462	Okay. How many times did he touch your cosa ?		
463		¿Cuantas veces te ha tocado tu parte, tu cosa? *How many times has he touched your part, your thing?*	
464	About-?		
465		Como.	

466			Como cuatro veces. *About four times*
467		About four times.	
468	About four times? Okay. What did he touch your cosa with?		
469		¿Con que te tocaba? *What did he touch you with?*	
470			Con las manos. *With his hands*
471		With his hands. (papers rustling)	

Obviously some of the effects of the interpreter cannot be seen in any transcript. Her presence changes the participant structure of the interview. Clearly this is no longer a dyadic interaction. And an analysis can show that it is also not merely a mediated dyadic interaction. What can be seen more easily in transcripts that are set up in this way, are the patterns of interaction within that participant structure and the movement of ideas as the interpreter changes the exchange from one language to another. Using this format, it was much easier to see exchanges between only the interviewer and the interpreter when they negotiated the meaning of a particular question, or exchanges between only the interviewer and the child when they negotiated meaning. It is also much easier to see occasions when the child directly responded to the interviewer in English rather than Spanish, completely skipping the move to the interpreter. These are all significant changes in the interactions. During the analysis stage, it is also possible to have additional columns in this type of format in which the researcher can keep track of coding or additional analytic remarks. There are drawbacks in this type of format, however. For example, while overlaps can still be marked with square brackets [] in the same way that they can be in other formats, it is a bit more difficult to visually see their timing. And, of course, this side-by-side column format can be a bit more unwieldy due to the narrower columns if one has to work on a typically sized sheet of paper.

Ochs (1979) provides an additional consideration in relation to transcripts of this type. She argues that the European culture of literacy socializes its members to encode ideas not only top to bottom but left to right. As such, "leftness" is linked with priority. Placing one person on the left may make that person seem dominant. The left-most position also indicates temporal priority, which can lead to assumptions that the left-most person chooses the topic and initiates conversation. That left-most utterance then becomes the frame within which other utterances are understood.

If we are including non-verbal behavior, we also need to think about where the non-verbals will be placed within the transcript. Representing both non-verbal and verbal behaviors in a transcript can be difficult. Consider Example 8.4 where Deckert was analyzing how children's testimonies were represented in an ABC television broadcast, *When Children Accuse. Who to Believe?* (West, 1997). Part of the broadcast involved interviews with two individuals, who are now young adults, and their mother. When the two young men were children, they had been involved in a very famous child abuse case, and they are now recounting their experiences.

Example 8.4

Visual	Audio
/¹/video footage of adult interview	/¹/Brenda K: And I said, "What kind of joke is this?" and they told me it wasn't a joke. And I told them, "Wait. I got a little boy in there in bed."
/²/shift to still photo of Brian Kniffen as a child: /³/ Shift to video footage of adult interview	/²/Brian K: And I remember my mom came in and woke me up, and she was crying. And she said, "Brian you're going to have to go with these men /³/ for a little while. You'll be—you know, just do whatever they tell you."
/⁴/Still photo of Brandon Kniffen as a child: /⁵/Shift to video footage of adult interview	/⁴/Brandon K: I didn't know what was going on. I was really scared, and I was crying, /⁵/too. I think I was crying, because I didn't know what was going on.

The show's producers chose the visuals that accompanied this interview. Therefore, keeping track of the visuals chosen and the timing of the visuals relative to the parts of the interview allows for an analysis of the roles the visuals play in the construction of the public presentation of this interview.

Another important consideration in working with transcripts is keeping close track of information related to the transcript. In one form or another, the researcher should provide the names of participants. Most often this is done using pseudonyms or initials. But keeping track of the date and time of the recording, sound file information, length of the recording, and the setting is also very useful. Many researchers keep track of this information in the first section of a transcript before the first line. This can be done by writing all of the information on the transcript itself or by giving the transcript a code number that correlates with this information in a separate file.

8.3.1 Transcription conventions

An important question a researcher must ask relates to how we make decisions about which transcription conventions to use. There are many possibilities for transcription conventions. As discussed earlier, the choice of detail needed for the analysis can determine the detail needed in the transcription, and this affects choices related to transcription conventions. However, it should also be noted that each area of study that addresses language use may have certain traditions for particular transcription conventions. For instance, if the researcher is engaged in conversation analysis, they might be expected to use conversation analytic conventions.

Du Bois, Schuetze-Coburn, Cumming, and Paolino (1993) suggest that researchers follow a transcription delicacy hierarchy to make systematic decisions about the detail that will be included in the transcript. However, there are some basic things that should be included. Of course, the names of the participants need to be included. The words have to be included. We must demarcate participant turns. It is also important to include pauses and places where the participants' talk overlaps. Let's take a look at Example 8.5 from Vickers' data of interactions between engineering students and consider some of the transcription conventions used.

Example 8.5
<1.14.03>
1	P:	hm: what are those little like uh <u>flat</u> battery cells
2	J:	oh lithiums
3	P:	yeah [lithiums]
4	J:	[we could] use lithiums..those are like three volts
5	P:	three volts?
6	J:	they ((xxx)) last a lo::ng time
7	P:	yeah
8	J:	they're perfect for portable digital circuits because they don't give
9		much current . . . and then these things are small
10	P:	mhm right
11	J:	so (1.2)
12	P:	so those are also three volts

This transcript follows several useful transcription conventions:

- Marking for time code: At the very beginning of this excerpt, there is a "<1.14.03>". In this case, this section of the sound file can be found beginning at approximately 1 minute, 14 seconds into the sound file. If this researcher had an additional question about this transcription, such as how intonation was being used in a certain line, she could go back to this time in the digital file. Keeping track of time markings is incredibly useful for any questions or clarifications a researcher has during their data analysis process. Time codes can also be useful to indicate how fast the interaction is progressing.
- Line numbers: We see that each line (in some transcripts each turn) is numbered. This allows for easier discussions of our findings in our writing. We can easily say, "In line 6, we see J discussing . . ." rather than something like, "Do you see where they are discussing the volts? Right after that, J discusses . . ."
- Initials or Names: In this example we see the first initial of each participant's pseudonym followed by a colon. Some transcripts may use full pseudonyms.
- Lengthening of sounds: In line 6, we see "hm:". This indicates that the "m" sound was lengthened. In Jefferson's transcript above, we see the use of colons to show the lengthening of the supportive "N o::::::.".
- Loudness: In line 6, we can also see "<u>flat</u>". This underlining shows that "flat" was pronounced a bit louder than the words surrounding it.
- Pauses: We can see pauses marked by a sequence of periods in line 4 "lithiums.." and line 9 "current . . .". The two dots indicate a short pause and the three dots a longer pause. Typically these pauses would be under 1 second with longer pauses represented by their actual timing. The "so (1.2)" in line 11, for example, indicates a pause of 1.2 seconds.
- Overlap: In lines 3 and 4, we can see that P and J were actually talking at the same time for a short period. The square brackets around P's "[lithium]" and J's "[we could]" show both the beginning point of the overlap marked with the "["bracket, and the end of the overlap marked with the "]" bracket. Since English speakers can vary the speed at which we speak for various purposes, including timing our stresses, the number of words for one speaker in an overlap may be quite different from the number of words in the second speaker's overlap. In that case, we try to line up the left side of the brackets and orient the right set of brackets as well as we can.
- Unintelligible speech: In line 6 of this transcript, we see "((xxx))". This indicates that the material in this section of the line was unintelligible to the transcriber despite listening to it several times.

The conventions that we have demonstrated here are not the only possible conventions, and there are a number of other features that we could have included. It is possible to show inhaling and exhaling, laughing, and making clicks with the tongue, to name a few. What is important in writing about the material from transcripts is providing readers with a transcription key. It would look something like this:

Transcription Key
.. indicates a short pause
. . . indicates a longer pause
(1.2) indicates a pause longer than 1 second
: indicates lengthening of a sound
<u>underline</u> indicates a sound said louder than its surrounding words
[ ] indicates overlap
((xxx)) indicates unintelligibility

A final point about transcribing is that it is a time-intensive process. The most time-intensive process of transcribing is in the number of repetitions of each phrase needed to clearly hear and type the data. There are programs available online, some of them free, that help with this process of transcription. Many of these programs allow for different audio playback speeds as well as preset amounts of times for repeated sections. The process of transcribing is also affected by the sound quality of the original sound file and the number of speakers. So care in setting up recording situations and choosing higher quality recording choices will pay off in both good sound files and time saved in transcribing.

8.4 Doing Sociolinguistics: Research Activity

Transcribe a 5-minute section of conversational data that you have collected. Experiment with different transcription layouts. What can you see in the one speaker above another format? What happens when you use a side-by-side format? What happens in the side-by-side format when you switch which column each speaker is in? Choose an element of conversation to analyze. Which of these formats is the most useful for your analysis and why?

In this section we have looked at many of the issues related to doing transcriptions. First we considered the connection between the type of analysis being made and the detail of the transcription. We then considered transcription conventions and the need to supply a reader with a key to the particular conventions used in a transcription. Finally, we addressed the reality that transcription is a time-consuming process affected by a number of variables.

8.4 Corpus linguistics

Corpus-based research has become highly influential throughout the discipline of linguistics since corpora provide databases of transcribed language as it is used in real social contexts. As McCarthy and Carter (2004) define it, a corpus is constituted by "a collection of texts, whether spoken or written, typically stored in computer-readable form and usually with some organizing or uniting feature" (p. 147). Some corpora, such as the Corpus of Spoken British English have a cumulative word count in the millions. Other corpora may be smaller but sufficiently large to enable the researcher to locate discernable patterns of language use, whether that be lexical items (Sinclair, 2001), figures of speech (McCarthy & Carter, 2004), metaphors (Stefanowitsch, 2006), verb phrase collocations (Wulff, 2006), register (Biber, 1995; 2003), discourse (Sinclair & Carter, 2004), discourse moves in narratives (Norrick, 2008), or even the different ways that disagreement is done in different contexts (Deckert & Yaeger-Dror, 1999; Yaeger-Dror, Hall-Lew, & Deckert, 2002), to name a very limited set of examples and ranges of corpus-based work. There are many corpora available, some of them can be accessed for free on the internet (e.g., MICASE), and there are a growing number of corpora representing increasingly diverse languages. Corpus-based approaches are of particular interest to sociolinguists because they allow both a quantitative and qualitative description of language use in social life. Scholars who engage in corpus-based research have shed new light on the connection between language use and identity. For instance, Reyes-Rodríguez (2008) engaged in corpus-based research to demonstrate the correlation between linguistic choice and left-wing political positioning. In this research, Reyes-Rodríguez collected speeches made by Fidel Castro, socialist leader of Cuba; Hugo Chavez, president of Venezuela; and Evo Morales a representative of "Movimiento al Socialismo" (Movement toward Socialism) in Bolivia. He then analyzed the stylistic choices made by these speakers in relation to a number of variables. Using this specific, focused corpus he was able to explore how these speakers used standard varieties of Spanish making particular style choices to engage their audiences.

There are various methods associated with a corpus-based approach to language analysis. One method is to engage in concordancing through the use of computer software. Concordancing allows the researcher to enter a particular word or combination of words in order to quantify the raw number of times that string is used within the corpus and to view each use of the string within its context of use. Consider as a specific example one element of a larger set of studies reported in Deckert and Yaeger-Dror (1999) and Yaeger-Dror, Hall-Lew, and Deckert (2002). The element under question in this study was variation in the distribution of contraction patterns for negatives. The Cognitive Prominence Principle (CPP) suggests that information that is semantically critical be given some dominance in discourse. However, the Social Agreement Principle (SAP) suggests that speakers be allowed to correct themselves rather than be corrected by their conversational partners. The use of negatives in verb phrases provides an interesting opportunity to examine how these two principles interact in conversations since negatives can take different forms. Consider, for example, the difference between:

> He is not (full negative form)
> He's not (auxiliary contraction)
> He isn't (not contraction)

"He is not" satisfies the CCP, but could be seen as somewhat confrontational and a potential breach of the SAP in certain situations. On the other hand, "He isn't" may be interpreted as downplaying the negative, which could satisfy the SAP, while creating possible difficulties with the CPP. Before conclusions could be drawn about the various types of corpora we wanted to compare, we needed to determine if the two contracted forms—auxiliary contraction and not contraction—were subject to regional variation. The Linguistics Data Consortium (LDC) has sound recordings and transcripts of different corpora of hundreds of telephone conversations. One of the corpora we used, "SWITCHBOARD2" contains conversations of middle-class American speakers of English having conversations with strangers. In order to view a wider range of conversation types, we also used a second LDC corpus, "CALLHOME" that contains conversations between family members. In order to begin our analysis of the conversations, we created a list of data for the concordancing program to look for. We won't include the entire list here, but to give you an idea, the list looked for each American English modal (including some phrasal modals) followed by not: may not, "must not", "might not" and so on to find full not forms. Included on the search parameters list were all versions of be and have followed by not; *n't, *'s not and *'re not, where the * was a wildcard for any word followed by "n't" and so on. Conc, the concordancing program we used, produced a list of instances that fit our search parameters and included a number of words on each side of the requested item. Each of these were examined separately, any extraneous productions were deleted, and the results were then tabulated. Altogether for this part of the study, 75 conversations were concordanced and tabulated from the CALLHOME corpus and more than 400 conversations from the SWITCHBOARD2 corpus. Since the SWITCHBOARD2 corpus included regional information for the speakers, it was possible to divide the speaker data into seven regions: west, north and south midlands, south, northern cities, New England, and New York City. Once we had the data tabulated, we were able to take a look at our results and determine percentages for the use of each type of negative form. In our examination of the percentage of auxiliary contraction for the verb *be*, for example, we found significant differences not only by type of conversation (those between family members and those between strangers), but also among all of the regions except New York City. We found that "These data show that for Middle Class American English phone conversations, auxiliary contraction is preferred over *not*-contraction for *be*, and *not*-contraction is preferred to full form for verbs other than *be*. They also indicate, contrary to our original assumption, that *'s not* is more typical than *isn't* across all the regions examined" (p. 56). So, for example, while Northern dialect speakers, like other regions, more typically used *'s not* is over *isn't*, their percentage of use of *isn't* was the highest of any region we examined.

What this study demonstrates is that using corpora of conversational language can reveal patterns in our language use that were unsuspected or that may even have run contrary to what we expected. It also showed that *full verb + not* combinations were lower in usage than all contracted forms. So we could conclude that in the registers we use for talking to families and to strangers, we tend to downplay negation. Another part of this same study showed that the register of presidential debates, however, reveals a very different pattern in how negatives are used.

Consider another corpus-based study related to the use of pronouns in French. In this study, (Waugh, Fonseca-Greber, Vickers, & Eröz, 2007) we "focus on smaller corpora with well-defined speech communities in well-defined speech events" (p. 122). One particularly striking quantitative empirical result of this study is the different understanding of the current uses of the French pronouns, *on* and *nous*. The study suggests that the meaning "we" is now given by *on*, rather than by *nous*, in the examined corpora of Everyday Conversational European French, which had approximately 194,000 words and represented the conversations of educated, middle-class speakers. This data suggests that *nous* has "all but disappeared from the spoken language as a subject pronoun" (Fonseca-Greber, 2000; Fonseca-Greber & Waugh, 2003a, 2003b, p. 126) as evidenced in the following excerpt from p. 126:

Example 8.6
(1) **on**-s'est mariés deux fois ouais . . . ici et aux Etats-U—ouais (S)
    '**we**.got.married twice yeah . . . here and in the United St—yeah'
[Note: according to our empirical results, all the subject pronouns studied here are actually prefixes and will be transcribed with a hyphen to show this status and glossed as part of the word in the English translation; 'United St—'indicates that in the French original, *Etats-U—*is an incomplete word]

Table 8.1 (from Table 3, p. 126) shows the number of tokens of *on* and *nous* with the overwhelming percentage of tokens of *on*.

Table 8.1 Loss of *nous* and replacement by *on* in ESEF

n. = 1348	Tokens	Percentage
Nous 'we'	13	1
On 'we'	1335	99

This is a highly significant empirical result—and, again, a surprising one, since when native speakers talk about the use of *on* for "we," they claim that it is a minor phenomenon and attribute it to uneducated, lower-class speech.

In this section, we have looked at how corpora and corpus-based analyses can be used to analyze examples of actual language use. Analyzing both large and sometimes, smaller, more focused corpora can provide insights into language and language use that can often be very surprising. The examples here show that speaker intuitions can often be misleading in contrast to actual examples of performed language.

8.5 Interactional sociolinguistics

According to John J. Gumperz (2001), the Interactional Sociolinguistics (IS) method originated in a criticism of earlier attempts in the Ethnography of Communication to explain cultural diversity in terms of differences between bounded language-culture systems. IS has its origins in the search for replicable methods of qualitative sociolinguistic analysis that can allow examinations of the linguistic and cultural diversity characteristic of modern, often urban, communicative environments. It views situated behavior as a site where both interactive forces and societal forces come into play. IS, then, examines how interaction depends on culturally informed inferential processes as well as on locally contextualized inferential processes. IS researchers examine how these processes play a role in speakers' interpretations of the types of activities or frames they are engaged in, and how these interpretations affect interactants' understandings of the ongoing interaction.

Consider, for example, the use of prosody in an utterance. Let's say that someone uses a sentence like "You're going to the wedding/" when talking to a friend about that friend going to the friend's ex's wedding. In this example utterance, the speaker is using rising intonation in the same way that one might in a yes/no question in English, as indicated by the transcription convention "/" at the end of the utterance. In this case, the speaker is using this rising intonation as a contextualization cue to signal to his interactant that the speaker is surprised his interactant will attend his ex's wedding. But also notice that the success of this use of prosody as a contextualization cue is based on the hearer's inferences that a statement said with rising intonation, can be used to signal surprise. Both the speaker and the hearer must share this cultural convention for this contextualization cue to be understood in line with the speaker's intent. The notion of context in this situation is a rather reflexive one because the context that is needed for the interpretation of the utterance depends on conventions that the speakers may or may not share. So for Interactional Sociolinguists, the notion of contextualization cues is an essential one for doing analyses.

One of the major strengths of Interactional Sociolinguistics is its insistence that participants may not share the same communicative background. It cannot be taken for granted that speakers and hearers share the same inferential procedures or contextualize cues in the same way. In fact, the question of whether cues are shared and interpreted in the same way is one of the main aims of an IS analysis.

To carry out IS, the researchers typically audiotape or videotape interactions between people. To find out how the interactions are the result of culturally based contextualization cues rather than possible individual differences or an atypical interaction, it is usual to record multiple interactions of the event in question involving several different sets of people. Researchers then transcribe the audio or videotape, and the transcription constitutes the data for linguistic analysis.

In analyzing the transcripts, researchers can identify important segments in the data. They may then conduct member checks by interviewing participants. In some instances, researchers may play important segments of the audio or videotape back to the participants to allow them to comment on their impressions of these segments of the interaction. The purpose of this type of participant feedback is for participants to provide researchers with further understandings of the participants' perspectives on the interaction in question. Analyses of the audio or video data, the transcript, and member checking information then allows the researcher to draw conclusions about the linguistic features that contribute to meaning making within that type of interaction.

Consider an example of IS research. Bailey (1997) and (2000) examined the relations between African American customers and Korean immigrant storekeepers in the Koreatown neighborhood of Los Angeles. This study was generated because Bailey noticed that African American customers of convenience stores in the Koreatown neighborhood of Los Angeles felt that they were being mistreated by Korean immigrant storekeepers. In particular, African American customers often complained that the Korean immigrant storekeepers treated them with a lack of respect. In this study, Bailey set out to identify interactional patterns that might explain this disconnect. In typical IS style, Bailey observed and videotaped service encounters in convenience stores. He conducted interviews with Korean immigrant storekeepers and with African American customers.

Example 8.7 from Bailey's study (2000, p. 98) is an excerpt from a transcript of an interaction between an African American customer and a Korean immigrant storekeeper and owner.

Example 8.7

Cust: . . . so I gotta go get another trade for them to pay me the money. So I'm gonna get another trade. But then like- after I get another trade they pay me (a sum) a lump sum of money? And I'm gonna do what I wanna do. ((.8))

Cust: they only gonna give me about sixty or seventy thousand. ((1.4))

Cust: plus- my schooling- ((1.0))

Cust: so- I got to take it easy for a little bit. ((Customer moves toward exit))

Cust: that's why I'm gonna buy enough of your liquor (so I can take it)

Own: alright, take care

Bailey explains the interaction as one in which the African American customer is engaging in an interactional strategy of personal involvement. The customer pauses at the end of his utterances, which indicates that he is turning the floor over to his interactant. If the storekeeper had shared an interactional style of involvement, the storekeeper would have taken the floor at that time and responded to the personal situation of the customer in some way. The storekeeper, however, is not working within the same interpretive frame and does not take a turn in which he or she responds to the personal revelation of the customer, rather the storekeeper works within a frame of what he or she considers to be the norm for service encounters of this type.

In his interviews with the Korean immigrant storekeepers, Bailey found that their interactional style in service encounters involved restraint, which clearly was an asymmetrical understanding to the African American customers who had an interactional style of involvement in service encounters. For the Korean American storekeepers, this meant that they had learned to expect a lot of social talk that they found not entirely relevant to the service encounter. As one Korean American described his perspective (Bailey, 2000, p. 93):

> If you express yourself you're too light. If you laugh or smile you don't have enough in your head. You're supposed to be stoic and expressionless which means you're thinking a lot. By saying "hi" you're putting yourself down to a lower level. (23-year old Korean American male)

This Korean American male expresses the interactional style of restraint that is typical of Korean immigrant storekeepers in the Koreatown neighborhood of Los Angeles. As the following African American customer reveals, however, this restraint interactional style is interpreted by African American customers as cold and uncaring (Bailey, 2000, pp. 91–92).

> you're tolerated. . . . I'm going in your store, paying my money and you're going to tol-erate me just because you want my money. I'm less than anything to you, just a vehicle. (African American man in his 50s)

The African American customer expresses dissatisfaction with the Korean immigrant storekeeper precisely because the storekeeper engages in the service encounter but not in the kind of interpersonal involvement that the African American customers tend to equate with a display of personal respect.

As this example demonstrates, IS provides a research methodology that allows the researchers to examine how groups of people make meaning through language. In understanding interactional styles that particular groups of people employ and what those styles mean to those people, we can also distinguish ways that groups differ in their meaning-making practices. This ability to pinpoint differences in meaning-making practices allows researchers to gain understandings of how such differences lead to tensions between groups of people with different ways of interpreting contextualization cues and different ways of making meaning.

8.5 Doing Sociolinguistics: Research Activity

Have you noticed interethnic tensions between groups of people where you live? Is there anything about the interactional styles of these groups of people that you think may cause the tension? Let's consider the interactional styles of men and women. Either in the conversations that you have already collected or in new conversations that you collect for this activity, consider how men and women interact with one another. Consider their interactional styles. Do you find any differences? Analyze whether these differences cause tension.

In this section, we have discussed IS as an approach to analyzing data. In examining how contextual cues can be different for different cultures and how these cues lead to interactant's interpretations of the interactional frame, IS allows for analysis of the way that different cultural groups interpret language.

8.6 Narrative analysis

In the various fields of inquiry that look at language in use, the analysis of narrative has been a central theme in examining identity as well as language and cultural ideologies. Sociolinguists typically concern themselves with narratives that are produced orally or signed, but written narratives such as those found in journals and other documents are also studied. Looking at narratives is important to studying how people communicate because much of the way that we communicate with each other is through oral narrative. We largely structure our life experience through narrative, making it fundamental to our way of understanding ourselves, others, and the world that we live in (Bruner, 1986).

As discussed in Chapter 4, the advancement of recording technologies, such as the portable tape recorder made it possible for some of the earliest sociolinguistic work conducted by William Labov and his colleagues in the 1960s. In order to mitigate the observers paradox, they wanted people to become engaged in telling stories. So the researchers asked people questions such as, "Were you ever in a situation where you were in serious danger of being killed?" (Labov & Waletzky, 1966). These are often called "danger of death" narratives. For the same reason, they asked people to talk about times when they got into fights to elicit engaged fight narratives, "Did you ever see anybody get beat up real bad?" or "What was the most important fight you remember?"

In Labov and Waletzky's (1966) seminal analysis of the structure of narratives, they collected and analyzed the narratives from a variety of places, and they proposed that narratives are not told in completely random ways. They argued that when analyzed together, the narratives they collected contained similar elements. In particular, they proposed:

> an *orientation*, that presents the basic who, what, where, when, and why information for the story;
>
> a *complicating action*, that describes what happened in a sequence of past-tense marked sentences;
>
> *evaluative* elements that provide a justification for the telling of the story and often address the "So what?" question of why the story is being told. They reveal as Labov and Waletzky put it, "the attitude of the narrator toward the narrative by emphasizing the relative importance of some narrative units as compared to others" (p. 37).
>
> a *resolution*, which provides an explanation of the event's outcome. Labov and Waltezky argued that resolutions are "that portion of the narrative sequence which follows the evaluation (p. 39); and
>
> a *coda* that signals the end of the story and serves as a "functional device for returning the verbal perspective to the present moment" (p. 39).

In Labov's (1972) seminal article on oral narrative, "The Transformation of Experience through Narrative Syntax," he further defines the basis for early understandings of the structure and functions of oral narratives. In particular, this work questions how children can acquire the ability to tell narratives, and it demonstrates that people become better storytellers as they grow older. Labov's (1972) work expands the earlier argument that oral narratives are structured in a particular way, proposing an additional element to the structure of narrative:

> an *abstract* tells the point of the narrative and lets the interlocutors know that the speaker is about to launch into narrative mode. So this element would typically appear as the first element in a narrative of this type.

In Example 8.8 we provide one of the example narratives analyzed in that paper. We have added line identifiers and speaker information (R=researcher and S=storyteller) to simplify our discussion of the narrative's structure.

Example 8.8 (from Narrative No. 6 in Labov & Waletzky, 1966)

R: Were you ever in a situation where you were in serious danger of being killed?

S: a. Yeah, I was in the Boy Scouts at the time.
   b. and we was doing the 50-yard dash,
   c. racing,
   d. but we was at the pier, marked off,
   e. and so we was doing the 50-yard dash.
   f. these was about eight or nine of us, you know, going down, coming back.
   g. and going down the <u>third</u> time, I caught cramps
   h. and I started yelling "Help!",
   i. but the fellows didn't believe me, you know.
   j. they thought I was just trying to catch up because I was going on or slowing down.
   k. so all of them kept going.
   l. they leave me.
   m. and so I started going down.
   n. Scoutmaster was up there.
   o. he was watching me.
   p. but he didn't pay me no attention either.
   q. And for no reason at all these was another guy, who had just walked up that minute. . .
   r. he just jumped over
   s. and grabbed me.

Let's use this narrative to further explore these structural issues. The *abstract* portion of this narrative is really taken up by the researcher's initial question. The *orientation* can be seen in lines a-f. We can see the introduction of the main character, the storyteller; the place, the pier; the time, when the speaker was in the Boy Scouts, and the general situation, a group of Boy Scouts in a swimming race. The *complicating action* is expressed in lines g through m: the action of the race, the struggle to stay up, the calls for help, being misunderstood and left, and finally beginning to drown. Although *evaluations* can occur throughout a narrative, there is a clear evaluative section in this narrative in lines n through p in which the story, in some sense, provides this storyteller's evaluation of this "life in danger" story by emphasizing the fact that he really was in danger at this moment. The *resolution* of this narrative is in lines q-s reporting how a complete stranger arrives at precisely this moment and saves the life of the narrator.

One interesting finding discussed in Labov (1972) is that as we grow older, we acquire the ability to tell increasingly more interesting narratives. What contributes to this is the ability to apply increasingly sophisticated evaluative devices. For instance, as Labov states, one way evaluation can be done throughout the narrative is "for the narrator to quote himself as addressing someone else" (p. 372). We see this in line h when the storyteller yells "Help!"

In a second type of analysis of the narrative above, we can see the way some of these sophisticated evaluative devices construct identity. Let's consider how the identities are constructed in this narrative. First, of course, is the identity of the narrator as a storyteller. In telling this story in a format that can be recognized as a narrative, this storyteller is constructing part of his identity as a narrator. The evaluation section, in particular, serves this purpose as well as emphasizing the real danger of the situation, and, by implication, the skills of storytelling in having chosen an appropriate story to tell. In this type of identity construction, the storyteller's appropriate choices in telling this story help construct an understanding of his proficiency at this storytelling form, and consequently construct him as a proficient storyteller. But this is not the only identity being constructed in this story. For example, we see his fellow Boy Scouts, who do not rescue him as might actually be expected from Boy Scouts, constructed not as "bad Boy Scouts," but as fellow racers who do not understand his dire situation for excusable reasons: they thought he was simply using this as a strategy to get them to slow down so that he could catch up. The Scoutmaster, on the other hand, is not constructed in a positive light. First, he isn't narrated into the story as a character until his constructed indifference becomes proof of the storyteller's danger. Second, he is constructed as aware of the situation, but as doing nothing. This construction is accomplished through direct statements: "He was watching me, but he didn't pay me no attention either." These statements go against typical categorizations of Scoutmasters. Part of the cultural categorization of "Scoutmasters" is someone who is responsible for the scouts under his care; someone who is aware of the events around him; and someone who is skilled at lifesaving techniques. These two statements construct the Scoutmaster as aware of the situation, and, yet, as someone who chooses to not carry out his relevant role of applying life-saving techniques. In fact, the story constructs a complete stranger, who it is assumed does not have the same social categorization expectations of "Scoutmaster," as arriving and carrying out the responsibilities of the Scoutmaster and saving the drowning swimmer. The actions of this individual serve as a counterpoint in the construction of the Scoutmaster's identity.

8.6.1 Narrative and identity analysis

Schiffrin (1996) points out "the ability of narrative to verbalize and situate experience as text provides a resources for the display of self and identity" (p. 168). Narrative, as seen in the analysis of the Boy Scout story above, provides an opportunity to examine how people situate themselves in relation to both larger social and cultural understandings and to more local contexts. This means that we can examine in narrative the performances that people embody as they position themselves in relation to certain stances essentially indexing and constructing certain aspects of identity.

This still leaves the question open about how we go about the process of analyzing identity in narrative. There is, of course, no one perfect way to analyze either narratives or the construction of identity, but since we know that identities are constructed in narratives, we can use the understandings we have about narrative as a place to begin an analysis of identity construction.

The following paragraphs provide a series, in no way complete, of methodological considerations and narrative elements we can explore to consider how interactants in conversation construct identities.

8.6.2 Analyzing narrative elements

Earlier in this chapter we examined some of the basic elements of the narratives discussed by Labov and Waletzky (1966) and Labov (1972) to explore the elements of the abstract, orientation, complicating action, evaluation, resolution, and coda. We can use the elements of stories as we have discussed them in this text to analyze narratives and the constructions of identity. For example, we can closely examine the complicating actions in a narrative to examine how individuals are constructed. We can examine evaluations within the narrative not only to decide if the narrator finds the narrative a valuable one, but also to see the narrator's stance toward the narrative and the individuals within the narrative.

Jefferson (1978) discusses how narratives are embedded in the ongoing interactions of a conversation and therefore, a conversational participant wanting to tell a story would provide a *preface* in which they indicated to their conversational partners that they are preparing to tell a story. This would be followed by a turn in which co-participants align themselves to the story letting the teller know whether they would like to hear the story or not; a longer turn, or series of turns, in which the storyteller tells the story; and a turn in which the hearers respond to the story. In each of these story elements, we can examine how identity is constructed. First, as discussed earlier in this chapter, by using narrative elements effectively or in negotiating a story effectively, storytellers are providing evidence that they are proficient storytellers. Second, each of these elements can be used in different ways to construct identities.

8.6.3 Narrative qualities

Ochs and Capps (2001) building on the work of Goffman's notions of the complex roles of both speaker and hearer, added further understanding of narratives by proposing that conversational narratives can be evaluated along a number of dimensions that are relevant to narratives. These included *tellership*, looking at whether there is a single or multiple active co-tellers; *tellability*, which relates to "the extent to which they convey a sequence of reportable events and make a point in a rhetoricaly effective manner" (p. 33), *embeddedness*, narratives that can be embedded in a single turn or told over multiple turns; *linearity*, which relates to the causality and temporal order of the story; and *moral stance*, in which speakers and hearers may relate certain or uncertain orientation. While each of these certainly can be analyzed in relation to identity, perhaps moral stance can most easily be seen in relation to identity. In examining narratives we can look for evidence or moral stances and each of these moral stances in turn can be said to be part of the construction of the individual taking the moral stance. It is also possible, of course, that a moral stance can be used to pass either positive or negative evaluation upon the character of another providing yet another possibility for analyzing identity construction.

8.6.4 Participant stances

We can examine the stances that participants take relative to one another. In understanding narratives in face-to-face interactions we can begin by analyzing the positions that individual participants take to one another. We can ask questions about their relationships and what effect this type of relationship has on the interaction in question. We can also examine the relationship that the narrator has to the individuals spoken about in the narrative. In an examination of the Boy Scout story above, for example, we find out that the adult who is constructed as standing by and not helping when the narrator needs help is the Scoutmaster. If the storyteller had merely said, "there was an adult there who didn't help," there would be a completely different construction of the identity of this individual. As hearers, we might think the individual didn't consider himself responsible or perhaps couldn't swim. But with the clarification that this person held a position of responsibility for the storyteller and as a Scoutmaster probably could swim, we see a completely different identity constructed for the individual.

8.6.5 Roles

Schiffrin (1996) examined stories told by mothers about their daughters and talked about how cultural understandings of this relationship shaped the stories. It's important to notice that part of analyzing the relationship between participants or between participants and individuals who are being talked about is the roles that come into play. Roles are part of the culturally dependant categories discussed in Chapter 5. In Sack's analysis of a little girl's narrative sentence, "the baby cried, the mother picked it up," for example, the assumption that the woman picking the baby up was the baby's mother hinges on the child's understanding of roles. The category of "mother" has the cultural notion that they are female, and have the responsibility for crying babies, so a female picking up a crying baby could satisfy these cultural understandings and lead to the identity construction of this particular individual in the child's narrative. In the same way we can examine how various elements of individuals' roles are indexed in a particular narrative to examine how a particular aspect of identity is constructed in the particular context of the given interaction.

8.6.6 Cultural themes

Narratives often invoke cultural themes, and quite often these cultural themes carry identity information and can be used to construct identities. Looking for and analyzing general themes in a narrative, themes including cultural ones, then, can be another way to examine how identity may be constructed in the process of an ongoing narrative. In examining language closely, we can also ask questions about what cultural notions are being indexed or what symbolic meanings are being used.

8.6.7 Language use

Clearly, since language is involved in narratives, we can do close examinations of the language that is being used. We must not only analyze what is there, but also analyze how it is being used. Speech Act Theory, as discussed in Chapter 5, reveals that speakers can deliver an utterance with the locutionary force of a question, for example, but be using the utterance with the illocutionary force of a polite suggestion. So we can carefully analyze the ongoing interaction to see if the interlocutor understood the purpose of the utterance—if the perlocutionary force, the force of utterance for the hearer, was the same as the illocutionary force resulting in a felicitous speech act. And if the speech act was felicitous, we can ask questions about its consequences and what it constructed in the conversation.

In examining the language closely we can also examine uses of metaphor or uses of repetition, for example, to find out their purposes. In many cultures using a story itself as a metaphor for giving advice to a co-participant is appropriate. Within these cultures, then, telling a narrative for this purpose is also constructing the co-participant as someone in need of advice and, at the same time, constructing the narrator as someone capable of giving advice and of giving it in a culturally appropriate way.

8.6.8 Indexicality

In analyzing aspects of identity in narratives, it is important to consider the process of indexing that was discussed in detail in Chapter 6. In the editors' introduction to Och's (1992) "Indexing Gender," they argue that in Och's work, "indexicality is depicted as a property of speech through which cultural contexts such as social identities (e.g. gender) and social activities (e.g. a gossip session) are constituted in particular stances and acts" (p. 335). An important point to review here is that there are, as Ochs (1992) points out, both direct indexical relations and constitutive, indirect indexical relations, and therefore, different types of indexical processes. There is no one-to-one relationship between particular linguistic forms and the status, age, race, or gender of a speaker, but there are tacit speaker understandings of how particular stances can be used to perform certain aspects of identity. This means that we can closely examine the interaction of individuals to determine the stances that they take relative to particular cultural contexts to perform aspects of social identity.

Finally, consider an example analysis by Deckert (2010) in which she examined how the identities of "victim," "witness," and "perpetrator" are constructed in the ongoing interactions of forensic interviews with children. To carry out this analysis she used Goffman's (1981) concepts of "animators," "authors," and "principals" to argue that aspects of the narratives and the identity construction processes were co-constructed in two different ways. Some elements were co-animated, and some elements were the result of single authorship on the part of the child. She used Labov's (1972) criteria to argue that some narratives were embedded narratives that occur within a single turn, and employed Ochs and Capps' (2001) narrative dimensions such as "tellership" and "embeddedness" to argue for the highly interactional accounts co-constructed across a number of turns. Finally she argued that these processes were used in different ways not only to construct the identities of witness, victim, and perpetrator, but also to construct children's identities as resistant to certain acts within the narrated events and within the interview event itself. This example shows that the analysis of narratives allows for very complex understandings of how identities are constructed and how a variety of different ways of looking at narrative can be useful in providing complex analyses of complex events.

8.6 Doing Sociolinguistics: Research Activity

Record the ongoing interactions of you and one of your friends or go through other data that you have collected. Find and analyze a narrative using some of the suggestions for analysis above. What aspects of identity do you find being co-constructed in the ongoing interaction?

In this section we have looked at many of the characteristics of narratives and discussed how these can be used as areas of focus when doing narrative analysis. We have discussed how narratives are not only very much a part of how we display our identities at the local level of the conversation and its context, but also at the larger social level.

8.7 Ethnography of communication

The Ethnography of Communication provides a systematic way of examining the intersection of language and social life. In the development of the Ethnography of Communication, Hymes (1974) stated that "the fundamental problem—to discover and explicate the competence that enables members of a community to conduct and interpret speech—cuts deeper than any schema any of us have so far developed" (p. 43). Hymes is interested in the communicative competence of members of a speech community. The concept of communicative competence entails that members of the speech community understand more than just the linguistic code; they understand speech events, genres, interactional strategies, among other issues related to language use in social life.

Moreover, the Ethnography of Communication is concerned with examining what it means to be communicatively competent in a certain speech community by gaining a thick description (Geertz, 1973) through ethnographic fieldwork in that speech community as well as the speech genres, speech events and speech situations that take place within that community. As Hymes (1974) states, "language as such is not everywhere equivalent in role and value; speech may have a different scope and functional load in the communicative economies of different societies" (p. 31). The Ethnography of Communication can benefit the study of sociolinguistics and identity by providing a framework to study interaction as embedded in a certain speech community and to discuss it as part of a particular speech event. As Philips (1998) states, "linguistic anthropologists and some cultural anthropologists equate practice with actual spoken discourse or language use" (p. 11). To understand how meaning is made in the speech community, it is necessary to study actual language use. In the Ethnography of Communication, there is a commitment to the study of language use as situated practice.

In the Ethnography of Communication, "ways of speaking" is used as the most general term. It is based on the idea that within certain communities, there are patterns of speech activity that are typical of that community. The communicative competence of persons is made up of the knowledge of such patterns and when to use them. Different communities can be expected to hold differing ideals of speaking for different sociolinguistic statuses, roles, and situations, for example. These ideals of speaking may be based on memorization, use specific improvisational rules, and involve other variables, such as use of pitch and quality of voice, for example.

Because of its recognition that language use is determined by different communities, the notion of *Speech Community* is a primary concept in the Ethnography of Communication. It's important to notice that a speech community is a social unit rather than a linguistic unit. Rather than starting with a language as the primary influence on the group, the Ethnography of

Communication starts with a social group and then begins to consider the organization of language within the group. In this analysis of speech communities and the knowledge of members of particular speech communities, *speech situations* are particular types of situations that are recognizable to members of the speech community. These situations have both verbal and nonverbal components. Members of the community would have competence, for example, in the appropriate ways of speaking, acting, and dressing at a summer picnic. In relation to their knowledge of speaking, speech situations, such as the picnic are made up of a variety of *speech events*, such as conversations as members move in and out of various social interactions. *Speech acts*, such as jokes, then, could be a part of a speech event that was itself one of the social interactions within the speech situation of the example picnic.

8.7.1 Doing ethnography of communication

In conducting an Ethnography of Communication, we can begin by identifying the speech community, the particular speech situations that may typically occur within the speech community, the speech events, and speech acts, and the normative language use that applies within these events and acts.

Ethnographic research involves collecting multiple types of data. These include data from participant observation and recorded field notes; audio or video recordings; open-ended ethnographic interviews; and document collection. Open-ended ethnographic interviews (Briggs, 1986) begin with general questions that become more specific based on the responses of the participants. In this way, these interviews require reflexivity and awareness on the part of the researcher. Analysis of these interviews allows researchers to gain a greater understanding of participants' perspectives on language use within their speech community. Ethnographic fieldwork may also involve the collection and analysis of documents in terms of the everyday interactions of the speech community (Hammersley & Atkinson, 2007).

Ethnographic analysis involves combining all data sources. It typically begins by categorizing the data. As the analyst gains knowledge of the data, common features are found by the researchers to constitute a pattern within the data, becoming categories. These are then given codes, which are in turn used to code the data. When a category (Code) is found repeatedly, especially across data sources, it then becomes a theme. The multiple data sources contribute to the validity of this finding, identified in multiple types of interactions involving many different participants.

Analysis then shifts to assessing the reliability of the categorized analysis. When examining ethnographic data, one does so by revisiting the data many times. This involves multiple coding and recoding with sessions occurring at least one month apart. Similar coding across different sessions increases coding scheme reliability.

Ethnographic research can be conducted in several different ways and on different scales. When we think of the classic ethnography in anthropology, we imagine the anthropologist deeply embedded within a community for a long period of time. Indeed, many linguistic anthropologists whose work is directly related to an understanding of sociolinguistics and identity have conducted such long-term ethnographies. However, it is also possible to use ethnographic methods in shorter-term projects.

8.7 Doing Sociolinguistics: Research Activity

Select 5 minutes of data. Familiarize yourself with the data. As you do this, consider possible categories that seem to recur. Write these down and assign a code to each of the tentative categories. Go through the data again, and code it with your tentative codes. You may find that you need to revise your codes as you go through this process. Go through the data three or four more times revising your categories and codes as necessary. Based on this activity, what conclusions can you draw about the categories that you found?

In this section we have discussed how the Ethnography of Communication allows for an examination of the competence people display of their appropriate language knowledge as it is situated in various speech communities. We discussed the idea that this form of research typically looks at multiple examples of speech situations, speech events, and speech acts to determine the typical patterns of knowledge speakers display as part of this language competence. Finally, we discussed how research in this area requires a deep familiarity with the data and multiple layers of coding before conclusions about practices can be reached.

8.8 Doing conversation analysis

Beginning with the work of Harvey Sacks, conversation analysis (CA) was developed out of the field of Sociology, and it was influenced by the work of both Erving Goffman and Harold Garfinkel.

Goffman is credited with the development of footing, frame, face, and interaction order as discussed in Chapter 5. For Goffman, talk is the basic means of communication, though he also focuses on the use of the body in interactions. Goffman approaches people's participation in interaction as one in which they play out particular roles. He argues that the roles that they play are not static over time, but are dependent upon the context of the interaction, including the other participants, the setting, and the topic.

Garfinkel's Ethnomethodology seeks to gain an understanding of people's practical reasoning and their common sense knowledge of the world. The argument is that people create meaning in context by using their background knowledge to make sense of even the most troublesome situations. In other words, people improvise their way through interactional events, making sense of the reality of that event as it unfolds.

Consonant with the idea that conversations are dependent on the contexts of unfolding events, conversation analysts began exploring how conversations could be ordered enough for participants to know how to negotiate through a constantly evolving interactive event. Conversation analysts have demonstrated that conversation in face-to-face interactions has an organized, sequential structure, and that beyond the sentence level, meaning is achieved through language in that organization (Sacks, Schegloff, & Jefferson, 1974). CA studies the sequential organization of conversation and how that organization unfolds on a turn-by-turn basis. CA has been employed to identify and study various types of conversational discourse, such as talk about troubles (Jefferson, 1981; 1984) and arguments among children (Goodwin, 1990) as well as talk unique to various institutional settings including the medical setting (Heath, 1992), the courtroom (Atkinson, 1992; Atkinson & Drew, 1979), the classroom (McHoul, 1978), and the media (Clayman & Heritage, 2002; Heritage, 1985). Conversation analysts understand any particular conversational event both as shaped by the context and as shaping the context. In order to understand the sequential organization for a particular type of talk, conversation analysts collect multiple forms of the type of talk in question and analyze the patterns found in the data. Since one of the elements of any conversation is the way that participants perform their own identities, their identities in particular contexts can be examined in the data.

CA's original focus was mundane conversation. The idea was to see how the conversation unfolded turn-by-turn, and how such turn-by-turn interaction defined the context of talk. Utterances within the conversation are seen as interdependent. This means that any particular utterance or even series of utterances must be interpreted in relation to the utterances within its context. This also means that an utterance taken out of its context can seem non-sensical. Consider, for instance, Example 8.9 from Sacks (1992, p. 757) in which the utterances might seem very strange in relation to one another.

Example 8.9
A: I have a fourteen year old son.
B: Well that's alright.
A: I also have a dog.
B: Oh I'm sorry.

This conversation might seem strange in isolation, but in the context of an interview for an apartment rental, it makes sense. A recognition that meaning is based in the interaction, calls into question the existence and predictability of ill-formed sequences.

In doing analyses, the basic unit of conversation is the *turn*. In analyzing transcripts of conversations, then, one place to start is to look for turn con-structional units. These are the points when a speaker turns the floor over to another speaker. Example 8.10 illustrates a turn constructional unit:

Example 8.10
A: I like riding horses
B: I've never ridden one

In this exchange, after A finishes the utterance, B takes the floor, making an utterance in relation to A's utterance. In active conversations, it's often the case that turn constructional units involve overlap. The same sequence about horses might have B beginning to comment during the end of A's utterance.

Example 8.11
A: I like riding [horses]
B: [I've] never ridden one

As noted in the transcription section above, the bracketed portions of A's and B's utterances are said at the same time as each other. They overlap. Not all overlaps are interruptive, of course. This kind of overlap at turn constructional units is quite common and can indicate an interactant's involvement with the conversation and a sense of affiliation between the interlocutors. On the other hand, in some contexts, overlap can also be hostile and indicate a disaffiliative move. This might be the case in the following example:

> Example 8.12
> A: I like [riding horses]
> B: [It's not your] turn to talk

In this case, B is clearly disaffiliating with A's identity as an appropriate speaker. We could identify the overlap in this case as an interruption. Notice, however, that much of what makes this move disaffiliative is the fact that B does not take up A's topic and, instead, makes a comment on the appropriateness of A's conversational move.

As this discussion indicates, any turn is contextualized within the turns that came before it and the ones that come after it. Within conversation, there is a *preference organization* in which certain kinds of next positioning are preferred. Let's take the case of a greeting, for instance. A typical greeting and response might look like the following:

> Example 8.13
> A: Hello. How are you?
> B: Fine. Thanks.

If, however, A greets B, and B walks by without acknowledging the greeting, that would be dispreferred, and A would probably interpret the act as hostile or rude. Consider another type of reply:

> Example 8.14
> A: Hello. How are you?
> B: Well, the nurse says my blood pressure is up.

B's response might seem quite strange in a context in which acquaintances greet each other on the street; however, it might seem more appropriate in a medical consultation when a familiar doctor enters the consultation room. There are many types of moves in which there is a preferred next position. Some very frequent ones include question-answer sequences or call-response sequences.

8.8 Doing Sociolinguistics: Thought Activity

Think of other situations in which there is a preferred next positioning. Can you think of a situation in which people might make dispreferred moves?

Preference organization relates not only to turn types, but also includes a social preference for agreement (Goffman, 1971; Sacks, 1992). The status of agreement as preferred can be seen in unfolding conversation. Typically, for example, if an interlocutor is making and agreement move, the turn is performed promptly and possibly emphatically. Disagreement, on the other hand, is dispreferred. Its status as dispreferred can be seen by the fact that speakers tend to delay and mitigate their negation in conversation. Consider Example 8.15 from Pomerantz (1984, p. 74) in which the second speaker, L, is trying to express disagreement with the first speaker's stance.

Example 8.15
(46) (MC:1.-22)
1. W: . . . the-the way I feel about it i:s, that as
         long as she cooperates, an'-an'she belie:ves
         that she's running my li:fe, or, you know, or
         directing it one way or anothuh, and she feels
         happy about it, I do whatever I please (h)any
         (h)wa(h).HHH! [(   )
2. L: [Yeah.
3. L: We::ll – eh-that's true: - I mean eh-that's
         alright, -- uhb-ut uh, ez long ez you do::.
         But h-it's-eh-to me::, -- after anyone . . .

L's response in turn 3 begin's with a stretched out "We::ll" a classic disagreement signal, followed by a proffered agreement before taking quite a bit of time to get to the disagreement "But h-it's-eh-to me::,". This display of a classic disagreement marker and the amount of time that it takes for the speaker to get to the actual disagreement statement demonstrates a speaker negotiating a dispreferred move.

Repair is another important conversational feature that has been identified in CA. Repair is defined as moments in the conversation when one of the participants cycles back through to an earlier point in the conversation to make a change to what was uttered. We can find *self repair* and *other repairs*. Due to the social need to save face (Brown & Levinson, 1987) there is a preference for a speaker's move to repair themselves (self repair) rather than for the other participant to do the repair (other repair). In the following example, A provides a self repair.

Example 8.16
A: Atlanta is in Alabama or I mean Georgia

A cycles back to an earlier point in the utterance to change the content of the contribution. Other repair occurs when a participant cycles back through the conversation to make a change to someone else's contribution. Example 8.17 demonstrates B doing an other repair:

Example 8.17
A: Atlanta is in Alabama
B: . . . no Atlanta is in Georgia unless there's an Atlanta in Alabama that I
      don't know
A: Yeah Georgia . . . what did I say?

In this case, B provides a repair to A's utterance. The dispreference for the other repair is evidenced in B's pause before making the repair. B also mitigates the repair, expressing the possibility that A's contribution may actually be correct.

To understand the nature of conversation, it is first critical to analyze the turn-by-turn construction by using conversation analytic methods. Particular sequences are defined not only in terms of one utterance or one turn but in terms of how that utterance or turn is ratified in the ongoing interaction. Conversation analysis allows for the turn-by-turn analysis of interaction, including a mechanism for describing how particular conversational sequences operate in the ongoing construction of meaning in interaction.

Audio recording or video recording of conversation is standard. Then a transcript of the recorded interaction is made. The analyst works from the transcript to employ CA methods.

Let's look at Example 8.18 taken from W. B. Smith (2010, pp. 9–10). This data is an excerpt from an interaction in which a California Highway Patrol officer (CHP) has pulled over a civilian motorist (CIV) and is in the process of issuing a ticket.

Example 8.18
1. CHP: How fast d'ya think you were goin'.
2. CIV: I's doin' about (.4) sixty, sixty five.
3. CHP: Sixty sixty fi:ve well fer one thing yer speedometer's
4. probly o::ff, (.4) number two: the speed limit's fifty five.
5. (.5)
6. CHP: So based upon yer own admission yer goin' over the
7. speed limit.

In this example we can see both self repair and other repair. In line 2, CIV self repairs the "sixty" to "sixty five," and this includes a small emphasis on the repaired "five".

The CHP officer engages in an other repair in lines 3 and 4. He cycles back through CIV's contribution, first repeating the "sixty sixty five" while further emphasizing the "fi::ve" by lengthening it. However, the CHP inserts the disaffiliative discourse marker, "well," before providing the repair, "yer speedomenter's probly o::ff". The next move is equally disaffiliative, "number two: the speed limit's fifty five" with its minor emphasis on the repaired element "fifty five", but this move is also mitigated by the 4-second pause that precedes it. In line 5, we see a turn constructional unit, where CIV could take a turn. But there is a .5-second pause, indicating that CIV does not take the turn. This move is dispreferred as indicated by the length of the pause before the CHP takes the turn in lines 6 and 7.

In this section we have looked at how CA theoretical perspectives on conversational structures lead to the ability to analyze interactions on a turn-by-turn basis. This focus on turn taking in conversation allows for analyses of conversational elements such as overlaps, pauses, and silence.

8.9 Doing Sociolinguistics: Research Activity

Analyze your own data in relation to the following:

Turn constructional units—How do you see the interactants constructing these units. Is it always done smoothly in a preferred way?

Next positioning—How do you see the interactants negotiating next positions within the interaction? Are there places where a dispreferred positioning is evident?

Silence and pausing—What role do these have in the ongoing interaction? What function can they be said to have in the particular contexts in which they occur?

Overlap—do you find this to be supportive and preferred or a more dispreferred form?

In this section we have looked at Conversation Analysis as an approach to examining the turn-by-turn interactions within ongoing conversations. In looking at turns, we discussed the interdependencies between utterances. This understanding allows for analyses of how particular turns are understood by hearers based on their performance in the next turn. It also allows for discussions of the qualities of what makes a turn preferred or dispreferred. These are based in part on the interaction itself, but they are also based on social principles.

8.9 Suggested further reading

Biber, D. (1995). *Dimensions of register variation: A cross-linguistic comparison*. Cambridge: Cambridge University Press.

Briggs, C. L. (1986). *Learning how to ask*. Cambridge: Cambridge University Press.

Bruner, J. (1986). *Actual minds, possible worlds*. Cambridge: Harvard University Press.

Du Bois, J. W., Schuetze-Coburn, S., Cumming, S., & Paolino, D. (1993). Outline of discourse transcription. In J. W. Du Bois, Schuetze-Coburn, S. Cumming & D. Paolino (Eds.), *Talking data: Transcription and coding in discourse research* (pp. 1–31 and 45–90). Hillsdale, NJ: Lawrence Erlbaum Associates.

Goffman, E. (1971). *Relations in public*. New York: Harper.

Gumperz, J. J. (1982). *Discourse strategies*. Cambridge: Cambridge University Press.

Hymes, D. (1974). *Foundations in sociolinguistics: An ethnographic approach*. Philadelphia: University of Pennsylvania Press.

Jefferson, G. (1978). Sequential aspects of story telling in conversation. In J. Schenkein (Ed.), *Language thought and culture: Advances in the study of cognition* (pp. 219–248). New York: Academic Press.

Labov, W. (1972). The transformation of experience in narrative syntax. *Language in the inner city* (pp. 134–166). Philadelphia: University of Pennsylvania.

Ochs, E. (1979). Transcription as theory. In E. Ochs & B. S. Schieffelin (Eds.), *Developmental pragmatics* (pp. 43–72). New York: Academic Press.

Ochs, E. (1992). Indexing Gender. In A. Duranti & C. Goodwin (Eds.), *Rethinking context: Language as an interactive phenomenon* (pp. 335–358). Cambridge: Cambridge University Press.

Ochs, E., & Capps, L. (2001). *Living narrative: Creating lives in everyday storytelling*. Cambridge, MA: Harvard University Press.

Philips, S. U. (1983). *The invisible culture: Communication in classroom and community on the Warm Springs Reservation*. Prospect Heights, IL: Waveland Press.

Sacks, H. (1992). *Lectures on conversation*. Oxford: Blackwell.

Sacks, H., Schegloff, E. A., & Jefferson, G. (1974). A simplest systematics for the organization of turn-taking for conversation. *Language, 50*, 696–735.

Schiffrin, D. (1996). Narrative as self-portrait: Sociolinguistic constructions of identity. *Language in Society, 25*(2), 167–203.

Smith, M. B. (2000). Moral foundations of research with human participants. In B. D. Sales & S. Folkman (Eds.), *Ethics in research with human participants* (pp. 3–10). Washington, D.C.: American Psychological Association.

References

Abu-Lughod, L. (1990). The romance of resistance: Tracing transformations of power through Bedouin Women. *American Ethnologist, 17*(1), 43–55.

Agar, M. (1985). Institutional discourse. *Text, 5*(1), 147–168.

Alim, H. S. (2004). *You know my steez: An ethnographic and sociolinguistic study of styleshifting in a Black American speech community.* Durham, NC: Duke University Press.

Anctil, G. (2007). 50th anniversary of On the Road – Kerouac wanted to write in French (Independence of Québec, Trans.) Le Devoir. Retrieved from <http://english.republiquelibre.org50th_anniversary_of_On_the_Road_Kerouac_wanted_to_write_in_French>.

Anderson, B. (2006). *Imagined communities: Reflections on the origin and spread of nationalism.* New York: Verso.

Anderson, E. S. (1990). *Speaking with style: The sociolinguistic skills of children.* London: Routledge.

Anderson, S. R. (2004). *How many languages are there in the world?* Washington, DC: Linguistic Society of America.

Antia, B. E., & Bertin, F. D. A. (2004). Multilingualism and healthcare in Nigeria: A management perspective. *Communication & Medicine, 1*(2), 107–117.

Atkinson, J. M. (1992). Displaying neutrality: Formal aspects of informal court proceedings. In P. Drew & J. Heritage (Eds.), *Talk at work: Interaction in institutional settings* (pp. 199–211). Cambridge: Cambridge University Press.

Atkinson, J. M., & Drew, P. (1979). The production of justifications and excuses by witnesses in cross-examination. In *Order in court: The organization of verbal interaction in judicial settings* (pp. 136–187). Atlantic Highlands: Humanities Press.

Auer, P. (2005). A postscript: Code-switching and social identity. *Journal of Pragmatics, 37*(4), 403–410.

Augé, M. (1995). *Non-places: Introduction to an anthropology of supermodernity* (J. Howe, Trans.). London: Verso.

Austin, J. L. (1975). *How to do things with words* (2nd ed.). Cambridge, MA: Harvard University Press.

Bailey, B. (1997). Communication of respect in interethnic service encounters. *Language in Society, 26,* 327–365.

Bailey, B. (2000). Communicative behavior and conflict between African-American customers and Korean immigrant retailers in Los Angeles. *Discourse & Society, 11*(1), 86–108.

Bailey, B. (2001). The language of multiple identities among Dominican Americans. *Journal of Linguistic Anthropology, 10*(2), 190–223.

Bamiro, E. (2006). The politics of code-switching: English versus Nigerian languages. *World Englishes*, *25*(1), 23–35.

Bardovi-Harlig, K., & Hartford, B. (1996). Input in an institutional setting. *Studies in Second Language Acquisition*, *18*(2), 171–188.

Bateson, G. (1972). *Steps to an ecology of mind*. New York: Ballantine.

Bell, A. (1984). Language style as audience design. *Language in Society*, *13*, 145–204.

Belz, J. (2002). The myth of the deficient communicator. *Language Teaching Research*, *6*(1), 59–82.

Berg, E. C., Hult, F. M., & King, K. A. (2001). Shaping the climate for language shift? English in Sweden's elite domains. *World Englishes*, *20*(3), 305–319.

Berk-Seligson, S. (1990). Bilingual court proceedings: The role of the court interpreter. In J. N. Levi & A. G. Walker (Eds.), *Language in the judicial process* (Vol. 5, pp. 155–201). New York: Plenum.

Berk-Seligson, S. (2000). Interpreting for the police: Issues in pre-trial phases of the judicial process. *Forensic Linguistics*, *7*(2), 212–237.

Bhabha, H. K. (1994). *The location of culture*. Abingdon: Routledge Classics.

Bhatt, R. M. (2002). Expert, dialects, and discourse. *International Journal of Applied Linguistics*, *12*(1), 74–109.

Bhatt, R. M. (2008). In other words: Language mixing, identity representations, and third space. *Journal of Sociolinguistics*, *12*(2), 177–220.

Biber, D. (1995). *Dimensions of register variation: A cross-linguistic comparison*. Cambridge: Cambridge University Press.

Biber, D. (2003). Variation among university spoken and written registers: A new multi-dimensional analysis. In P. Leityna & C. F. Meyer (Eds.), *Corpus analysis: Language structure and language use* (pp. 47–70). Amsterdam: Rodopi.

Birdsong, D. (2005). Nativelikeness and non-nativelikeness in L2A research. *International Review of Applied Linguistics*, *43*(4), 319–328.

Blommaert, J. (2005). Situating language rights: English and Swahili in Tanzania revisited. *Journal of Sociolinguistics*, *9*(4), 390–417.

Blommaert, J. (2009). Language, asylum, and the national order. *Current Anthropology*, *50*(415–441).

Bourdieu, P. (1977a). The economics of linguistic exchanges. *Social Science Information*, *16*, 645–668.

Bourdieu, P. (1977b). *Reproduction in education, society and culture*. London: Sage.

Bourdieu, P., & Nice, R. (1980). The production of belief: Contribution to an economy of symbolic goods. *Media, Culture and Society*, *2*(3), 262–293.

Bovingdon, R. (2004). From language to ethnolect: Maltese to Maltratjan. *Current Issues in Language Planning*, *5*(2), 166–175.

Briggs, C. L. (1986). *Learning how to ask*. Cambridge: Cambridge University Press.

Briggs, C. L. (1988). *Competence in performance: The creativity of tradition in Mexicano verbal art*. Philadelphia: University of Pennsylvania Press.

Brown, P., & Levinson, S. C. (1987). *Politeness: Some universals in language usage* (2nd ed.). Cambridge, MA: Cambridge University Press.

Bruner, J. (1986). *Actual minds, possible worlds*. Cambridge, MA: Harvard University Press.

Bucholtz, M., Bermudez, N., Fung, V., Edwards, L., & Vargas, R. (2007). Hella Nor Cal or totally So Cal?: The perceptual dialectology of California. *Journal of English Linguistics*, *35*(4), 325–352.

Bucholtz, M., Liang, A. C., & Sutton, L. A. (Eds.). (1999). *Reinventing identities: The gendered self in discourse.* New York: Oxford University Press.

Butler, J. (1993). *Bodies that matter.* New York: Routledge.

Butler, J. (1997). *Excitable speech: A politics of the performative.* New York: Routledge.

Canagarajah, S. (2007). Lingua Franca English, multilingual communities, and language acquisition. *The Modern Language Journal, 91*(Focal Issue), 923–939.

Carmona, R. H. (2007). Improving language access: A personal and national agenda. *Journal of General Internal Medicine, 22*(Supplement 2), 277–278.

Cedergren, H. J., & Sankoff, D. (1974). Variable rules: Performance as a statistical reflection of competence. *Language, 50*(2), 333–355.

Cenoz, J., & Gorter, D. (2006). Linguistic landscape and minority languages. *International Journal of Multilingualism, 3*(1), 67–80.

Chang, G. C., & Mehan, H. B. (2008). Why we must attack Iraq: Bush's reasoning practices and argumentation system. *Discourse & Society, 19*(453–482).

Chen, R. (2005). Universalism vs. particularism: Whither pragmatics? *Modern Foreign Languages, 28*(1), 120–128.

Chen, R. (2010). Pragmatics East and West: Similar or different? In A. Trosborg (Ed.), *Handbook of Pragmatics* (Vol. 7, pp. 167–188). Berlin: Mouton de Gruyter.

Cicourel, A. V. (2005). Bureaucratic rituals in health care delivery. *Journal of Applied Linguistics, 2*(3), 357–370.

Clayman, S., & Heritage, J. (2002). *The news interview: Journalists and public figures on the air.* Cambridge: Cambridge University Press.

Conley, J. M., & O'Barr, W. M. (1990). *Rules versus relationships: The ethnography of legal discourse.* Chicago: University of Chicago Press.

Cook, V. (1991). The poverty-of-the-stimulus argument and multicompetence. *Second Language Research, 7*(2), 103–117.

Cook, V. (1992). Evidence for multicompetence. *Language Learning, 42*(4), 557–591.

Cook, V. (1999). Going beyond the native speaker in language teaching. *TESOL Quarterly, 33*(2), 185–209.

Coutin, S., & Chock, P. (1995). Your friend, the illegal: Definition and paradox in newspaper accounts of U.S. immigration reform. *Identities, 2*(1–2), 123–148.

Cumming, A., & Abdolmehdi, R. (2000). Building models of adult second-language writing instruction. *Learning and Instruction, 10*(2), 55–71.

Cutler, C. (2007). The co-construction of whiteness in an MC battle. *Pragmatics, 17*(1), 9–22.

Danet, B. (1980). "Baby" or "fetus"? Language and the construction of reality in a manslaughter trial. *Semiotica, 32*(3–4), 187–219.

Davidson, B. (2001). Questions in cross-linguistic medical encounters: The role of the hospital interpreter. *Anthropological Quarterly, 74*(4), 170–178.

Deckert, S. K. (2006). *The construction of functional identities in forensic interviews with children* (Doctoral dissertation). Available from Dissertations and Theses database. (UMI No. 3219750).

Deckert, S. K. (2010a). Co-animation of and resistance to the construction of witness, victim, and perpetrator identities in forensic interviews with children. *Critical Inquiry in Language Studies, 7*(2–3), 197–206.

Deckert, S. K. (2010b). Task-based materials, ownership, and identity construction. In H. P. Widodo & L. Savova (Eds.), *Materials design & development in English language teaching: Theory & practice* (pp. 194–294). München, Germany: Lincom Europa.

Deckert, S., & Yaeger-Dror, M. (1999). Disagreement, contraction and prosody: Evidence from a large corpus of American English. *CLIC: Crossroads of Language, Interaction, and Culture, 2,* 49–59.

de Klerk, V. (2006). Codeswitching, borrowing and mixing in a corpus of Xhosa English. *International Journal of Bilingual Education, 9*(5), 597–614.

Di Paolo, M., & Green, G. (1990). Jurors' beliefs about the interpretation of speaking style. *American Speech, 65*(4), 304–322.

Doke, C., & Vilakazi, B. W. (1958). *Zulu-English dictionary* (2nd ed.). London: Oxford.

Dominguez, V. (1986). *White by definition: Social classification in Creole Louisiana.* New Brunswick: Rutgers University Press.

Du Bois, J. W., Schuetze-Coburn, S., Cumming, S., & Paolino, D. (1993). Outline of discourse transcription. In J. W. Du Bois, Schuetze-Coburn, S. Cumming & D. Paolino (Eds.), *Talking data: Transcription and coding in discourse research* (pp. 1–31 and 45–90). Hillsdale, NJ: Lawrence Erlbaum Associates.

Eades, D., Fraser, H., Siegel, J., McNamara, T., & Baker, B. (2003). Linguistic identification in the determination of nationality: A preliminary report. *Language Policy, 2*(2), 179–199.

Eckert, P. (2000a). *Jocks and Burnouts: Social categories and identity in the high school.* New York: Teacher's College Press.

Eckert, P. (2000b). *Linguistic variation as social practice.* Oxford: Blackwell Publishers.

Erickson, F., & Shultz, J. (1982). *The counselor as gatekeeper: Social interaction in interviews.* New York: Academic Press.

Fairclough, N. (1989). Discourse and power. In C. N. Candlin (Ed.), *Language and power* (2nd ed., pp. 43–108). London: Longman.

Fillmore, C. (1997). *Lectures on deixis.* Stanford: Center for the Study of Language and Information.

Firth, A., & Wagner, J. (1997). On Discourse, communication, and (some) fundamental concepts in SLA research. *The Modern Language Journal, 81*(3), 285–300.

Fishman, J. (1967). Bilingualism with and without diglossia: Diglossia with and without bilingualism. *Journal of Social Issues, 23*(2), 29–38.

Fonseca-Greber, B. (2000). *The change from pronoun to clitic to prefix and the rise of null subjects in spoken Swiss French* (Doctoral dissertation). Available from Dissertations and Theses database. (UMI No. 9992079).

Fonseca-Greber, B., & Waugh, L. R. (2003a). On the radical difference between the subject personal pronouns in written and spoken European French. In P. Leityna & C. F. Meyer (Eds.), *Corpus analysis: Language structure and language use* (pp. 225–240). Amsterdam/New York: Rodopi.

Fonseca-Greber, B., & Waugh, L. R. (2003b). The subject clitics of European conversational French: Morphologization, grammatical change, semantic change, and change in progress.

In R. Núñez-Cedeño, L. López & R. Cameron (Eds.), *A romance perspective on language knowledge and use* (pp. 99–118). Amsterdam & Philadelphia, PA: John Benjamins.

Fought, C. (2006). *Language and ethnicity*. Cambridge: Cambridge University Press.

French, B. M. (2001). The symbolic capital of social identities: The genre of bargaining in an urban Guatemalan market. *Journal of Linguistic Anthropology, 10*(2), 155–189.

Friginal, E. (2009). Threats to the sustainability of the outsourced call center industry in the Philippines: Implications for language policy. *Language Policy, 8*(1), 51–68.

Gal, S. (1979). *Language shift*. New York: Academic Press.

Gal, S. (1987). Codeswitching and consciousness in the European periphery. *American Ethnologist, 14*(4), 637–653.

Gal, S. (1989). Language and political economy. *Annual Review of Anthropology, 18*, 345–367.

Gallagher, S., & Marcel, A. J. (1999). The self in contextualized action. *Journal of Consciousness Studies, 6*(4), 4–39.

Garfinkel, H. (1967). *Studies in ethnomethodology*. Englewood Cliffs: Prentice-Hall.

Garrett, P. B., & Baquedano-Lopez, P. (2002). Language socialization: Reproduction and continuity, transformation and change. *Annual Review of Anthropology, 31*, 339–361.

Gaudio, R. (1997). Not talking straight in Hausa. In A. Livia & K. Hall (Eds.), *Queerly phrased: language, gender, and sexuality* (pp. 416–419). New York: Oxford University Press.

Geertz, C. (1973). *The interpretation of cultures*. New York: Basic Books.

Goffman, E. (1959). *The presentation of self in everyday life*. New York: Anchor Books.

Goffman, E. (1967). *Interaction ritual*. New York: Pantheon.

Goffman, E. (1971). *Relations in public*. New York: Harper.

Goffman, E. (1974). *Frame analysis: An essay on the organization of experience*. Boston: Northeastern University Press.

Goffman, E. (1981). *Forms of talk*. Philadelphia: University of Pennsylvania.

Goodwin, C., & Heritage, J. (1990). Conversation analysis. *Annual Review of Anthropology, 19*, 283–307.

Goodwin, M. H. (1990). *He-said-she-said: Talk as social organization among black children*. Bloomington: Indiana University Press.

Gramsci, A. (1971). State and civil society. In A. Gramsci (Ed.), *Selections from the prison notebooks* (pp. 206–276). New York: International Press.

Greatbatch, D., Luff, P., Heath, C., & Campion, P. (1993). Interpersonal communication and human-computer interaction: An examination of the use of computers in medical consultations. *Interacting with computers, 5*(2), 193–216.

Greenfield, P. M. (1984). A theory of the teacher in the learning activities of everyday life. In B. Rogoff & J. Lave (Eds.), *Everyday cognition: Its development in social contexts* (pp. 117–138). Cambridge, MA Harvard University Press.

Groce, N. E. (1985). *Everyone here spoke sign language: Hereditary deafness on Martha's Vineyard*. Cambridge: Harvard University Press.

Gumperz, J., Jupp, T. C., & Roberts, C. (1979). *Crosstalk. Background materials and notes to accompany the B.B.C. film*. London: National Centre for Industrial Language Training.

Gumperz, J., & Roberts, C. (1991). Understanding in intercultural encounters. In J. Blommaert & J. Verschueren (Eds.), *The pragmatics of intercultural and international communication* (pp. 51–90). Philadelphia: John Benjamins.

Gumperz, J. J. (1982). *Discourse strategies.* Cambridge: Cambridge University.

Gumperz, J. J. (2001). Interactional sociolinguistics: A personal perspective. In D. Schriffrin, D. Tannen & H. Hamilton, E. (Eds.), *The handbook of discourse analysis* (pp. 215–228). Malden, MA: Blackwell Publishers.

Gumperz, J. J., & Cook-Gumperz, J. (2008). Studying language, culture, and society: Sociolinguistics or linguistic anthropology? *Journal of Sociolinguistics, 12*(4), 532–545.

Hall, J. K., Cheng, A., & Carlson, M. T. (2006). Reconceptualizing multicompetence as a theory of language knowledge. *Applied Linguistics, 27*(2), 220–240.

Hall, K., & Bucholtz, M. (1995). *Gender articulated: Language and the socially constructed self.* New York: Routledge.

Halmari, H., & Smith, W. B. (1994). Code-switching and register shift: Evidence from Finnish-English child bilingual conversation. *Journal of Pragmatics, 21*(4), 427–445.

Hammersley, M., & Atkinson, P. (2007). *Ethnography: Principles in practice.* London: Routledge.

Hanauer, D. I. (2009). Non-place identity: Britain's response to migration in the age of supermodernity. In G. Delanty, P. Jones & R. Wodak (Eds.), *Migrant voices: Discourses of belonging and exclusion* (pp.198–207). Liverpool, UK: Liverpool University Press.

Hanauer, D., & Englander, K. (in press). *Scientific writing in a second language.* West Lafayette: Parlor Press.

Hanks, W. F. (2009). Fieldwork on deixis. *Journal of Pragmatics, 41*(1), 10–24.

Heath, C. (1992). The delivery and reception of diagnosis in the general practice consultation. In P. Drew & J. Heritage (Eds.), *Talk at work: Interaction in institutional settings* (pp. 235–267). Cambridge: Cambridge University Press.

Hedegaard, M. (2001). *Learning in classrooms: A cultural-historical approach.* Aarhus: Aarhus University Press.

Heller, M. (1992). The politics of codeswitching and language choice. In C. Eastman (Ed.), *Codeswitching* (pp. 123–132). Clevedon: Multilingual Matters.

Heritage, J. (1985). Analyzing news interviews: Aspects of the production of talk for an overhearing audience. In T. van Dijk (ed.), *Handbook of discourse analysis: Dimensions of discourse* (vol. 3, pp. 95–117). London: Academic press.

Hill, J. H. (1993). Junk Spanish, covert racism, and the (leaky) boundary between public and private spheres. *Pragmatics, 5*(2), 197–212.

Hill, J. H. (1995). *Mock Spanish: A site for the indexical reproduction of racism in America.* Paper presented at the Language and Culture: Symposium 2.

Hill, J. H. (1998). Language, race, and white public space. *American Anthropologist, 100*(3), 680–689.

Hower, T. R. (1997). Brown University's anti harrassment code: The case of Douglas A. Hann. In M. Heumann & T. Church, W (Eds.), *Hate speech on campus* (pp. 149–169). Boston: Northeastern University Press.

Hoyle, S. M. (1991). Children's competence in the specialized register of sportscasting. *Journal of Child Language, 18*(2), 435–450.

Hutchby, I. (1999). Frame attunement and footing in the organization of talk radio openings. *Journal of Sociolinguistics, 3*(1), 41–63.

Hutchby, I., & O'Reilly, M. (2010). Children's participation and the familial moral order in family therapy. *Discourse Studies, 12*(1), 49–64.

Huysmans, J., & Buonfino, A. (2008). Politics of exception and unease: Immigration, asylum and terrorism in parliamentary debates in the UK. *Political Studies, 56*(4), 766–788.

Hymes, D. (1972). Models of the interaction of language and social life. In J. Gumperz & D. Hymes (Eds.), *Directions in sociolinguistics: The ethnography of communication* (pp. 35–71). New York: Holt, Rinehart, and Winston.

Hymes, D. (1974). *Foundations in sociolinguistics: An ethnographic approach.* Philadelphia: University of Pennsylvania Press.

Ide, S. (1989). Formal forms and discernment: Two neglected aspects of linguistic politeness. *Multilingua, 8*(2), 223–248.

Irvine, J. T. (1998). Ideologies of honorific language. In B. B. Schieffelin, K. A. Woolard & P. V. Kroskrity (Eds.), *Language ideologies: Practice and theory* (pp. 51–67). Oxford: Oxford University Press.

Jacoby, S., & Gonzales, P. (1991). The constitution of expert-novice in scientific discourse. *Issues in Applied Linguistics, 2*(2), 149–181.

Jacoby, S., & Ochs, E. (1995). Co-construction: An introduction. *Research on Language & Social Interaction, 23*(3), 171–183.

Jefferson, G. (1978). Sequential aspects of story telling in conversation. In J. Schenkein (Ed.), *Language, thought and culture: Advances in the study of cognition* (pp. 219–248). New York: Academic Press.

Jefferson, G. (1981). The rejection of advice: Managing the problematic convergence of a "troubles-telling" and "service encounter." *Journal of Pragmatics, 5*(4), 399–422.

Jefferson, G. (1984). On the organization of laughter in talk about troubles. In J. Atkinson & J. Heritage (Eds.), *Structures of social action* (pp. 399–422). Cambridge: Cambridge University Press.

Jefferson, G. (2002). Is "no" an acknowledgment token? Comparing American and British uses of (+)/(-) tokens. *Journal of Pragmatics, 34*(10/11), 1345–1383.

Johnstone, B., & Kiesling, S. F. (2008). Indexicality and experience: Exploring the meanings of /aw/-monophthongization in Pittsburgh. *Journal of Sociolinguistics, 12*(1), 5–33.

Jones, R., & Thornborrow, J. (2004). Floors, talk and the organization of classroom activities. *Language in Society, 33,* 399–423.

Kachru, B. (1986). The power and politics of English. *World Englishes, 5*(2/3), 121–140.

Kachru, B. (1994). Englishization and contact linguistics. *World Englishes, 13*(2), 241–255.

Kachru, Y. (1994). Monolingual bias in SLA research. *TESOL Quarterly, 28*(4), 795–800.

Kanahele-Stutz, N. (2009). *United States mainland speakers' use of Hawai'ian Creole English and Standard American English across social situations* (Master's thesis). California State University, San Bernardino.

Kendall, S. (2008). The balancing act: Framing gendered parental identities at dinnertime. *Language in Society, 37*(4), 539–568.

King, K. A. (2009). Global connections: Language policies and international call centers. *Language Policy, 8*(1), 1–3.

Koerner, E. F. K. (2002). *Toward a history of American Linguistics.* London: Routledge.

Kramsch, C. (2000). Social discursive constructions of self in L2 learning. In J. P. Lantolf (Ed.), *Sociocultural theory and second language learning* (pp. 133–153). New York: Oxford University Press.

Kremer-Sadlik, T., & Kim, J. L. (2007). Lessons from sports: Children's socialization to values through family interaction during sports activities. *Discourse & Society, 18*(1), 35–52.

Krzyzanowski, M., & Wodak, R. (2008). Multiple identities, migration and belonging: "Voices of migrants." In C. R. Caldas-Coulthard & R. Iedema (Eds.), *Identity trouble: Critical discourse and contested identities* (pp. 95–119). Basingstoke: Palgrave MacMillan.

Kulyk, V. (2010). Ideologies of language use in post-Soviet Ukrainian media. *International Journal of the Sociology of Language, 201*(1), 79–104.

Labov, W. (1963). The social motivation of a sound change. *Word, 19,* 273–209.

Labov, W. (1966). *The social stratification of English in New York City.* Washington, D.C.: Center for Applied Linguistics.

Labov, W. (1972). *Sociolinguistic patterns.* Philadelphia: University of Pennsylvania Press.

Labov, W. (1982). Objectivity and commitment in linguistic science: The case of the Black English trial in Ann Arbor. *Language in Society, 11*(2), 165–201.

Labov, W. (2007). Transmission and diffusion. *Language, 83*(2), 344–387.

Labov, W., & Waletzky, J. (1966). Narrative analysis and oral versions of personal experience. In J. Helm (Ed.), *Essays on the verbal and visual arts: Proceedings of the 1966 annual spring meeting of the American Ethnological Society* (pp. 12–45). Seattle: University of Washington Press.

Lakoff, R. (1975). *Language and woman's place.* New York: Harper and Row.

Landry, R., & Bourhis, R. Y. (1997). Linguistic landscape and ethnolinguistic vitality: An empirical study. *Journal of Language and Social Psychology, 16*(1), 23–49.

Lave, J., & Wenger, E. (1991). *Situated learning: Legitimate peripheral participation.* Cambridge: Cambridge University Press.

Lazarus-Black, M. (1994). *Legitimate acts and illegal encounters: Law and society in Barbuda and Antigua.* Washington, D.C.: Smithsonian Institution Press.

Lippi-Green, R. (1997a). *English with an accent: Language, ideology, and discrimination in the United States.* London: Routledge.

Lippi-Green, R. (1997b). Teaching children how to discriminate: What we learn from the Big Bad Wolf. In R. Lippi-Green (Ed.), *English with an accent: Language, ideology, and discrimination in the United States* (pp. 79–103). New York: Routledge.

Livia, A., & Hall, K. (Eds.) (1997). *Queerly phrased: Language, gender, and sexuality.* New York: Oxford University Press.

Loftus, E. F. (1979). *Eyewitness testimony.* Cambridge, MA: Harvard University Press.

Low, B., Sarkar, M., & Winer, L. (2009). "Ch'us mon propre Bescherelle": Challenges from the Hip-Hop nation to the Quebec nation. *Journal of Sociolinguistics, 13*(1), 59–82.

Lucas, C. (Ed.). (2001). *Sociolinguistics of sign languages.* Cambridge: Cambridge University Press.

Lucas, C., Bayley, R., Valli, C., Rose, M., & Wulf, A. (2001). Sociolinguistic variation. In C. Lucas (Ed.), *Sociolinguistics of sign languages* (pp. 61–111). Cambridge: Cambridge University Press.

Majewicz, A. E. (1996). Kashubian choices, Kashubian prospects: A minority language situation in northern Poland. *International Journal of the Sociology of Language, 120*(1), 39–53.

Mao, R. L. (1994). Beyond politeness theory: "Face" revisited and renewed. *Journal of Pragmatics, 21*(5), 451–486.

Martinez, G. (2008). Language-in-healthcare policy, interaction patterns, and unequal care on the U.S.-Mexico border. *Language Policy, 7*(3), 345–363.

Matoesian, G. M. (1993). *Reproducing rape: Domination through talk in the courtroom.* Chicago: The University of Chicago Press.

Matoesian, G. M. (2001). *Law and the language of identity: Discourse in the William Kennedy Smith rape trial.* Oxford: Oxford University Press.

Matsuda, P. K. (2003). Proud to be a nonnative English Speaker. *TESOL Matters, 13*(4), 15.

Matsumoto, Y. (1989). Politeness and conversational universals: Observations from Japanese. *Multilingua, 8*(2), 207–221.

McCarthy, M., & Carter, R. (2004). "There's millions of them": Hyperbole in everyday conversation. *Journal of Pragmatics, 36*(2), 149–184.

McHoul, A. (1978). The organization of turns at formal talk in the classroom. *Language in Society, 7*(2), 183–213.

Mead, G. H. (1934). The social foundations and functions of thought and communication. In *Mind, self, and society* (pp. 253–260). Chicago: Chicago University Press.

Meek, B. A. (2006). And the Injun goes "How!": Representations of American Indian English in white public space. *Language in Society, 35*(1), 93–128.

Mehan, H. (1997). The discourse of the illegal immigration debate: A case study in the politics of representation. *Discourse in Society, 8*(2), 249–270.

Mendoza-Denton, N. (2008). *Homegirls: Language and cultural practice among Latina youth gangs.* Malden, MA: Blackwell.

Mertz, E. (1988). The uses of history: Language, ideology, and law in the United States and South America. *Law and Society Review, 22*(4), 661–685.

Messing, J. (2007). Ideologies of public and private uses of language in Tlaxcala, Mexico. *International Journal of Sociology of Language, 2007*(187–188), 211–227.

Milroy, J., & Lesley, M. (1985). Linguistic change, social network and speaker innovation. *Journal of Linguistics, 21*(2), 339–384.

Milroy, L. (1987). *Observing and analyzing natural language.* Oxford: Blackwell.

Morgan, B., & Ramanathan, V. (2009). Outsourcing, globalizing economics, and shifting language policies: Issues in managing Indian call centres. *Language Policy, 8*(1), 69–80.

Myers-Scotton, C. (1993). *Social motivations for codeswitching: Evidence from Africa.* Oxford: Oxford University Press.

Norrick, N. R. (2008). Using large corpora of conversation to investigate narrative: The case of interjections in conversational storytelling performance. *International Journal of Corpus Linguistics, 13*(4), 438–464.

O'Barr, W. M. (1982). Speech styles in the courtroom. In D. Black (Ed.), *Linguistic evidence: Language, power, and strategy in the courtroom* (1st ed., pp. 61–187). New York, NY: Academic Press.

O'Barr, W. M., & Atkins, B. K. (1980). "Women's language" or "powerless language?" In S. McConnell-Ginet, R. Borker & N. Furman (Eds.), *Women and language in literature and society* (pp. 93–110). New York: Praeger.

Ochs, E. (1979). Transcription as theory. In E. Ochs & B. S. Schieffelin (Eds.), *Developmental pragmatics* (pp. 43–72). New York: Academic Press.

Ochs, E. (1992). Indexing gender. In A. Duranti & C. Goodwin (Eds.), *Rethinking context: Language as an interactive phenomenon* (pp. 335–358). Cambridge: Cambridge University Press.

Ochs, E. (1993). Constructing social identity: A language socialization perspective *Research on Language and Social Interaction, 26*(3), 287–306.

Ochs, E., & Capps, L. (2001). *Living narrative: Creating lives in everyday storytelling.* Cambridge, MA: Harvard University Press.

Ochs, E., & Kremer-Sadlik, T. (2007). Introduction: Morality as family practice. *Discourse & Society, 18*(1), 5–10.

Olsson, J. (2008). *Forensic linguistics* (2nd ed.). London: Continuum International Publishing Group.

Olsson, J. (2009). *Word crimes.* London: Continuum International Publishing Group.

Ortega, L. (2010). *The bilingual turn in SLA.* Paper presented at the Annual Conference of the American Association for Applied Linguistics, Atlanta, GA.

Otheguy, R., Zentella, A. C., & Livert, D. (2007). Language and dialect contact in Spanish in New York: Toward the formation of a speech community. *Language, 83*(1), 770–802.

Owens, T. J. (2003). Self and identity. In J. D. DeLamater (Ed.), *Handbook of social psychology* (pp. 205–232). New York: Kluwwer Academic/Plenum Publishers.

Pan, Y. (2000). Facework in Chinese service encounters. *Journal of Asian-Pacific Communication, 10*(1), 25–61.

Panayiotou, A. (2004). Switching codes, switching code: Bilinguals' emotional responses in English and Greek. *Journal of Multicultural and Multilingual Development, 25*(2/3), 124–139.

Paredes, L., & Valdes, M. L. (2008). Language contact and change: Direct object leísmo in Andean-Spanish. In M. Westmoreland & T. J. Antonio (Eds.), *Selected proceedings of the 4th workshop on Spanish sociolinguistics.* Somerville, MA: Cascadilla Proceedings Project.

Pavlenko, A. (2002). "We have room for but one language here": Language and national identity in the US at the turn of the 20th century. *Multilingua, 21*, 163–196.

Pavlenko, A. (2003). "I never knew I was a bilingual": Reimagining teacher identities in TESOL. *Journal of Language, Identity, and Education, 2*(4), 251–268.

Philips, S. U. (1972). Participant structures and communicative competence: Warm Springs children in community and classroom. In C. B. Cazden, V. John-Steiner & D. Hymes (Eds.), *Functions of language in the classroom* (pp. 370–394). New York: Teacher's College Press.

Philips, S. U. (1982). On the use of Wh questions in American courtroom discourse: A study of the relation between language form and language function. In L. Kedar (Ed.), *Power through discourse* (pp. 83–111). Norwood, NJ: Ablex Publishing Company.

Philips, S. U. (1983). *The invisible culture: Communication in classroom and community on the Warm Springs Indian Reservation.* Prospect Heights, IL: Waveland Press.

Philips, S. U. (1985). Strategies of clarification in judges' use of language: From the written to the spoken. *Discourse Processes, 8,* 421–436.

Philips, S. U. (1998). *Ideology in the language of judges: How judges practice law, politics, and courtroom control.* New York: Oxford University Press.

Philips, S. U. (2006). Language and social inequality. In A. Duranti (Ed.), *A companion to linguistic anthropology* (pp. 474–495). Malden, MA: Blackwell.

Pomerantz, A. (1984). Agreeing and disagreeing with assessments: Some features of preferred/dispreferred turn shapes. In J. M. Atkinson & J. Heritage (Eds.), *Structures of social action: Studies in conversation analysis* (pp. 57–101). Cambridge: Press Syndicate of the University of Cambridge.

Quinto-Pozos, D., & Mehta, S. (2010). Register variation in mimetic gestural complements to signed language. *Journal of Pragmatics, 42,* 577–584.

Radwanska-Williams, J. (2008). The "native speaker" as a metaphorical construct. In E. A. Berendt (Ed.), *Metaphors for learning: Cross-cultural perspectives* (pp. 139–156). Amsterdam: John Benjamins.

Rampton, B. (1995). Language crossing and the problematisation of ethnicity and socialisation. *Pragmatics, 5*(485–513).

Rampton, B. (2005). *Crossing: Language and ethnicity among adolescents.* London: Longman.

Rampton, B. (2009). Interaction ritual and not just artful performance in crossing and stylization. *Language in Society, 38*(2), 149–176.

Regan, T. (2001). Language planning and policy. In C. Lucas (Ed.), *The sociolinguistics of sign language* (pp. 145–180). Cambridge: Cambridge University Press.

Reyes-Rodríguez, A. (2008). Political discourse and its sociolinguistic variables. *Critical Inquiry in Language Studies, 5*(4), 225–242.

Roberts, C., & Sayers, P. (1998). Keeping the gate: How judgements are made in interethnic interviews. In P. Trudgill & J. Cheshire (Eds.), *The sociolinguistics reader: Multilingualism and variation* (pp. 25–43). New York: Arnold.

Romaine, S. (1999). Changing attitudes to Hawai'i Creole English. In J. R. Rickford & S. Romaine (Eds.), *Creole genesis, attitudes and discourse* (pp. 287–301). Philadelphia: John Benjamins.

Sacks, H. (1984). Notes on methodology. In J. M. Atkinson & J. Heritage (Eds.), *Structures of social action: Studies in conversation analysis* (pp. 21–27). Cambridge: Cambridge University Press.

Sacks, H. (1992). *Lectures on conversation.* Oxford: Blackwell.

Sacks, H., Schegloff, E. A., & Jefferson, G. (1974). A simplest systematics for the organization of turn-taking for conversation. *Language, 50,* 696–735.

Sakoda, K., & Siegel, J. (2003). *Pidgin grammar: An introduction to the Creole English of Hawai'i.* Honolulu: Bess Press, Inc.

Sankoff, D. (1978). Probability and linguistic variation. Synthese, 37, 217–238.

Schieffelin, B. B., Woolard, K. A., & Kroskrity, P. V. (1998). *Language ideologies: Practice and theory.* Oxford: Oxford University Press.

Schiffrin, D. (1996). Narrative as self-portrait: Sociolinguistic constructions of identity. *Language in Society, 25*(2), 167–203.

Schutz, A. (1970). Intersubjectivity and understanding. In A. Schutz (Ed.), *On phenomenology and social relations* (pp. 163–184). Chicago: University of Chicago Press.

Scott-Jones, D. (2000). Moral foundations of research with human participants. In B. D. Sales & S. Folkman (Eds.), *Ethics in research with human participants* (pp. 27–34). Washington, D.C.: American Psychological Association.

Searle, J. R. (1990a). Indirect speech acts. In A. P. Martinich (Ed.), *The philosophy of language* (2nd ed.) (pp. 161–175). New York, NY: Oxford University Press.

Searle, J. R. (1990b). What is a speech act? In A. P. Martinich (Ed.), *The philosophy of language* (2nd ed., pp. 115–125). New York, NY: Oxford University Press.

Sebba, M. (1997). *Contact languages: Pidgins and creoles.* London: Macmillan.

Seidlhofer, B. (2001). Closing a conceptual gap: The case for a description of English as a Lingua Franca. *International Journal of Applied Linguistics, 11*(2), 133–158.

Seidlhofer, B. (2004). Research perspectives on teaching English as a Lingua Franca. *Annual Review of Applied Linguistics, 29*, 209–239.

Shonkoff, J. P., & Phillips, D. A. (2000). *From neurons to neighborhoods: The science of early childhood development.* Washington, D.C.: National Academies Press.

Shuy, R. W. (1987). Conversational power in FBI covert tape recordings. In L. Kedar (Ed.), *Power through discourse* (pp. 43–56). Newark, NJ: Ablex Publishing Corporation.

Shuy, R. W. (1993). *Language crimes: The use and abuse of language evidence in the courtroom.* Cambridge, MA: Blackwell.

Sinclair, J. (2001). Data-derived multilingual lexicons. *International Journal of Corpus Linguistics, 6*(SI), 79–94.

Sinclair, J., & Carter, R. (2004). *Trust the text: Language, corpus and discourse.* London: Routledge.

skynews. (2009). Hillary's hissy fit: An unexpected outburst from Mrs Clinton. Retrieved June 6, 2010, from http://www.youtube.com/watch?v=xIVYRYVB5b8.

Smith, M. B. (2000). Moral foundations of research with human participants. In B. D. Sales & S. Folkman (Eds.), *Ethics in research with human participants* (pp. 3–10). Washington, D.C.: American Psychological Association.

Smith, W. B. (2010). Footing, resistance and control: Negotiating a traffic citation. *Critical Inquiry in Language Studies, 7*(2–3), 1–14.

Spitulnik, D. (1998). Mediating unity and diversity: The production of language ideologies in Zambian broadcasting. In B. B. Schieffelin, K. A. Woolard & P. V. Kroskrity (Eds.), *Language ideologies: Practice and theory* (pp. 163–188). Oxford: Oxford University Press.

Stefanowitsch, A. (2006). Words and their metaphors: A corpus-based approach. In A. Stefanowitsch & S. T. Gries (Eds.), *Corpus-based approaches to metaphor and metonymy* (pp. 63–105). Berlin: Mouton de Gruyter.

Swisher, M. V. (1989). The sociolinguistic situation of natural sign languages. *Applied Linguistics, 10*(3), 294–312.

Tannen, D. (1990). *You just don't understand: Women and men in conversation.* New York: Morrow.

Tannen, D. (1994). *Gender and discourse.* Oxford: Oxford University Press.

Toklaw. (2007). King Juan Carlos to Chávez: "Shut up." Retrieved June 6, 2010, from http://www.youtube.com/watch?v=X3Kzbo7tNLg.

tpmtv. (2008). John McCain at the 2nd Presidential Debate, October 7, 2008, from http://www.youtube.com/watch?v=lNzA9LfMlmU.

Trew, T. (1979). Theory and ideology at work. In R. Fowler, B. Hodge, G. Kress & T. Trew (Eds.), *Language and control* (pp. 94–116). London: Routledge & Kegan Paul.

Trinch, S. L. (2003). *Latina's narratives of domestic abuse: Discrepant versions of violence.* Amsterdam and Philadelphia: John Benjamins.

Trudgill, P. (1972). Sex, covert prestige and linguistic change in the urban British English of Norwich. *Language in Society, 1*(2), 179–195.

Tyler, A. (1995). The coconstruction of cross-cultural miscommunication: Conflicts in perception, negotiation and enactment of participant role and status. *Studies in Second Language Acquisition, 17*(2), 129–152.

Valdés, G. (2005). Heritage language learners, and SLA research: Opportunities lost or seized. *The Modern Language Journal, 89*(3), 410–426.

van Dijk, T. A. (2006). Discourse and manipulation. *Discourse & Society, 17*(3), 359–383.

Vickers, C. (2004). *Interactional accommodation and the construction of social roles among culturally diverse undergraduates* (Doctoral dissertation). Available from Dissertations and Thesis database. (UMI No. 3145144).

Vickers, C. H. (2007). Second language socialization through team interaction among electrical and computer engineering students. *The Modern Language Journal, 91*(4), 621–640.

Vickers, C. H. (2010a). Language competence and the construction of expert-novice in NS-NNS interaction. *Journal of Pragmatics, 42*(1), 116–138.

Vickers, C. H. (2010b). The local construction of the asymmetrical power relationship in teamwork among engineers. *Critical Inquiry in Language Studies, 7*(2–3), 131–151.

Vygotsky, L. S. (1978). Interaction between learning and development. In M. Cole, V. John-Steiner, S. Scribner & E. Souberman (Eds.), *Mind in society: The development of higher psychological processes* (pp. 79–91). Cambridge, MA: Harvard University Press.

Walker, S. (1994). *Hate speech: The history of an American controversy.* Lincoln, NE: University of Nebraska Press.

Watson-Gegeo, K. A. (2004). Mind, language, and epistemology: Toward a language socialization paradigm for SLA. *The Modern Language Journal, 88,* 331–350.

Watson-Gegeo, K. A., & Gegeo, D. W. (1999). (Re)modeling culture in Kwara'ae: The role of discourse in children's cognitive development. *Discourse Studies, 1*(2), 227–246.

Waugh, L. R. (2010). Power and prejudice: Their effects on the co-construction of linguistic and national identities. *Critical Inquiry in Language Studies, 7*(2/3), 112–130.

Waugh, L. R., Fonseca-Greber, B., Vickers, C., & Eröz, B. (2007). Multiple empirical approaches to a complex analysis of discourse. In M. Gonzalez-Marquez, M. Spivey, I. Mittelberg & S. Coulson (Eds.), *Methods in cognitive linguistics* (pp. 120–148). Amsterdam: John Benjamins.

Wenger, E. (1998). *Communities of practice: Learning, meaning, and identity.* Cambridge: Cambridge University Press.

Wenger, E., McDermott, R., & Snyder, W. (2002). *Cultivating communities of practice: A guide to managing knowledge.* Cambridge, MA: Harvard Business School Press.

Wertsch, J. V. (1985). *Vygotsky and the social formation of mind.* Cambridge, MA: Harvard University Press.

West, B. (1997). *When children accuse: Who to believe?* (Transcript #201 ed.). New York: American Broadcasting Company Inc.

Widdowson, H. G. (2003). *Defining issues in English language teaching.* Oxford: Oxford University Press.

Wierzbicka, A. (1985). Different cultures, different languages, different speech acts. *Journal of Pragmatics, 9*(2), 145–178.

Wierzbicka, A. (1992). *Semantics, culture, and cognition: Universal human concepts in cultural-specific configurations.* New York: Oxford University Press.

Wingard, L. (2007). Constructing time and prioritizing activities in parent–child interaction. *Discourse & Society, 18*(1), 75–91.

Woolard, K. A. (1985). Language variation and cultural hegemony: Toward an integration of sociolinguistic and social theory. *American Ethnologist, 40,* 738–748.

Woolard, K. A. (1998). Introduction: Language ideology as a field of inquiry. In B. B. Schieffelin, K. A. Woolard & P. V. Kroskrity (Eds.), *Language ideologies: Practice and theory* (pp. 3–47). Oxford: Oxford University Press.

Wulff, S. (2006). Go-V vs. go-and-V in English: A case of constructional synonymy? In S. T. Gries & A. Stefanowitsch (Eds.), *Corpora in cognitive linguistics: Corpus-based approaches to syntax and lexis* (pp. 101–126). Berlin: Mouton de Gruyter.

Yaeger-Dror, M., Hall-Lew, L., & Deckert, S. (2002). It's not or isn't it? Using large corpora to determine the influences on contraction strategies. *Language Variation and Change, 14,* 79–118.

Index